Fun with the Family™ Oregon

Praise for the *Fun with the Family*™ series

"Enables parents to turn family travel into an exploration."

—Alexandra Kennedy, Editor, *Family Fun*

"Bound to lead you and your kids to fun-filled days,
those times that help compose the
memories of childhood."

—Dorothy Jordon, *Family Travel Times*

Help Us Keep This Guide Up to Date

Every effort has been made by the authors and editors to make this guide as accurate and useful as possible. However, many changes can occur after a guide is published—establishments close, phone numbers change, hiking trails are rerouted, facilities come under new management, etc.

We would love to hear from you concerning your experiences with this guide and how you feel it could be improved and be kept up to date. While we may not be able to respond to all comments and suggestions, we'll take them to heart, and we'll make certain to share them with the authors. Please send your comments and suggestions to the following address:

The Globe Pequot Press
Reader Response/Editorial Department
P.O. Box 480
Guilford, CT 06437

Or you may e-mail us at: editorial@GlobePequot.com

Thanks for your input, and happy travels!

INSIDERS' GUIDE®

FUN WITH THE FAMILY™ SERIES

fun WITH the Family™

OREGON

HUNDREDS OF IDEAS FOR DAY TRIPS WITH THE KIDS

CHERYL MCLEAN

REVISED AND UPDATED BY LEE JUILLERAT

FIFTH EDITION

INSIDERS' GUIDE®

GUILFORD, CONNECTICUT
AN IMPRINT OF THE GLOBE PEQUOT PRESS

The prices, rates, and hours listed in this guidebook
were confirmed at press time. We recommend, however, that you
call establishments to obtain current information before traveling.

To buy books in quantity for corporate use
or incentives, call **(800) 962–0973**
or e-mail **premiums@GlobePequot.com.**

Text design by Nancy Freeborn and Linda R. Loiewski
Maps by Rusty Nelson © Morris Book Publishing, LLC
Spot photography throughout © Photodisc and © RubberBall Productions

ISSN 1540-4366
ISBN 978-0-7627-4396-4

Manufactured in the United States of America
Fifth Edition/First Printing

To our children, and their children, that they will savor and protect
the glorious and diverse beauty that is Oregon's

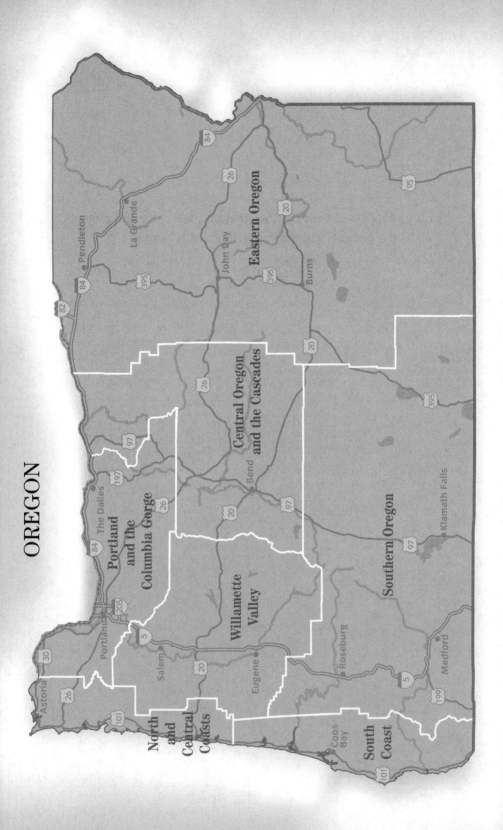

OREGON

Eastern Oregon

Central Oregon
and the Cascades

Southern Oregon

Portland
and the
Columbia Gorge

Willamette
Valley

North
and
Central
Coasts

South
Coast

Pendleton

La Grande

John Day

Burns

The Dalles

Bend

Klamath Falls

Portland

Salem

Eugene

Roseburg

Medford

Astoria

Coos
Bay

84

26

20

95

395

20

26

395

97

197

26

20

97

97

84

82

205

5

30

26

101

20

5

199

101

Contents

Preface
to the Fifth Edition

Oregon is a surprising state with an incredible diversity of offerings, from some of the world's most beautiful beaches, rugged lava-chewed terrains, and snow-frosted mountains to expansive high desert and a network of streams and rivers that are sometimes soothingly peaceful and sometimes full of thundering white water.

Because of its diversity, Oregon is a place to be enjoyed by people of all ages, interests, and abilities, but especially by families. Whether camping in the forested Cascades or enjoying performances at the Oregon Shakespeare Festival or taking in views of the Willamette River from a comfortable berth in a paddle wheeler, there's something for everyone, and for every family.

While the basic attractions remain the same—places like Crater Lake and Cannon Beach, and events like the Pendleton Round-Up and Eugene Celebration—there are always new or modified attractions, motels, and restaurants that open and close. One of the goals of this fifth edition was to significantly update information to make it easier and more tempting to pile the whole family in the minivan or SUV and enjoy Oregon's many possibilities.

The Web is increasingly an important player for people searching for detailed information. But unless you're planning to tote along a laptop, it's not capable of providing the portability of a travel guide like this one. Try using this guide, and others, for both long-range planning and last-minute impulse decisions.

Sources for Oregon **Information**

Welcome to Oregon Web site: www.el.com/to/oregon. This site also has city pages with links to various local attractions.

Travel Oregon: (800) 547–7842, www.traveloregon.com.

State Park Campsite Reservations and Information: (800) 452–5687 for reservations; (800) 551–6949 for general information; www.oregonstateparks.org.

Bureau of Land Management in Oregon: www.or.blm.gov/recreation.htm

Junior **Rangers**

The Oregon State Parks and Recreation Department likes to keep kids interested in nature, and its Junior Ranger program provides activities to help stimulate the imagination while teaching kids to protect and enjoy our natural resources. Children ages six to twelve can participate in programs offered at most campgrounds and selected day-use parks that have staff or hosts on hand. A complete list of sites and more details about activities can be found online at www.oregonstateparks.org/juniorrangers.php, or call the general information line at (800) 551–6949.

Take advantage of visitor bureaus and chamber offices. The staff in these organizations are inevitably helpful and personable, and they are usually ready to provide suggestions on the best places to eat, stay overnight, or visit.

Researching the fifth edition has been inspiring because it serves as a reminder of all that's available, including places my family and I have enjoyed and places I realize we need to revisit or, more temptingly, sample for the first time.

—Lee Juillerat

Introduction

I've lived in Oregon most of my life and traveled extensively along its highways and back roads, yet I still have more to discover. I've always marveled at the variety to be found in this state—ocean, mountains, gently rolling pastures, verdant valleys, giant old-growth forests, sagebrush deserts, mesas and canyon lands, and wide stretches of volcanic wasteland. The opportunities for family adventure are just as varied and vast as the landscapes.

Oregon has far more attractions, amusements, and family fun opportunities than can possibly be covered in a book this size, but in the following pages I've included those that have stood the test of time—or the test of Cassidy, my daughter.

In addition to the specific attractions listed in the book, here are some ideas for family fun in just about any town in Oregon:

- Head over to family swim time at the local pool.
- Visit the police department, fire station, and city or county government center or courthouse (call first to see if they'll give you a tour).
- Join family hour at the roller-skating rink.
- Grab a lane at the bowling alley (most now have inflatable gutter guards to help little ones play).
- Tour a recycling center, local industry, fast-food franchise restaurant, hospital, post office, or television or radio station (call in advance).
- Visit a U-pick farm and gather berries, beans, or whatever's in season.
- In winter grab your mittens and scarves, don your warmest coats, and head for the nearest snow hill with sleds, inner tubes, or just a cardboard box.
- In summer find a swimming hole at the nearest stream, river, or lake (there are plenty in just about every corner of Oregon).
- Find a wide open space (no overhead wires and few trees) where you can fly a kite on a windy day.

We're looking forward to going back to many places and making more discoveries for family adventure in Oregon. I hope you'll contribute your ideas and experiences for future editions. Meanwhile, have fun!

—Cheryl McLean

RATES FOR LODGING	**RATES FOR RESTAURANTS**	**RATES FOR ATTRACTIONS**
$ up to $60	$ most selections $5 or less than $6	$ up to $5.99
$$ $61 to $80		$$ $6.00 to $10.99
$$$ $81 to $100	$$ most $6 to $10	$$$ $11 to $20
$$$$ $101 and up	$$$ most $11 to $20	$$$$ more than $20
	$$$$ most more than $20	

All prices and hours of operation are subject to change.

Attractions Key

The following is a key to the icons found throughout the text.

SWIMMING		**FOOD**	
BOATING / BOAT TOUR		**LODGING**	
HISTORIC SITE		**CAMPING**	
HIKING / WALKING		**MUSEUM**	
FISHING		**PERFORMING ARTS**	
BIKING		**SPORTS/ATHLETICS**	
AMUSEMENT PARK		**PICNICKING**	
HORSEBACK RIDING		**PLAYGROUND**	
SKIING/WINTER SPORTS		**SHOPPING**	
PARK		**PLANTS / GARDENS / NATURE TRAILS**	
ANIMAL VIEWING		**FARM**	

the North and Central Coasts

Oregon's Pacific Coast National Scenic Byway (U.S. Highway 101) follows the entire 400-mile coastal edge. To get a sense of the whole, plan at least four days to explore the many parks, waysides, lighthouses, and public beaches found along the north and central coasts. Within this stretch of broad sandy beaches and rocky headlands, you and your kids can experience the power of the Pacific Ocean, the lush natural beauty of coastal rain forests, and the fascinating animal and plant life found in tide pool wonderlands. Thanks to the foresight of the state legislature and the leadership of the late governor Tom McCall, who in 1967 enacted the Beach Bill, all of Oregon's beaches are open to the public. No individual can own any of the beaches in the state, so you're free to roam and explore. Oregon's shoreline is among the least populated in the country, too, so you can frequently find long stretches of beach where you're the only person in sight.

The Oregon coast is a popular vacation spot in the summer for locals and out-of-state travelers. Traffic on the winding scenic highway sometimes seems to crawl in the early afternoon. Try leaving for your destination by 9:00 A.M. to avoid waiting in traffic or in lines at tourist attractions. During the fall and winter, the coastal highway is less congested, lines shrink in restaurants and on beaches, and life gets a little more laid-back. Winter is also the best time to view the gray whale migration and to visit the many historical museums that enrich Oregon's coastal communities. And your kids might end up having the entire beach to themselves.

This region provides the backdrop for all kinds of family fun, but you should carry some essential ingredients with you: Frisbees and other things to toss to one another; simple pails with shovels for building sand castles and digging clams; kites to fly on blustery coastal days; blankets for relaxing on the sand; towels for drying off; snacks to replace the energy kids expend running on the beach; binoculars for spotting whales, birds, and other kinds of wildlife; and, of course, a bag of marshmallows for roasting when the sun goes down.

In several places along the coast, the position of the tide will make a difference in both enjoyment and safety. Pick up a tide table when you get to the area and use it to plan your tide-pooling, beachcombing, and hiking to ensure the maximum fun for your family.

THE NORTH AND CENTRAL COASTS

Astoria

Seaside

Cannon Beach

Manzanita

Rockaway Beach

Garibaldi

Tillamook

Lincoln City

Gleneden Beach

Depoe Bay

Newport

Waldport

Yachats

Safe Fun on the Beach

Keep in mind the following guidelines for beach safety and conservation. "Sneaker," or "rogue," waves are especially dangerous in areas such as jetties and rocky head-lands where obstructions cause waves to crash with greater force. Riptides and undertows can pull children as well as adults underwater and out to sea.

Driftwood also can present dangers. If you see a log drifting in the surf, stay well away, and keep away from piles of logs on shore when waves are nearby. It's legal to build fires on the beach, but remember: Never build a fire in a large pile of driftwood or near grassy slopes that could keep burning after you leave. Before you go, douse the fire with water or wet sand. Don't bury hot coals, because someone walking along shortly after you've gone could be burned. More safety tips can be found online at www.visittheoregoncoast.com; click on "Beach Safety."

Preserving the Coast for Everyone

The Oregon coast is a popular destination for tourists because of its natural beauty and the many recreational opportunities to enjoy along its shores. Explain to your children the importance of leaving everything as they find it. As the saying goes, take nothing with you but memories; leave nothing but your footprints in the sand.

The North Coast
Astoria

Astoria was the first settlement west of the Rocky Mountains, famous for being the place where Lewis and Clark ended their 3,700-mile journey. It remains an important shipping port. Huge ships pass daily under the bridge that crosses the 4.1-mile-wide Columbia River to Washington. On the waterfront you'll find piers to walk on and shops to browse in. At **Smith Point** you can watch the shipping activity from a large viewing deck just west of Pier 1. Kids love watching the enormous cranes at work, lift-ing whole railroad cars onto ships that make everything else in the vicinity seem minuscule.

Take a **Stroll**

The Riverfront Walkway at the historic Astoria Waterfront features an ever-changing parade of sea lions, birds, freighters, tugboats, and fishing vessels. It's the perfect place for a predinner walk with your active tod-dlers and preschoolers.

Top Astoria **Events**

April

Astoria-Warrenton Crab & Seafood Festival. This celebration of the sea's bounty is held at Hammond Mooring Basin. (800) 875–6807 or (503) 325–6311.

June

Scandinavian Midsummer Festival. This festival includes dances, food and craft booths, a beer garden, and performances by traditionally garbed singers and dancers. www.astoriascanfest.com.

June through July

Astoria Music Festival. This festival is held at the historic Liberty Theater in downtown Astoria and sponsored by River Theater. (503) 325–7487.

August

Clatsop County Fair. The fair is located in the Astoria fairgrounds and features carnival rides, games, exhibitions, and a tempting array of foods. (503) 325–4600.

Astoria Regatta. The century-old regatta is a week full of activities along the waterfront. Kids enjoy the demolition derby, Coast Guard drills, and boat races. (800) 875–6807; www.astoriaregatta.org.

October

Fort Stevens War Reenactment. People in period costumes reenact battles and camp life at the Fort Stevens Historic Area. (503) 861–2000; www.oldoregon.com.

November

St. Lucia Festival of Lights. The festival, held the day after Thanksgiving, celebrates the holiday season with an evening program honoring St. Lucia and featuring a dance. For information call (503) 325–6135 or visit www.astoriascanfest.com.

For information on Astoria events, call (800) 875–6807 or (503) 325–6311 or visit www.oldoregon.com.

Astoria Column (ages 5 and up)

**Reach Coxcomb Hill by driving south on Jerome Avenue and turning east onto Fif-
teenth Avenue; then continue to the park entrance at Coxcomb; (503) 325–2963;
www.oldoregon.com/Pages/AstoriaColumn.htm. Open daily dawn to dusk. $1.00 per
car donation.**

Built in 1926 for $32,550, this 125-foot landmark tower standing on the hill above the
town is a favorite with children. The mural painted on the monument's outside walls
tells the history of the area as it spirals upward. To get a good view of the other community landmarks, climb the 164 winding steps.

Heritage Museum (ages 8 and up)

**1618 Exchange Street; (503) 325–2203; www.clatsophistoricalsociety.com. Open daily
May through September 10:00 A.M.–5:00 P.M.; Tuesday through Saturday October
through April 11:00 A.M.–4:00 P.M. $ adults and children ages 6–17, under 6 free.**

The museum, run by the Clatsop County Historical Society, is housed in the 1904 City
Hall. The exhibits encompass all ingredients of the area's history—Native Americans,
fur traders, pioneer settlers, geology and natural history, and timber and maritime
industries.

Flavel House (ages 8 and up)

**441 Eighth Street and Duane Avenue; (503) 325–2203. Open daily May through Sep-
tember 10:00 A.M.–5:00 P.M., October through April 11:00 A.M.–4:00 P.M. $ adults and
children ages 6–17; $$$ family (up to three adults and four children).**

The Flavel House was built in 1885–87 by Captain George Flavel, the state's best-
known Columbia River bar pilot. You'll start your tour in the rehabilitated Carriage
House, which is now an interpretive center.

Fun Fact

The Astoria Column is the only large piece of memorial architecture
made of reinforced concrete. It was patterned after the famous Tra-
jan's Column in Rome. The pictorial frieze illustrates the history of the
Northwest Territory, from its discovery by Captain Gray to the arrival
of the Great Northern Railroad.

Fun Fact

The Columbia River bar is one of the most dangerous crossings in the world. When oceangoing vessels arrive at the river, they rely on the expert local river pilots to guide them across the bar.

Uppertown Fire Fighters Museum and Astoria Children's Museum (ages 5 and up)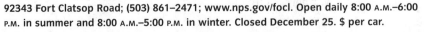

Thirtieth Street and Marine Drive; (503) 325–2203; www.ears.net/museum. Open Wednesday through Saturday 11:00 A.M.–2:00 P.M. $ adults and children ages 6–17, $$$ family, under 6 free.

The Uppertown Fire Fighters Museum has lots of kid appeal with its extensive collection of old firefighting equipment, including a horse-drawn fire wagon in use here in 1877.

Astoria Aquatic Center (ages 5 and up)

Twentieth Street and Marine Drive; (503) 325–7027; www.swimastoria.com. Open daily except Sunday; call for swim times. $ adults and children ages 2–17, $$$ family, under 2 free.

Opened in 1998, the Aquatic Center has four pools filled with nearly 200,000 gallons of water. Locker rooms are available for men and women, and parents with small children will appreciate the family changing rooms. The center also has a weight room, concession stand, waterslide, and "lazy river."

Columbia River Maritime Museum (ages 5 and up)

Seventeenth Street and Marine Drive; (503) 325–2323; www.crmm.org. Open daily 9:30 A.M.–5:00 P.M. $$ adults, $ children ages 6–17, under 6 free.

Founded in 1962, the museum was recently renovated, adding interactive exhibits and oral histories that bring maritime history to life. The museum houses many miniature ships and several full-size vessels, including a WWII navy destroyer. Call for information on monthly children's programs.

Fort Clatsop National Memorial (all ages)

92343 Fort Clatsop Road; (503) 861–2471; www.nps.gov/focl. Open daily 8:00 A.M.–6:00 P.M. in summer and 8:00 A.M.–5:00 P.M. in winter. Closed December 25. $ per car.

Transport your kids back to the early nineteenth century with a visit to Fort Clatsop, which contains an exact replica of the stockade used by explorers Lewis and Clark when they led their Corps of Discovery into this area in 1805.

An Adventure to Remember

Fort Clatsop National Memorial gives a lively lesson in nineteenth-century history and many rich details about the courageous Lewis and Clark expedition. From mid-June through Labor Day, buckskin-clad rangers demonstrate the art of candle making and canoe building and describe the trials of the thirty-three-member party who camped here in the winter of 1805–6. A replica of the explorers' 50-foot-by-50-foot fort is the center-piece of this 125-acre park. The rustic fort, a historic canoe landing, and a natural spring are surrounded by lush coastal forests and wetlands that merge with the Columbia River estuary. There is a visitor center with exhibits and audiovisual programs. Walking trails, which connect the visi-tor center, fort, and canoe landing, are about 1 mile in length and easy for preschoolers to navigate. Allow one to two hours to visit Fort Clatsop. At $5.00 per family, this is a best buy.

Fort Stevens State Park and Fort Stevens Historic Area (all ages)

Located 10 miles west of Astoria off US 101 at 100 Peter Iredale Road; (800) 551–6949 or (503) 861–3170; (800) 452–8657 for reservations; www.oregonstateparks.org. His-toric area open daily 10:00 A.M.–6:00 P.M. in summer and 10:00 A.M.–4:00 P.M. the rest of the year. Park hours vary. $ daily use fee or $$$$ annual permit for all state park day-use areas. Tours available for a nominal fee; call (503) 861–2000.

Fort Stevens State Park and the adjacent Fort Stevens Historic Area, which stretch north to the mouth of the Columbia River at Clatsop Spit, are well worth a visit, espe-cially in the summer months, when living history programs are offered.

Fort Stevens State Park encompasses sandy beaches, wetlands, forested areas of spruce and pine, and several shallow lakes. The largest of these, Coffenbury Lake, is popular with sailboarders, hikers, swimmers, and anglers. You can circle the lake on a 2-mile trail. The park's 8-mile system of paved bicycle trails is a real treat for par-ents with active children.

Fort Stevens Historic Area is the only mainland military installation to receive enemy fire since the War of 1812. An interpretive center displays photographs of the fort's guns in action. Access to the still-visible 1906 shipwreck of the four-masted British ship *Peter Iredale* is through the park campground, at the end of a 1-mile road and a trail that both lead to the beach.

Astoria Riverfront Trolley (ages 3 and up) 🏛

On the Columbia riverfront between the Port of Astoria and the East End Mooring Basin; (503) 861–1031; www.old300.org. Hours vary; generally 3:00–9:00 P.M. weekdays and noon–9:00 P.M. weekends. $.

Old Number 300, built in 1913 and restored as part of a long-term loan from the San Antonio Museum of Art, now carries passengers along the riverfront. A sheltered deck at the end of Sixth Street and the dock at Seventeenth Street provide views of the river and two Coast Guard cutters. The Fourteenth Street ferry dock includes interpretive displays.

Eco Cruises on the Columbia River Estuary (ages 10 and up) 🔺

354 Industry Street, on the docks at the west-end marina adjacent to the Red Lion Inn; (503) 325–6700 or (877) 717–1206. Two-hour waterfront and river cruise $$$$ adults, $$$ children 5–16, 4 and under free. Three-hour tours of the lower estuary and Cape Disappointment "Graveyard of the Pacific" or of the upper estuary and Lewis & Clark Wildlife Refuge $$$$ adults and ages 13–16, $$$ children 5–12, 4 and under free.

Fully narrated tours explore the rich local history and wildlife of the lower Columbia River estuary. The charter vessel *Shamrock* offers waterfront and river excursions every day beginning at 9:00 A.M. Sunset cruises leave the dock at 7:00 P.M.

Seaside

Seaside has been a haven for families since pioneer settlers in the Tillamook Bay area stopped over for a rest on their way home from Portland. In 1920 Seaside built the **Promenade,** now a pedestrian walkway atop a concrete wall, paralleling an 8,000-foot stretch of beach. At the center of the Promenade, or Prom, the **Turnaround** marks the point where Lewis and Clark ended their westward journey.

From the Turnaround, Broadway is lined with amusements such as bumper cars, shooting galleries, and video arcades. Locals refer to this street as "Million Dollar Walk," no doubt because of the millions of quarters that kids have wheedled out of their parents over the years.

Seaside **Pony Rides**

Faraway Farms (ages 10 and under). On Hamlet Road off US 101, immediately south of Seaside; (503) 738–6336. Call for appointments and prices.

Fun Fact

On December 8, 1905, Captains Meriwether Lewis and William Clark set up their winter quarters at Fort Clatsop, where they began preparations for the trip home. On December 28 Lewis and Clark sent five men to find a site for mining salt along the seacoast. Five days later the men set up camp at a site 15 miles southwest of the fort. The stones they stacked to create a furnace are all that remain of the site, and their authenticity was documented by the Oregon Historical Society in 1900. To reach the saltworks site, turn west on Avenue G from US 101 and follow the green signs to South Beach Drive and Lewis & Clark Way.

Seaside Aquarium (all ages)

200 North Promenade; (503) 738–6211; www.seasideaquarium.com. Open daily at 9:00 A.M.; call or check the Web site for closing times. $$ adults, $ ages 6–13, $$$ family (up to six), under 6 free with paid adult.

The aquarium is home to a room full of rowdy harbor seals. You can buy a bag of fish to throw to the barking, baying bunch. Touch tanks give kids an opportunity to get close to the tide pool denizens. There's also a rubbing table and an interpretive center.

The Seaside Museum and Historical Society (ages 5 and up)

570 Necanicum Drive at Fifth Street; (503) 738–7065; www.seasidemuseum.org/. Open daily the third weekend in March through October 10:00 A.M.–4:00 P.M., Sunday noon–3:00 P.M.; November until late March noon–3:00 P.M. $ adults and students 13–20, 12 and under free.

Lewis and Clark exhibits, along with Native American displays and depictions of the town's development as the ultimate family beach resort, charm parents and children alike. Kids love the photographs of Seaside's early bathing beauties.

Prom Bike Shop (all ages)

622 Twelfth Avenue; (503) 738–8251. Open daily 10:30 A.M.–5:30 P.M. Rental prices vary.

Explore Seaside on wheels—bicycles or in-line skates. You'll be amazed at the variety of transportation modes available from this rental shop—bikes, tandems, adult two-seater trikes, infant seats, strollers, skates, Rollerblades, scooters, and surreys (four-person pedal carts).

Seaside **Amusements** (ages 6 and up)

Amusement rides and arcades are found along Broadway—bumper cars, a carousel, and video arcades. A few miles south of town off US 101, you'll find miniature golf and go-carts. In addition, more fun can be found at these locations:

- **Outdoor Fun For All.** 407 South Holladay Drive; (503) 738–8447. Rollerblades and skates, electric bikes, lowriders, Seaside chariots, kayaks, trikes, and electric cars.

- **Interstate Amusement Co.** 110 Broadway; (503) 738–5540. Bumper cars, tilt-a-whirl, miniature golf, ice cream, and snacks.

- **Seaside Heli-Tours with Captain Jack.** Just south of Seaside on US 101; (503) 717–9796 or (503) 648–2831. Operated by Hillsboro Aviation.

- **Funland Entertainment Center.** 201 Broadway; (503) 738–7361. Saltwater aquarium, video games, pinball, shooting gallery, air hockey, pizza restaurant, and big-screen TV.

- **Town Center Mall.** 300 Broadway; (503) 738–6728. Indoor carousel.

- **Cannes Cinema.** 1026 Twelfth Avenue; (503) 738–0671. Local movie house.

- **Evergreen Lanes and Coffee Shop.** 3578 US 101 North; (503) 738–5333.

- **Sunset Empire Park & Recreation.** 1140 Broadway; (503) 738–3311. Year-round swimming pool, spa, recreation programs, and playground equipment.

Broadway Park (all ages) 🚻🌲

Located off Broadway at the east end of town along the banks of Neawanna Creek; (800) 444–6740. Free.

You'll find covered picnic shelters and plenty of games for your family to play here. In summer, as part of Lewis and Clark historical reenactments, you can participate in the forgotten art of salt making on the beach (at the end of Avenue U).

Top Seaside **Events**

February

Chocolate Lover's Festival. Pie-eating contest, dessert competition, chocolate carving, and lots of tasting.

July

Miss Oregon Pageant. This annual event charms many families who have never witnessed a beauty pageant live. (800) 394–3003.

Prom Walk & Beach Run. This midsummer event includes sand games and a Kids Downtown Bash.

September

Lewis & Clark Kite Exposition. Watch amazing stunt-kite demonstrations or try your hand at kite flying.

Sand Castle Contest. Two-day beach sculpting for both amateurs and pros.

For more information on these Seaside events, call (888) 306–2326 or (503) 738–3097.

Cannon Beach

Cannon Beach, like Rockaway Beach to the south, developed as a resort community. The town combines quaint old-time charm with a thriving cultural community, good restaurants, and interesting shops—all within view of the most picturesque stretches of beach in the state.

Haystack Rock (ages 5 and up)

One-half mile south of Cannon Beach off US 101; (503) 436–2623; www.cannonbeach .org (click on "Haystack Rock"). Always open, though cut off from land at high tide. Free.

This ocean landmark has graced many a calendar and coffee-table book. A designated marine garden and bird sanctuary, the 235-foot Cannon Beach Haystack is one of the world's largest freestanding monoliths. Enjoy the tide pools around its base, which are accessible at low tide. In summer, interpretive guides are on hand to help identify the many marine species visible at low tide.

Top Cannon Beach **Events**

April

Puffin Kite Festival. This festival includes a workshop for kids on how to make and fly kites. (800) 547–6100; www.surfsand.com.

June

Cannon Beach Sand Castle Day. Bring your sand-carving tools to this international event that offers cash prizes. (503) 436–2623, ext. 3; www.cannonbeach.org.

July through Labor Day

Sunday Concerts in the Park. Cannon Beach City Park, Second and Spruce Streets. Bring a picnic, spread out a blanket, and kick back and enjoy the music. (503) 436–2623; www.cannonbeach.org.

All Year

Coaster Theatre. 108 North Hemlock. This theater company hosts many productions with kids in mind. (503) 436–1242; www.coastertheatre.com.

Ecola State Park (all ages) 🛏️ 🚻
Two miles north of Cannon Beach just off US 101; (800) 551–6949; www.oregonstate parks.org. Open until dusk. Summer day-use fee $ or $$$$ annual state park pass.

This day-use area provides an incredible view from the picnic tables, where brazen seagulls will beg your kids for handouts. Children love exploring **Indian Beach,** a tiny cove littered with driftwood and rocks.

Fun Fact

Just a few miles north of Cannon Beach at the US 101 and State Highway 26 junction is the world's tallest Sitka spruce. Located in an old-growth fir and spruce forest in Klootchy Creek Park, the 216-foot-high tree has a trunk that is 52 feet in circumference. It's believed to be more than seven centuries old.

Other Things to See and Do
in Cannon Beach

It's almost impossible to visit Cannon Beach without wandering through its many attractive stores. Kids can buy trinkets and treasures at **Geppetto's Toy Shoppe,** 200 North Hemlock Street (503–436–2467), or experience some science fun at the **ExploraStore,** 164 North Hemlock Street (503–436–1844). You might even lure the children through some of the many art galleries in town with the promise of a stop at **Bruce's Candy Kitchen,** 256 North Hemlock (503–436–2641), where watching the taffy-pulling machines is mouthwatering, or the **Picnic Basket,** 162 Second Street at Hemlock (503–436–1470), where kids can enjoy ice-cream cones while you get a lift from a shot of espresso.

Sea Ranch Stables (ages 10 and up)

415 Fir Street at the back of Sea Ranch RV Park; (503) 436–2815; e-mail: searanch@ seasurf.net. Rides offered daily mid-June through Labor Day, 9:00 A.M.–4:30 P.M. $$$$ (prices vary by length of ride, forty-five minutes to two hours).

Reservations must be made in person at the stables. All rides are led by competent, experienced guides who strive to make each trip enjoyable and memorable. Horses are not available to take out on your own. Reservations are recommended, but walk-ins are welcome on a first-come, first-served basis. Rides vary from trips to Haystack Rock to special night excursions.

Mike's Bike Shop (all ages)

West of City Park on Spruce Street; (503) 436–1266 or (800) 492–1266; www.mikes bike.com. $$ to $$$ per hour; $$$$ weekly rates. Open daily 9:00 A.M.–6:00 P.M. mid-March through mid-September, 10:00 A.M.–5:30 P.M. daily except Wednesday the rest of the year.

You can rent bikes for all ages (infant trailers or bike seats for kids under three)—mountain bikes, tandems, and the classic whitewall "cruisers," as well as recumbent three-wheel tricycles that are great for use on the beach (only available during low tide). Younger children pedal their own tagalong "bikes" attached behind Mom or Dad. Mike's even rents strollers for use around town when the little ones are worn out.

Hug Point State Recreation Site (all ages) ⊕

Located 5 miles south of Cannon Beach off US 101; (800) 551–6949; www.oregonstate parks.org. Always open. Free.

This park, named for the way pioneers traveling the beach "highway" had to hug the point at low tide in order to pass, has caves and sections of the old road carved out of rock to explore, though these are cut off when the tide comes in.

Manzanita

One of the most delightful beaches on this stretch of the north coast is the lesser-known Manzanita, a small community that sits a few miles off US 101. Walk the beach in relative solitude, or blend the sound of pounding horse hooves with the pounding surf on a horseback ride along the shore (call **Pearl Creek Stables** at 503–368–5267). The solitude makes this a nice place to stay. Cafes, a few stores, and a small library are all nearby when you want to wander away from the beach.

Neahkahnie Mountain (ages 8 and up) ⊛

The trailhead is 0.5 mile off US 101, 1.5 miles north of Manzanita to hiker sign; turn east on rocky access road 0.5 mile to trailhead. Neahkahnie Mountain is in Oswald West State Park, which stretches to the north beyond Cape Falcon and Smuggler's Cove; (800) 551–6949; www.oregonstateparks.org. Free.

To get a bird's-eye view of the beach and bay, walk to the top of Neahkahnie Mountain, which rises 1,631 feet above the surf. The 1.5-mile trail takes you through forest and, in spring, beautiful wildflower meadows. Legend tells of buried treasure on the mountain, an enticing tidbit to entertain kids along the way. During World War II a Coast Guard sentry watched from the mountaintop for invaders. Allow an hour to get to the rocky summit, where children must use caution.

Oswald West State Park (ages 5 and up) ⊛ ⊛ ⊕

Located 10 miles south of Cannon Beach off US 101; (800) 551–6949; www.oregon stateparks.org. Free.

Strewn with red needles, the path through this enchanting rain forest is so peaceful that you can easily forget the ocean waves crashing on the cape just beyond. The trees form such a dense canopy that even if it's raining, you'll hardly notice. From the **Short Sand Beach** parking lot, follow a trail that parallels Short Sand Creek to where it merges with Necarney Creek at the ocean shore. Camping is for tents only because the sites are 0.25 mile away from the parking area. Wheelbarrows are provided for transporting your gear along paved pathways.

Fishing in Nehalem Bay

Nehalem Bay, according to locals, is one of the richest estuaries for both clamming and crabbing. If you don't have your own equipment, the following outlets can get you set up with buckets, shovels, and such.

Nehalem Bay fisheries (ages 10 and up). Rent crab rings or clam shovels as well as boats and motors from either of these fisheries:

Brighton Marina, 29200 North US 101, 3.5 miles south of Wheeler; (503) 368–5745. Call for hours. $$ for baited crab ring rentals to use on the dock. Boat rentals $$$$ for three hours and three baited crab rings.

Wheeler Marina, 580 Marina Drive, 2 miles south of Nehalem off US 101; (503) 368–5780. Call for hours. Boat rental $$$$ for three hours, $$ each additional hour; $ for crab rings; $ for bait.

Wheeler Marina (ages 10 and up)

580 Marine Drive, Wheeler; (503) 368–5858. Open daily year-round 8:00 A.M.–7:00 P.M. Single or double kayaks $$$ per hour, $$$$ half day and full day. Discounts available after 5:00 P.M. until dark and November through March. Price includes kayak, paddle, and life vest; shuttle service $$ per person per trip. Call for guided tour prices.

Beginners are welcome to try their hand at paddling the Nehalem Bay estuary. You'll receive brief training in how to safely get in and out of the kayak, how to paddle, and—most desirably—how to stay upright. You can paddle from the dock or be shuttled to a point upriver, then use the current to help you drift back to the marina.

Rockaway Beach and Garibaldi

Rockaway and Garibaldi are small towns whose livelihoods depend on the sea, but in very different ways. Rockaway grew up as a resort community, while Garibaldi, one of the earliest settlements on the coast, is very much a working community.

Rockaway Beach State Park (ages 5 and up) (⚓) (🏃)
Located right in the center of Garibaldi; (800) 551–6949; www.oregonstateparks.org. Call for hours and fees.

Rockaway Beach State Park is a great family spot for beachcombing, kite flying, and long walks.

Oregon **Coast Pass**

This multiagency pass covers entry, vehicle parking, and day-use fees at all state and federal fee sites along the entire Oregon coast. You can buy an annual pass valid for the calendar year for $25 or a twenty-four-month pass for $40. For more information or to purchase your pass by phone, call the Oregon State Parks Information Center at (800) 551–6949.

The passport covers entry for the following locations:

- Fort Stevens State Park
- Ecola State Park
- Nehalem Bay State Park
- Cape Lookout State Park
- Fogarty Creek State Recreation Area
- Heceta Head Lighthouse Viewpoint
- Honeyman State Park
- Shore Acres State Park
- Fort Clatsop National Memorial

- Oregon Dunes National Recreation Area
- Sutton Recreation Area
- Cape Perpetua Scenic Area
- Sand Lake Recreation Area
- Marys Peak Recreation Area
- Drift Creek Falls Trail
- Yaquina Head Outstanding Natural Area
- Hebo Lake

Fun Fact

Garibaldi was once the site of a Tillamook Indian whaling village. It was later explored by Captains Drake, Meares, and Cook and became a major lumber port and fishing village.

Garibaldi Marina and Boat Rentals (ages 8 and up) 🚲⛺
302 Mooring Basin Road; (800) 383–3828 or (503) 322–3312. Open daily 5:00 A.M.–5:00 P.M. $ for crab ring rentals; $$$$ for three-hour boat rentals, $$ each additional hour.

Rent crab rings at the Garibaldi Marina and catch your own appetizers. Boat rentals let you get out on the bay, and charters are available for deep-sea fishing.

Barview Jetty County Park (ages 8 and up) 🚲⛺
Located just north of Garibaldi off US 101; (503) 322–3522, (503) 322–0301 (chamber); www.garibaldichamber.com. Always open. Free.

This 160-acre park is a great place for surf fishing, and the beach to the north of the jetty gives the kids a place to roam. There are campsites available year-round as well.

Top Rockaway Beach and Garibaldi
Events

May
Rockaway Kite Festival. During the day kids get help from the Oregon Kiters Association in making their own kites. A teddy bear drop and hobby horse races add to lots of family-oriented fun. When the weather's right, a lighted kite flight in the evening requires blankets for snuggling together on the beach.

July
Garibaldi Days Festival. Includes fishing derby, crabbing derby, antique car show, dancing in the street, parade, and children's games in the park. (503) 322–0301; www.garibaldi.com.

September
Valley Annual Autumn Festival and Sand Castle Contest. This isn't a pros-only contest—kids are expected to join in. (503) 355–8108.

Memorial Lumberman's Park (ages 5 and up) 🏕️ 🏛️
Third and American Streets, Garibaldi; (503) 322–0301. Always open. Free.

For a picnic and a bit of local industrial history, stop by this park. Old logging donkeys and railroad equipment placed throughout the park invite children to climb.

Tillamook

Most Oregonians know about Tillamook, if only because of the delicious cheddar cheese to be found in every grocery store cold case. Tillamook is a small community, well inland from the ocean but enjoying the generally mild climate associated with the coast.

Tillamook Cheese Factory (all ages) 🍴
4175 US 101 North; (503) 815–1300; www.tillamookcheese.com. Open daily 8:00 A.M.– 8:00 P.M. in summer; 8:00 A.M.–6:00 P.M. the rest of the year. Free.

The Tillamook Cheese Factory is a favorite for all ages, with its free offerings of cheese samples. Be sure to take a quick tour to learn about the cheese-making process. Then stop by the deli to purchase a variety of packaged cheeses for vacation snacks or to send home, or choose from up to forty flavors of Tillamook ice cream.

Blue Heron Cheese and Wine Company (all ages) 🍴
Located 1 mile north of Tillamook off US 101; (503) 842–8281 or (800) 275–0639; www .blueheronoregon.com. Summer hours 8:00 A.M.–8:00 P.M.; winter hours 9:00 A.M.–6:00 P.M. Free.

Blue Heron is a less well-known (and less crowded) cheese company in the area that offers equally delicious samples of creamy Bries as well as home-smoked sausages. Blue Heron sells its products at an on-site deli-restaurant. Have a snack, then head for the petting farm on the premises, filled with goats, llamas, ducks, rabbits, cows, and sheep.

Money-Saving **Travel Tips**

- Be sure to ask if a complimentary breakfast is included in the hotel rate. Enjoying a simple continental breakfast with the children in the room is often more relaxing than dining out first thing in the morning.

- A room with a small refrigerator saves money when you load it up with fruit, juice, and yogurt for the kids to snack on.

Tillamook County Pioneer Museum (ages 5 and up)

2106 Second Street; (503) 842–4553; www.tcpm.com. Open Tuesday through Saturday 8:00 A.M.–5:00 P.M., Sunday 11:00 A.M.–5:00 P.M. $ adults and children.

This large museum contains more than 35,000 artifacts of pioneers and Native Americans who lived in this area and features a replica of the original stump house where Tillamook's first settler lived.

Tillamook Naval Air Station Museum (ages 5 and up)

6030 Hangar Road, 2 miles south of Tillamook off US 101; (503) 842–1130; www.tillamookair.com. Open daily year-round 9:00 A.M.–5:00 P.M. Adults $$, children 7–17 $, under 7 free.

This museum is enclosed inside a World War II blimp hangar, with fighter planes and blimps that are fascinating for kids. The largest clear-span wood building in the world, the hangar is as wide as a football field is long and stretches 1,072 feet from end to end. The ceiling is fifteen stories high—195 feet—making everything inside seem tiny by comparison. The hangar housed blimps that patrolled the ocean for enemy submarines during the war.

Cape Lookout State Park (all ages)

Located 12 miles southwest of Tillamook on Whiskey Creek Road; (800) 551–6949 or (503) 842–3182; (800) 452–5687 for camping reservations; www.oregonstateparks.org. Open daily year-round; $ day-use fee.

This is part of the **Three Capes Loop drive,** which takes you off US 101 for about 35 miles between Tillamook and Neskowin to view three outstanding natural areas. The park extends north along the Netarts Spit, which forms the boundary of Netarts Bay. Many campsites have ocean views or direct beach access. Yurts—canvas-walled circular buildings—and tepees are available to campers who aren't traveling with their own tents.

Cape Meares State Scenic Viewpoint (ages 5 and up)

Located 9 miles northwest of Tillamook via Whiskey Creek Road; (800) 551–6949; www.oregonstateparks.org or www.capemeareslighthouse.org. Open daily May through September 7:00 A.M. to dusk; lighthouse usually open 11:00 A.M.–4:00 P.M. April through October, weather permitting. Free.

The 1890 **Cape Meares Lighthouse** and the nearby giant spruce **Octopus Tree** are perennial favorites of kids. Oregon's largest seabird colonies thrive at **Three Arch Rocks National Wildlife Refuge** offshore, where species include common murre, tufted puffin, storm petrel, and pigeon guillemot.

Cape Kiwanda State Natural Area (ages 5 and up) 🏕️

Located south of Cape Lookout, 15 miles southwest of Tillamook on Whiskey Creek Road; (800) 551–6949; www.oregonstateparks.org. Day use only. Free.

You can watch Pacific City dories launch if you're here early in the morning, but it's even more fun to be standing on the beach just south of the park when they're heading for shore. They head straight for the sand, riding to ground on high waves.

Munson Creek Falls (ages 5 and up) 🚶

Located about 6.5 miles south of Tillamook on US 101; (503) 842–7525. Always open. Free.

Here you'll find a trailhead that takes you through old-growth forest to the highest waterfall (266 feet) in the Oregon Coast Range. The 1.5-mile road into the small parking area is pretty rough, but the 0.25-mile walk to the falls is worth the ride. Another 0.5-mile trail leads to an upper viewpoint.

The Central Coast

Lincoln City

The largest of the coastal resort towns, Lincoln City has almost 8 miles of wide-open sands where families can walk, fly kites, jump over waves, and soak up the sun or—since this is, after all, the Oregon coast—the rain. With fifteen beach access spots in town, you'll have no problem finding your way onto the sand.

Devil's Lake has an interesting history, according to Indian folklore. Once known as Indian Bay, the lake was supposedly inhabited by an evil spirit, and sometimes Siletz warriors mysteriously disappeared in it. The legend remains that if a boat crosses the moon's reflection in the center of the lake, the passengers will feel a chill of fear rise up from the water.

Connie Hansen Gardens (ages 8 and up) 🚶

1931 Northwest Thirty-third Street; (541) 994–6338; www.conniehansengarden.com. Open daily 9:00 A.M.–5:00 P.M. Free, but donations appreciated.

Constance P. Hansen was well-known within the regional horticultural community. She moved to Lincoln City in 1973 and developed a one-acre plot with her own hybrid and exotic plants, converting an overgrown marshland meadow and creek into a showcase for more than 300 varieties of rare rhododendrons as well as azaleas, primroses, Siberian and Japanese irises, and hardy perennials. She trained as a botanist at UC Berkeley. Today the Connie Hansen Garden Conservancy, a group of

Fun Facts

Lincoln City is the Kite Capital of the World, because kites are frequent sky decorations, especially along the beach around the D River. **Catch the Wind Kite Shop,** 266 Southeast US 101 (541–994–9500; www.catch thewind.com), south of the D River wayside, sells kites of all shapes and sizes for parents and kids who want to try their own hand at kite flying.

The D River is the world's shortest river, flowing from Devil's Lake a brief 120 feet to the ocean.

dedicated volunteers, continues to plant and tend the garden, guides visitors, and conducts horticulture classes.

Lincoln City Skateboard Park (ages 10 and up)

Behind Kirtsis Field on Northeast Twenty-second Street and US 101; (541) 994–8378 or (800) 452–2151. Always open. Free.

Lincoln City's skateboarders' oasis in Kirtsis Park has been named one of the "gnarliest" parks in the United States. The 8,000-square-foot facility has more than a hundred lines and a unique 9-foot bowl to challenge boarders of all levels. It is the site of the Board Games Skateboard Tournament, a competition for professionals, amateurs, and beginners held in September and October. A second park, a short distance from the first, is currently underway and is covered to enable boarding in bad weather.

Pacific Northwest Surfing Museum (ages 12 and up)

Located inside the Lincoln City Surf Shop at 4792 Southeast US 101; (541) 996–7433. Free.

If your li'l dudes are into hanging ten, they'll enjoy a quick stop at this in-store museum, which has some twenty-five surfboards on display, along with newspaper articles, posters, books, videos, club jackets, and other paraphernalia from the history of surfing in the Northwest.

Fun Fact

Cascade Head is home to the Oregon silverspot butterfly, listed as a threatened species. It's known to only five other locations in the world.

North Lincoln County Historical Museum (ages 5 and up) 🐘
4907 Southwest US 101; (541) 996–6614; www.northlincolncountyhistoricalmuseum
.org. Call for times. Free, but donations accepted.

Housed in the old fire hall, the museum's rooms are set up as they would have looked in the early days of the pioneers. Displays include a variety of Native American baskets and beadwork as well as a hands-on table with pioneer and Native American artifacts that kids can handle, plus puppets and coloring activities. Most summer Thursday afternoons offer oral history or film archive presentations.

Devil's Lake **Parks** (all ages)

Six parks offer recreation on Devil's Lake, from fishing and boating (in daylight, of course) to camping and picnicking. Call for hours and fees: (800) 551–6949, (541) 994–8378, or (541) 994–2131.

Blue Heron Landing, 4006 West Devil's Lake Road (541–994–4708), has plenty of choices for water play. Canoes, paddleboats, bumper boats, and motorboats are available for rent by the day or by the hour.

Regatta Park is located on Devil's Lake, 0.75 mile east off US 101 on Regatta Park Road. You can take advantage of a 0.5-mile exercise and jogging path while your kids try out the playground equipment, then visit the Interpretive Center or explore the walking trails.

Sand Point Park, located off East Devil's Lake Road on a point of land jutting into the lake, has a swimming beach and picnic tables.

Devil's Lake State Park, 1452 Northeast Sixth Drive, has camping facilities straddled between the lake and the ocean. It's open year-round, and you can make reservations in advance by calling (800) 452–8657. Check out the new wetland ecology trail, still being developed.

Holmes Road Park, on Holmes Road, 8 blocks off US 101. A small dock allows access to the lake, and the picnic tables in this little park have a great view.

East Devil's Lake Park, located near the southern tip of the lake on East Devil's Lake Road near the Factory Stores @ Lincoln City. There's a boat dock here, and a moderately difficult 0.5-mile hike takes you through natural forestland.

Top Lincoln City **Events**

June
Cascade Head Music Festival. Held at St. Peter the Fisherman Lutheran Church. Classical music; no children under 5. (541) 994–5333 or (877) 994–5333; www.cascadeheadmusic.org.

Summer Kite Festival. Another kite extravaganza that offers prizes for the best children's kites, among other categories.

Late Summer
Sand Castle Competition. Fun in the sand for the whole family. If you aren't up to sculpting your own, you can watch the pros at work.

October
Fall Kite Festival. D River Wayside. The biggest and most spectacular of Lincoln City's annual events. Kids are thrilled by skydivers gliding on gigantic kitelike, colorful parachutes; kite battles and team choreography; and nighttime lighted kite flying.

October through May
Glass Float Search. From October through Memorial Day, handblown glass floats by local artisans are hidden above the high-tide level. If you find one, take it to the Visitor Center (801 Southwest US 101) for a certificate and description of the artist.

For information about Lincoln City events, call (800) 452–2151 or (541) 996–1274; www.oregoncoast.org.

Ocean Trails Riding Stables (ages 8 and up)
Located in Neskowin, 8 miles north of Lincoln City; (541) 994–4849 or (503) 392–5841. Beach rides June through September $$$$ per hour; pony walks year-round $ for fifteen minutes or $$$ per hour.

Call a few days ahead of time for reservations. Rides are offered year-round, and a new indoor arena provides space for lessons and winter pony rides.

Super Shopping
Factory Stores @ Lincoln City

US 101 at East Devil's Lake Road; (541) 996–5000 or (866) 665–8680; www.tangeroutlet.com. Open Monday through Saturday 10:00 A.M.–8:00 P.M., Sunday 10:00 A.M.–6:00 P.M.; daily 10:00 A.M.–6:00 P.M. January and February. No discussion of activities in Lincoln City can ignore the presence of this mammoth shopping center. The collection of big-name factory stores includes at least a few to keep the kids happy: **K.B. Toy Liquidators, OshKosh B'Gosh, Carter's Childrenswear, Children's Place Outlet, Gap Kids,** and the **Book Warehouse.** There's also an ice-cream shop tucked in the mall, offering rewards for patience and good behavior!

Cascade Head (ages 5 and up)

Located 4 miles north of Lincoln City at the west end of Three Rocks Road; (503) 392–3161 or (541) 994–5564; http://nature.org. Open dawn to dusk. Free.

An area of outstanding scenic beauty just 4 miles north of Lincoln City, Cascade Head is a haven for rare plants and offers hiking trails to suit all ages. Within the **Cascade Head Experimental Forest and Scenic Research Area,** two trails maintained by the Nature Conservancy and two USDA Forest Service trails take you through a variety of ecosystems, and on one a self-guiding brochure lets your child be the guide, pointing out old-growth Sitka spruce or the scars left by forest fires.

Taft Waterfront Park (all ages)

Located at the mouth of the Siletz River, off Fifty-first Street on the south side of town. Open dawn to dusk. Free.

Sea lions often congregate here and across the river on the northern edge of the Salishan Spit, which forms the south edge of the Siletz River mouth. A small parking area has restrooms, and **Mo's Restaurant** (541–996–2535), famous for its clam chowder, lies just up the street. Crabbing is good October through February, off the public crabbing dock adjacent to the restaurant. Rent crab rings from **Eleanor's Undertow** (541–996–3800), a restaurant and take-out at 869 Southwest Fifty-first Street, for $10 for twenty-four hours, including bait, bucket, and gauge.

Gleneden Beach

Here you'll find a small marketplace ideal for browsing or picking up picnic supplies, a golf course, and a resort that makes any trip to the coast very special. **Westin Salishan Lodge** (888–725–4742 or 503–764–3600; www.salishan.com), a well-known five-star resort, has something for the whole family: tennis courts, swimming pool, exercise room, large whirlpool spa, sauna, nature walks, jogging path, playground, and video arcade.

Depoe Bay

A little fishing village that claims the world's smallest harbor, Depoe Bay sits midway between the larger towns of Lincoln City and Newport. From the bridge it's fun to watch the boats navigate the narrow, rocky channel that leads into the tiny harbor. Your kids will be more fascinated by the spouting horns, a pair of ocean-driven geysers that spout plumes of water with the crashing of the waves, especially at high tide or after a storm. Watch out, though—if the waves are strong, you're in for a dousing!

Tradewinds Charters (all ages)

Located at north end of the bridge in Depoe Bay; (800) 445–8730 or (541) 765–2345; www.tradewindscharters.com. Whale-watching tour: $$$ adults and teens, $$ ages 5–12, under 5 free.

To experience the passage from the deck of a boat, try a whale-watching or fishing charter trip.

Fogarty Creek State Recreation Area (all ages)

Two miles north of Depoe Bay on US 101; (800) 551–6949; www.oregonstateparks .com. Day use only. $ fee or $$$$ annual state park pass.

This is a beautiful spot to spend the day. You can walk on the path alongside the creek as it lazily winds through the park, crossing picturesque arched footbridges at several points. Spread out a picnic feast at the charming cove where Fogarty Creek meets the sea, and explore the tide pools at low tide.

Top Depoe Bay **Event**

September
Depoe Bay Annual Indian Style Salmon Bake. Sample delicious salmon prepared on alder stakes over open fire pits. The Siletz Dancers often perform traditional tribal dances for this event. (877) 485–8348 or (541) 765–2836.

Super Shopping
Siletz Tribal Smokehouse

272 US 101 South in Depoe Bay; (541) 765–3349; www.oregonsmoked foods.com. You can purchase mouthwatering smoked chinook or coho salmon as well as a variety of other foods and gift items here.

Rocky Creek State Park (ages 5 and up) 🐘 🛖 🚫
Two miles south of Depoe Bay; (800) 551–6949. Call for hours and fees.

Rocky Creek offers an excellent viewpoint for whale watching. Sitting on a bluff over the ocean, the day-use park has picnic facilities as well as broad areas of grass where the kids can run and play.

Newport

This central Oregon coast community has developed a successful tourist industry that works hard to give people experiences worth coming back for. Fishing, centered at the **Newport Bayfront,** is still one of the town's economic mainstays. **Nye Beach,** which became a beloved vacation spot at the turn of the twentieth century, still has the lingering feel of an old-fashioned neighborhood and boasts several small cafes and shops to explore.

Oregon Coast Aquarium (ages 5 and up) 🐘
2820 Southeast Ferry Slip Road; (541) 867–3474; www.aquarium.org. Open daily 9:00 A.M.– 6:00 P.M. in summer and 10:00 A.M.–5:00 P.M. in winter. $$ ages 4 and older, children under 4 free. Behind-the-scenes tours $$ ages 14 and older, $ children 4–13.

The twenty-nine-acre state-of-the-art aquarium is an impressive complex nestled on the south shore of Yaquina Bay. Everything is geared to give your children an educa-

Super Shopping

On Saturdays May through October, you can pick up fresh organic produce, cut flowers, catch-of-the-day seafood, and local arts and crafts at the Newport Saturday Market. Open 9:00 A.M.–1:00 P.M. in the Armory parking lot behind City Hall; park on Ninth Street. (541) 574–4040.

tional experience they'll only remember as fun. A favorite with kids of all ages is watching the otters float on their backs as they dine on crustaceans and other goodies at feeding time. On busy summer weekends it's a good idea to reserve tickets in advance or purchase them at the Lincoln City Visitors Center (801 US 101 South).

Aquarium Village (all ages) 🅐⊖

Located just south of the Oregon Coast Aquarium and east of US 101; (800) 867–6531 or (541) 867–6531; e-mail: aqvill@charterinternet.com.

Renovated industrial units have been transformed into a unique collection of specialty shops and artist studios for live glassblowing demonstrations to candle making, award-winning gourmet chocolates to clothing and antiques. Here are a few family favorites:

Pyromania Glass Studio. (541) 867–4650; daily 10:00 A.M.–6:00 P.M. Watch glassblowing demonstrations then browse through the Gallery of Contemporary Glass Works, featuring a variety of blown, kiln-formed, and lamp-worked glass pieces from various West Coast artists.

Pegasus European Style Gourmet Chocolates. (541) 867–3855; open Tuesday through Saturday 10:00 A.M.–5:00 P.M. Homemade candies and chocolate delicacies.

Alex's Cafe. (541) 867–6002; open weekdays 7:00 A.M.–2:00 P.M., weekends 8:00 A.M.–2:00 P.M. Country breakfast all day, plus burgers, chowder, and fish and chips for lunch.

Top Newport **Events**

May

Loyalty Days and Sea Fare. This gala four-day event celebrates patriotism with a carnival, a parade, military ship tours, and lots of food and fun.

Glastonbury Renaissance Faire. Held in South Beach State Park, this annual event is sponsored by the Oregon Coast Cultural Association. (888) 701–7123 or (541) 265–9231.

July

Rope in some good-old family fun at the annual **Lincoln County Fair and Rodeo.**

For information on these and other Newport events, call (888) 628–2101 or (541) 574–2679 or visit www.newportchamber.org.

Whale-Watching Sites

Volunteers are usually stationed at the sites below to help you spot migrating whales during the peak migration seasons—the last two weeks in March and late December through early January. For specific dates and more information on the giants of the ocean, visit www.whalespoken .org or call (541) 765–3407 or (800) 551–6949.

- Ecola State Park
- Neahkahnie Mountain Historic Marker on US 101
- Cape Meares State Scenic Viewpoint
- Cape Lookout State Park (2.5-mile hike to site at the tip of the cape)
- Inn at Spanish Head lobby on the tenth floor
- Boiler Bay State Scenic Viewpoint
- Depoe Bay Sea Wall
- Rocky Creek State Scenic Viewpoint
- Cape Foulweather
- Devil's Punchbowl (Otter Rock) State Natural Area
- Yaquina Head Lighthouse
- Yaquina Bay State Recreation Site
- Seal Rock State Recreation Site
- Yachats State Park
- Devil's Churn Viewpoint

- Cape Perpetua Overlook
- Cape Perpetua Interpretive Center
- Sea Lion Caves Turnout (large US 101 turnout south of tunnel)
- Umpqua Lighthouse, near Umpqua Lighthouse State Park
- Shore Acres State Park
- Face Rock Wayside State Scenic Viewpoint
- Cape Blanco Lighthouse, near Cape Blanco State Park
- Battle Rock Wayfinding Point, Port Orford
- Cape Sebastian
- Cape Ferrelo
- Harris Beach State Park, Brookings

Mark O. Hatfield Marine Science Center (ages 5 and up)
2030 Southeast Marine Science Drive, south side of Yaquina Bay and east of US 101; (541) 867–0271; hmsc.orst.edu/visitor. Open daily 10:00 A.M.–5:00 P.M. in summer and 10:00 A.M.–4:00 P.M. the rest of the year. Free, but donations appreciated.

This is a terrific, long-beloved option for coastal education. Your children will love the touching pool, where they can have close encounters with starfish, sea urchins, anemones, sculpins, and the deliciously yucky sea cucumber. The resident octopus is another favorite.

Ripley's Believe It Or Not (ages 7 and up)
Wax Works (ages 7 and up)
Undersea Gardens (ages 8 and up)
Located at Mariner Square, 250 Southwest Bay Boulevard; (541) 265–2206; www .marinersquare.com. All open daily 9:00 A.M.–8:00 P.M. July and August, 10:00 A.M.– 6:00 P.M. June and September, generally 10:00 A.M.–5:00 P.M. the rest of the year. Admission to each center: $$ adults, $ ages 5–12, under 4 free. Combo rates for all three: $$$ adults, $$ children.

You can pay one admission price to enjoy all three attractions or pick a favorite. Our family's favorite has always been the **Undersea Gardens,** located across the street on the bayfront. Call ahead to find out the schedule for the diver who adds an extra dimension to the show.

Bike Newport (ages 5 and up)
152 Northeast 6th Street; (541) 265–9917; www.bikenewport.net. Hours are10:00 A.M.– 6:00 P.M. year-round; closed Sunday. Basic rental rates $$ per hour, $$$$ per day; discounts for rentals of three or more days and weekly rates available.

This bike shop is close to the beach access at Nye Beach and features fun cycles, fat-tire strollers for the beach, road bikes, tandems, mountain bikes, freestyle bikes, and helmets for trail riding, touring, or sightseeing. The shop can help fit bikes for all ages and sizes.

Yaquina Head Outstanding Natural Area (ages 6 and up)
Two miles north of Newport off US 101; (541) 574–3129; www.yaquinalights.org. Open dawn to dusk daily. Lighthouse and Interpretive Center open 10:00 A.M.– 4:00 P.M. daily. $$.

Visitors are in for a real treat here. During whale migrations there's often a park ranger on hand with strong binoculars or a spotting scope to help you see them. During summer some resident gray whales have taken to feeding offshore. You can also get a look at a wandering sea lion or, on the rocks below, some offshore bird species, such as the elusive tufted puffin or the endangered guillemot. Wheelchair-accessible tide pools and an interpretive center make this a place for everyone to enjoy. The **Yaquina Head Lighthouse** is a 93-foot-high tower that stands 162 feet above sea level, making it Oregon's tallest lighthouse. You can tour the authentically refurbished 1873 lighthouse year-round, weather permitting.

Marine Discovery Tours (ages 8 and up) ⚠ 🐘

345 Southwest Bay Boulevard; (541) 265–6200 or (800) 903–2628; www.marinediscovery .com. Call for hours. (The Chamber of Commerce can provide a list of other charter services; call 800–262–7844 or visit www.coastvisitor.com.) Two-hour Discover tour Sealite cruise $$$$ adults, $$$ ages 4–16, under 4 free. More adventuresome *Oregon Rocket* one-hour wave-jumping tour $$$$ adults; $$$ ages 8–16.

To see the whales up close, a number of tour operators take charter trips into the ocean for whale watching and offer both a one-hour bay tour and a two-hour whale-watching cruise. Marine Discovery Tours has a naturalist on board who leads the kids in fun learning activities during the two-hour ride.

Free Things to Do in Newport

Clamming (ages 8 and up)

South Beach Marina. Under the bridge adjacent to the marina. Clamming is popular in the bay's tide flats during spring and summer minus tides (check the tide tables). This spot gives the best access to gaper clams. Grab a shovel and bucket, roll up your jeans, and get ready to have a ball and make a mess. Be sure to check that there isn't a red tide, a rare occurrence in Oregon but potentially fatal.

Beachcombing (ages 5 and up)

Agate Beach. Located on the north edge of town off Ocean View Road. Agates are commonly found among the loose gravel on top of the sand, especially in off-season months, from October to April. From Agate Beach you've got a clear stretch of beach leading north to **Yaquina Head** or south to **Yaquina Bay.**

Yaquina Bay State Park. Located at the north end of Yaquina Bay, just west of US 101. Park on the bluff below the historic lighthouse, then enjoy a picnic, walk the trail down to the beach, or throw a fishing line into the surf off the north jetty (be very watchful of children on the jetty—sneaker waves can be dangerous).

Newport Marina at South Beach (ages 8 and up) 🦀

2122 Southeast Marine Science Drive; (541) 867–4470. Open daily 7:00 A.M.–6:00 P.M. $ per day for crab rings; $$$$ for four-hour boat rental with three crab rings, $$$$ for full day.

This South Beach marina rents crab rings at its store and at the fuel dock. The long public pier adjacent to the marina is a perfect place to toss your rings into the water and wait for those delicious Dungeness crabs to take the bait.

Newport Visual Arts Center (ages 8 and up) 🎵

777 Nye Beach Turnaround; (888) 701–7123 or (541) 265–6540; www.coastarts.org. Open Tuesday through Sunday 11:00 A.M.–6:00 P.M. April through October, 11:00 A.M.–5:00 P.M. the rest of the year. Free, but donations welcome.

The center looks out over a renovated beach access area, with benches and an attractive walkway to Nye Beach. It offers exhibits of local artists, touring exhibits, and frequent workshops.

Newport Performing Arts Center (ages 8 and up) 🎵

777 West Olive; (541) 265–2787, (541) 265–9231, or (888) 701–7123; www.coast arts.org. Call for hours, prices, and schedule of events.

The Newport Performing Arts Center brings touring companies into the community and also presents local productions, with several directed at family audiences.

Oregon Coast History Center (ages 5 and up) 🏛

545 Southwest Ninth Street; (541) 265–7509. Open Tuesday through Sunday 10:00 A.M.–5:00 P.M. in summer, 11:00 A.M.–4:00 P.M. in winter. Free, but donations appreciated.

The Lincoln County Historical Society operates both the **Log Cabin Museum** and the **Burrows House.** The 1895 Victorian Burrows House includes Native American, maritime, and coastal settlement exhibits. The professionally designed exhibits draw from some 40,000 artifacts in the center's collection.

U.S. Coast Guard Station (ages 8 and up) 🏛

Located on the east end of Bay Boulevard on the Newport waterfront; (541) 265–5381. Open daily 1:00–4:00 P.M. Free.

You will get a strong sense of the Coast Guard's role on the Oregon coast here, both past and present. It's also a great chance for your kids to learn about ocean safety as well as the Coast Guard's dramatic rescue capabilities.

Fun Fact

At Yaquina Head, you'll see the world's first barrier-free tidal zone. It was constructed in an old quarry site, with gently sloping paths winding around the tide pools, the perfect alternative for parents with strollers as well as for people who are physically challenged.

Yaquina Bay Lighthouse/State Park (all ages) 🚻 🏛

8465 Southwest Government Street at the north end of the bay bridge; (541) 867–7451, (541) 574–3129, or (800) 551–6949; www.yaquinalights.org. Lighthouse open 11:00 A.M.– 5:00 P.M. daily in summer and on weekends, noon–4:00 P.M. the rest of the year. Park is day use only. Free, but donations are welcome for the lighthouse.

Built in 1871, the lighthouse is Newport's oldest building. It operated for only three years before giving way to the more powerful lighthouse at Yaquina Head. Your kids will appreciate the tale of the lighthouse "ghost"; look for a pamphlet at the museum that tells the story.

Devil's Punchbowl State Natural Area (ages 8 and up) 🚶 🍴

Located 8 miles north of Newport off US 101; (800) 551–6949; www.oregonstateparks .org. Day use only. Free.

This park is on Crest Loop Drive and has picnic facilities and a walking trail to a view of the punchbowl, a wave-carved rock bowl that fills from a cavern below as the tide thunders in. Another trail leads to the marine gardens, an area of tide pools that is perfect for exploring during low or minus tides (indicated with a minus sign on the tide table). It can be hazardous during high tides, however, so keep an eye on the water level. This is also a popular whale-watching site.

Seal Rock State Recreation Site (ages 8 and up) 🌊 🐃

Located 10 miles south of Newport on US 101; (800) 551–6949 or (888) 628–2101. Free.

This lovely park sits atop a bluff next to Seal Rock, a large basalt sea stack just offshore. Picnic tables are nestled along narrow forest paths that lead to the beach below.

Waldport

Waldport means "port of the woods" in German. The early settlers in this Alsea River basin were Germans who came for the brief gold rush and then stayed to develop the timber industry.

Alsea Bay Bridge Interpretive Center (ages 8 and up)

620 Northwest Spring Street, on US 101 just south of the Alsea Bay Bridge; (541) 563–2002 or (800) 551–6949; www.oregonstateparks.org. Open daily in summer, Wednesday through Sunday the rest of the year, 9:00 A.M.–5:00 P.M. Daily bridge tours at 2:00 P.M. Free.

In the center you'll learn the old bridge's story through photographs and a short video. Once the longest cement-poured bridge in the world, it was torn down in 1992 and rebuilt to be more structurally sound.

Attractions kids will appreciate include a model replica of the old bridge, displays on the history of transportation, a powerful viewing scope trained on the new bridge, and exhibits about the Alsi Indians who once lived in this area. You can also participate in clamming and crabbing demonstrations; times and locations vary with the tides.

Top Waldport **Events**

June
Beachcomber Days. These fun-filled days include a sand castle contest, a treasure hunt, slug races, and a parade.

September
Valley Alsea Bay Crab Festival. This event features a crab-ring toss, a crab-catching contest, crab races, and, of course, a crab feed.

For information call (541) 563–2133 or visit www.waldport.org.

Fantastic Facts about Oregon

- Nearly half of Oregon's 97,073 square miles is forested.

- Oregon has more than 5,800 registered campsites. (Call 800–551–6949 for a copy of the state campground guide.)

- Oregon is one of the very few states that still has no sales tax—it's a shopper's paradise for visitors.

- Oregon is one of only two states (New Jersey is the other one) that don't allow motorists to pump their own gasoline—so sit back, relax, and let someone else do the work!

Yachats

Practice pronouncing the name of this tiny coastal town before you venture any questions to the locals. It's "YAH-hots," and it comes from the local tribe of Chinook Indians and is said to mean "dark waters at the foot of the mountain."

Little Log Church Museum (ages 5 and up) 🏛️

Corner of Third and Pontiac Streets; (541) 547–3976. Open daily except Thursday, noon–3:00 P.M. weekdays, 10:00 A.M.–4:00 P.M. Saturday and Sunday. Free, **although donations are welcome.**

This tiny museum houses an interesting collection of Native American artifacts as well as pioneer tools and household items, such as a one-hundred-year-old crazy quilt, teddy bears, fossils, and a molar from a wooly mammoth.

Yachats Ocean Road State Natural Site (ages 5 and up) 🚶

Located immediately south of Yachats, 500 feet off US 101; (800) 551–6949; www .oregonstateparks.org. Day-use area. Free.

Access to a wide sandy beach begins here along a 1-mile loop road. Tide-pooling is great on the rocks that edge the ocean shore. But be very careful, and venture onto these rocks only when the tide is well out. Sneaker waves—especially during winter months—can be deadly, and the rocks can be slippery.

Smelt Sands State Recreation Site (ages 5 and up) 🚶

Located at the north end of Yachats; (800) 551–6949. Day-use area. Free.

Both a whale-watching viewpoint and a great kids-oriented hiking trail, this area is located about 0.5 mile north of town along the oceanfront. From the parking area you can take the **Yachats 804 Trail,** 0.75 mile one way. The trail is wheelchair accessible, so even your youngest will manage the easy, level terrain. It leads along a cliff top above odd-shaped rocks that eroded from the twenty-five-million-year-old Yaquina Formation. The beach is not quite a mile from the trailhead.

Cape Perpetua Scenic Area (ages 5 and up) (⚇)

Three miles south of Yachats; (541) 547–3289; www.fs.fed.us/r6/siuslaw. Visitor center open daily 9:00 A.M.–5:00 P.M. in summer. Call for winter hours and whale-watching information. Day-use fee is $ per vehicle; covers Oregon Dunes National Recreation Area and all of Cape Perpetua.

One of the most beautiful areas on the coast—and the highest point along the Oregon coast—Cape Perpetua winds along coastal cliffs that jut straight up from the ocean. Stop by the **visitor center,** which contains exhibits that explain local geological features, give whale-watching tips, present local history, and describe Native American culture. Maps are available for the area's 23 miles of hiking trails. The **Giant Spruce Trail** leads for 1 mile to a massive 500-year-old Sitka spruce.

Devil's Churn Viewpoint, just north of the junction at Cape Perpetua Road and US 101, is a day-use area with trails near the viewpoint that take you down to the rocks below, where the surf at high tide churns in the deep chasm and crashes onto the rocks, throwing sea spray onto everything around—including tourists who get too close! Enjoy the view at high tide from above, which is now a wheelchair-accessible viewpoint. Several other scenic overlooks and turnoffs in this area give you access to sandy beaches, picnic spots, tide pools, and hiking trails.

Family Favorites on the North and Central Coasts

1. Astoria Aquatics Center
2. Fort Clatsop National Memorial, Astoria
3. Haystack Rock Marine Garden, Cannon Beach
4. Tillamook Cheese Factory
5. Tillamook County Pioneer Museum
6. Cascade Head, near Lincoln City
7. Oregon Coast Aquarium, Newport
8. Yaquina Bay Lighthouse, near Newport
9. Cape Perpetua Scenic Area, near Yachats
10. Devil's Churn Viewpoint, near Yachats

Where to Eat

IN ASTORIA

Mr. Fultano's Pizza. 620 Olney; (503) 325–2855. Fultano's has old-fashioned pizzas, Italian and Mexican dishes, hamburgers, and a salad bar. They'll even deliver to your hotel room. $$

Pier 11 Restaurant & Lounge. 77 Eleventh Street; (503) 325–0279. Almost all tables here offer a view of the river and frolicking sea lions and seals. Seafood specialties; breakfast, lunch, and dinner; children's menu. $–$$$

IN CANNON BEACH

Cannon Beach Bakery. 240 North Hemlock; (503) 436–0399. Danish family traditions are kept alive and featured at this bakery. Try the eight-grain and crusty Haystack breads. There is also a daily offering of sweet treats. $–$$

Dooger's Seafood & Grill. 1371 South Hemlock Street; (503) 436–2225. Casual dining well-suited for families with young children. Pick up a clam chowder kit to take the tastes of Cannon Beach home with you. $–$$

Lazy Susan Cafe. 126 North Hemlock Street; (503) 436–2816. A cheerful cafe in a brick courtyard off the main street in downtown Cannon Beach. Highly recommended for breakfast waffles and omelettes. $–$$

IN AND AROUND LINCOLN CITY

McMenamin's Lighthouse Brewery Pub and Restaurant. Located in the Roads End shopping center, 5157 North US 101; (541) 994–7238. The Lighthouse Brewery has burgers, fish and chips, and other kid-oriented fare on the children's menu as well as local ales for Mom and Dad to try. $–$$$

Mo's Restaurant. 860 Southwest Fifty-first Street at Taft Waterfront Park; (541) 996–2535. This popular seafood coastal chain is a can't-miss with little ones. $–$$

60s Cafe. 4157 Northwest US 101, #139; (541) 996–6898. Nostalgic diner with good burgers. $

IN MANZANITA

Big Wave Café. Highway 101 and Laneda Avenue; (503) 368–9283. The Wave offers a wide variety of tasty favorites. It's favored by locals, who especially appreciate the meat loaf served each Wednesday. $–$$

Marzano's Pizza Pie. 60 Laneda; (503) 368–3663. Gourmet fresh pizzas featuring house-made Italian sausage and dough made fresh daily. $–$$

IN NEWPORT

April's at Nye Beach. 749 Northwest Third; (541) 265–6855. Fresh ingredients and great homemade desserts are a plus for this casual restaurant with an ocean view. $$–$$$

Chowder Bowl at Nye Beach. 728 Northwest Beach Drive; (541) 265–7477. Heaping bowls of chowder make this the perfect stop for lunch. $–$$

Georgie's Beachside Grill. 744 Southwest Elizabeth Street; (541) 265–9800; www.georgiesbeachsidegrill.com. The grill offers great oceanfront views, and its tasty breakfast menu ranges from the traditional to tasty surprises. $–$$

Rogue Ales Public House. 748 Southwest Bay Boulevard; (541) 265–3188. Although technically a pub, families are welcome during meal hours. There's a special menu for kids, and adults can enjoy tasting some local microbrews. The brewery and another restaurant are located under the bridge on the south side of the bay. $–$$

IN SEASIDE

Dooger's Seafood & Grill. 505 Broadway; (503) 738–3773. Famous for its rich clam chowder. Wonderful desserts might extend the dinner hour for your family. Breakfast, lunch, and dinner. Children's menu available. $$–$$$

Vista Sea Cafe. 150 Broadway; (503) 738–8108. Casual lunch and dinner fare for the whole family. Pizza, soup, and sandwiches are the specialties here. Clam chowder is a local favorite, but beware—they run out early. $–$$

IN YACHATS

The Joe's Java Depot Creation. 262 US 101 North; (541) 547–4287. You'll find fresh-baked muffins and scones and homemade soups at this breakfast and lunch spot. $–$$

The Landmark Restaurant. 256 Ocean View Drive; (541) 547–3215. Open for breakfast, lunch, and dinner with a sweeping view of the surf, this restaurant was selected as one of twenty-three "best fish dives" in the nation by *Coastal Living* magazine. $–$$$

Where to Stay

IN AND AROUND ASTORIA

Crest Motel. 5366 Leif Erickson Drive; (503) 325–3141 or (800) 421–3141 (for reservations only); www.crestmotelastoria .com. Forty rooms on a picturesque hilltop overlooking the Columbia River. Continental breakfast, spa, coin laundry. $$–$$$

Fort Stevens Campground. Ten miles west of Astoria off US 101; (800) 452–5687; www.oregonstateparks.org. Oregon's third–largest campground. $–$$

Rosebriar Hotel. 636 Fourteenth Street; (800) 487–0224 or (503) 325–7427; www.rosebriar.net. This small historic hotel overlooking the Columbia River was once a convent. Some kitchenettes, complimentary breakfast. $$–$$$

Shilo Inn. 1609 East Harbor Drive, Warrenton; (800) 222–2244 or (503) 861–2181; www.shiloinns.com. Restaurant, some kitchenettes, indoor swimming pool, hot tub, sauna, and fitness center. $$–$$$$

IN CANNON BEACH

Blue Gull Inn. 632 South Hemlock Street; (800) 507–2714 or (503) 436–2714; www .bluegullinn.com. Just a few steps away from the beach. Two-bedroom suites and cottages are ideal for families. $$$–$$$$

McBee Motel Cottages. Check in at the Sandtrap Inn at 539 South Hemlock Street; (866) 262–2336 or (503) 436–2569; www .mcbeecottages.com. Cottages a block from the beach and a short walk to downtown. Some kitchens and fireplaces. Well-mannered pets are welcome. $$–$$$

RV Resort at Cannon Beach. 345 Elk Creek Road; (800) 847–2231 or (503) 436–2231; www.cbrvresort.com; e-mail: info@cbrvresort.com. This facility offers the closest camping in the Cannon Beach area and has a kids' playground, an indoor pool and spa, and summer Saturday night weenie roasts. $

Schooner's Cove Inn. 188 North Larch Street; (800) 843–0128 or (503) 436–2300; www.schoonerscove.com. Beach access and ocean views from private decks. A variety of rooms and suites with fireplaces, fully equipped kitchens, and VCRs. Oceanfront lawn features gas barbecues, picnic tables, and chaise lounges. $$$$

Sea Ranch RV Park. 415 Fir Street; (503) 436–2815; e-mail: searanch@seasurf.net. Horseback riding is available in the summer at Sea Ranch. Set in a grassy park. Some cabins available. $–$$

The Waves Motel. 188 West Second Street; (800) 822–2468 or (503) 436–2205; www.the wavesmotel.com. Above the beach in the heart of town. Kitchens, fireplaces, and views. $$$–$$$$

Vacation Rentals:
An Alternative to Motels

All along the Oregon coast, you can find a home away from home through a variety of vacation rental agencies. You'll be amazed at the options—from small beach cottages and condos to oceanfront luxury homes. These privately owned homes are furnished, have well-stocked kitchens so you don't have to eat all your meals in restaurants, and are often equipped with family fun extras, such as games, bicycles, hot tubs, and barbecues. Here are several agencies, organized from north to south.

- **Oceanside Vacation Rentals.** 43 North Holladay, Seaside; (800) 840–7764; www.oceanside1.com; e-mail: oceanside@freedomnw.com.

- **Cannon Beach Vacation Rentals.** 3363 South Hemlock, Cannon Beach; (866) 436–0940 or (503) 436–0940; www.visitcb.com; e-mail: info@visit cb.com.

- **Manzanita Rental Company.** 686 Manzanita Avenue, Manzanita; (800) 579–9801 or (503) 368–6797; www.manzanitarentals.com; e-mail: mrc@nehalemtel.net.

- **Ocean Paradise Vacation Rentals, Inc.** P.O. Box 535, Lincoln City, 97367; (800) 362–5229 or (541) 994–7028.

- **Dolphin Real Estate.** 547 Southwest Seventh Street, Newport; (800) 365–6638 or (541) 265–6638.

- **Bayshore Rentals, Inc.** 2214 Northwest Bayshore Drive, Waldport; (800) 752–6321 or (541) 563–3162; www.bayshorerentals.com; e-mail: rentals@bayshore-rentals.com.

- **Ocean Odyssey Vacation Rentals.** 261 North US 101, Yachats; (800) 800–1915 or (541) 547–3637; www.odysseyvacations.org; e-mail: yachats@odysseyvacations.org.

IN GARIBALDI

Bayshore Inn. 227 Garibaldi Avenue; (503) 322–2552 or (877) 537–2121; e-mail: information@bayshoreinn.org. Refrigerators, microwaves, and free movies. Pets welcome. $$

IN GLENEDEN BEACH

The Westin Salishan. 7760 US 101 North; (800) 452–2300 or (541) 764–2371; www .salishan.com; e-mail: reservations@ salishan.com. Ocean beaches about 0.5 mile away. Pets allowed. Five-star golf resort on 750 acres with tennis courts, swimming pool, exercise room, large whirlpool spa, sauna, nature walks, jogging path, playground, and video arcade. Three restaurants offer the best in Oregon coast cuisine. $$$$

IN LINCOLN CITY

Lakeshore. 4006 Devil's Lake Road; (541) 994–4702. Next door to Blue Heron Landing, this is the only lodging on Devil's Lake. Kitchenettes and lake views. $–$$

Oceanfront Inn. 2855 Northwest Inlet; (541) 994–8901 or (800) 889–7037. Oceanfront lodging on miles of walking beach with low access. Budget-priced rooms and apartments. Balconies, fireplaces, kitchenettes. Walking distance to restaurants, casinos, shops. Pets allowed. $$–$$$$

Seagull Motel. 1511 Northwest Harbor; (541) 994–2948 or (800) 422–0219; www.seagullmoteloregon.com; e-mail: seagullmotel@charterinternet.com. Oceanfront motel with low beach access. Large variety of rooms with kitchens and private spas. Small pets welcome. $$–$$$$

IN MANZANITA

Nehalem Bay State Park. Nehalem Bay; (800) 452–5687; www.oregonstateparks .org. A children's playground, showers, and a boat ramp into the bay are among Nehalem Bay State Park's amenities. On the beach you can walk 6 miles to the end of the spit at the mouth of the river, where you might see Roosevelt elk, migrating whistler swans, or harbor seals. $

Spindrift. 114 Laneda; (877) 368–1001 or (503) 368–1001; www.spindrift-inn.com. This charming inn is just a block from the beach. Some kitchenettes; pets welcome. Cafe has varied menu. $–$$

IN NEWPORT

Beverly Beach State Park. Located 7 miles north of Newport on the landward side of US 101; (800) 452–5687 for reservations; (541) 265–9278 or (800) 551–6949 for information; www.oregonstateparks .org. Primitive campsites and facilities for electrical or full hookup. Yurt camping available. Open year-round. $

Shilo Oceanfront Resort. 536 Elizabeth Street; (800) 222–2244 or (541) 265–7701. Offers a wide variety of rooms and sizes, all with ocean views. Pets welcome. In-room refrigerator, microwave, coffeemaker. $$–$$$$

South Beach State Park. About 2 miles south of Newport; (800) 452–5687 or (541) 867–4715; www.oregonstateparks .org. Hiker/biker sites and facilities for electrical or full hookup. Yurt camping also available. $

Viking's Condominiums and Cottages. 729 Northwest Coast Street; (800) 480–2477 or (541) 265–2477; www.vikings oregoncoast.com. Twenty-four condominiums and fourteen cottages. Kitchenettes, oceanfront rooms, family units. Stairs to beach, heated outdoor pool, and spa. $$$–$$$$

The Waves of Newport Motel and Vacation Rental Houses. 820 Northwest Coast Street; (800) 282–6993 or (541) 265–

4661; www.wavesofnewport.com; e-mail: info@wavesofnewport.com. Some kitchens, ocean view, close beach access, skateboard park across the street, and free continental breakfast, coffee/tea, fruit, and popcorn. $$–$$$

IN ROCKAWAY BEACH

Jetty Fishery RV Park & Marina. 27550 US 101 North; (800) 821–7697 or (503) 368–5746; www.jettyfishery.com; e-mail: jettyfishery@nehalemtel.net. Riverside park at the mouth of the Nehalem River. Boat and canoe rentals year-round. $

Tradewinds Motel. 523 North Pacific Street; (503) 355–2112 or (800) 824–0938; www.tradewinds-motel.com. Fifty feet from edge of the beach. Children's playground on beach side of motel. Oceanfront rooms have fireplaces, refrigerators, and coffeemakers. Pets allowed. $$–$$$

IN WALDPORT

Beachside State Recreation Site. Located about 3 miles south of Waldport off US 101; (800) 452–5687 for reservations; (800) 551–6949 or (541) 563–3220 for information; www.oregonstateparks .org. Open mid-March through October, this park provides sheltered campsites with a measure of privacy not always found in coastal campgrounds. A separate day-use picnic area lies across a small stream. A section of the Oregon Coast Trail, connecting Yachats and Waldport, passes through the campground. Yurts also available. $

Cliff House Bed and Breakfast. 1450 Adahi Street; (541) 563–2506; www.cliff houseoregon.com; e-mail: innkeeper@cliff houseoregon.com. Located south of Waldport just off US 101, this beautiful little house sits atop the cliff, with decks and a sunroom and even an all-glass gazebo, where you can enjoy your morning coffee

with an incredible view but without being buffeted by the coastal winds. $$$–$$$$

IN YACHATS

Fireside Resort Motel. P.O. Box 313, 1881 US 101 North; (800) 336–3573 or (541) 547–3636. Kitchenettes; coffeemaker and fridge in all rooms. Oceanfront rooms. $$–$$$

Shamrock Lodgettes Resort and Spa. 105 US 101 South, next to the Yachats Ocean Road Wayside; (800) 845–5028 or (541) 547–3312; www.shamrocklodgettes .com. Offers family-size cabins nestled on parklike grounds near the ocean. Each cabin has a fireplace, and some are equipped with kitchens or Jacuzzi tubs. Spa, sauna, and exercise room. Pets accepted. $$–$$$$

Wayside Lodge. 5773 US 101 North; (541) 547–3450; www.casco.net/~wayside. All units a stone's throw from the beach. Kitchenettes. Swings and large lawn area make this inexpensive spot ideal for families with young kids. $$–$$$

For More Information

Astoria-Warrenton Area Chamber of Commerce. P.O. Box 176, 111 West Marine Drive, Astoria, OR 97103; (800) 875–6807 or (503) 325–6311; www.old oregon.com; e-mail: awacc@seasurf.com.

Astoria-Warrenton Highway 101 Visitor Center. 143 South US 101, Warrenton, OR 97146; (503) 861–1031.

Cannon Beach Chamber of Commerce. P.O. Box 64, Second and Spruce Streets, Cannon Beach, OR 97110; (503) 436–2623; www.cannonbeach.org; e-mail: chamber@ cannonbeach.org.

Central Oregon Coast Association. P.O. Box 2094, Newport, OR 97365; (800) 767–2064 or (541) 265–2064; www.coastvisitor .com; e-mail: coca@coastvisitor.com.

The Confederated Tribes of Siletz Indians. 201 Southeast Swan Avenue, Siletz, OR 97380; (800) 922–1399 or (541) 444–2532; www.ctsi.nsn.us.

Depoe Bay Chamber of Commerce. P.O. Box 21, 70 Northwest US 101, Depoe Bay, OR 97341; (541) 765–2836 or (877) 485–8348; www.depoebaychamber.org; e-mail: dbchamber@newportnet.com.

Garibaldi Chamber of Commerce. P.O. Box 915, 235 Garibaldi Avenue, Garibaldi, OR 97118; (503) 322–0301; www.garibaldi chamber.com; e-mail: info@garibaldi chamber.com.

Greater Newport Chamber of Commerce. 555 Southwest Coast Highway, Newport, OR 97365; (800) 262–7844 or (541) 265–8801; www.newportchamber .org; e-mail: chamber@newportnet.com.

Lincoln City Visitor & Convention Suite Bureau. 801 Southwest US 101, Suite 1, Lincoln City, OR 97367; (800) 452–2151 or (541) 996–1274; www.oregoncoast.org; e-mail: info@oregoncoast.org.

Oregon Coast Visitors Association. P.O. Box 74, 137 Northeast First Street, Newport, OR 97365; (888) 628–2101 or (541) 574–2679; www.visittheoregoncoast.com; e-mail: info@visittheoregoncoast.com.

Rockaway Beach Chamber of Commerce. P.O. Box 198, 103 South First Street, Rockaway Beach, OR 97136; (503) 355–8108; www.rockawaybeach.net; e-mail: info@rockawaybeach.net.

Seaside Visitors Bureau. 7 North Roosevelt, Seaside, OR 97138-6825; (888) 306–2326 or (503) 738–3097; www.seasideor .com; e-mail: visit@seasideor.com.

Tillamook Chamber of Commerce. 3705 US 101 North, Tillamook, OR 97141; (503) 842–7525; www.tillamookchamber.org; e-mail: tillchamber@oregoncoast.com.

Waldport Chamber of Commerce and Visitors Center. P.O. Box 669, 620 Northeast Spring Street, Waldport, OR 97394; (541) 563–2133; www.waldport-chamber .com; e-mail: chamber@peak.org.

Yachats Area Chamber of Commerce and Visitors Center. P.O. Box 728, 241 US 101, Yachats, OR 97498; (800) 929–0477 or (541) 547–3530; www.yachats.org; e-mail: info@yachats.org.

the
South
Coast

The dramatic scenery of Oregon's south coast varies from the vast dunes around Florence to the sandstone cliffs south of Coos Bay and the myriad sea stacks dotting the shore near Brookings, the state's "Banana Belt." Less populated than the north or central parts of the coast, this area is ideal for family getaways. Your adventures can take you on dune-buggy rides, hikes through redwood and old-growth myrtlewood forests, and visits to a wildlife petting park, a dinosaur-infested rain forest, and a garden where the plants themselves are carnivores.

Originally populated by adventurers seeking gold dust that washed ashore or was swept down mountain streams, the towns on the south coast quickly turned to the ocean and the forests for economic viability. Tourism now joins these primary industries as communities develop the resources that attract visitors from around the country. Even the weather has become a drawing card: Brookings, just 6 miles from the California border, claims the mildest, sunniest weather on the Oregon coast, while Bandon touts itself as the "Storm Watching Capital" to encourage wintertime visits.

Florence

In the last several years, Florence's Old Town has been revitalized with an influx of boutiques, cafes, restaurants, and other attractions. Around Florence you can enjoy all kinds of recreation on more than a dozen lakes covering some 10,000 acres and on several hiking trails.

Westward Ho! Sternwheeler (ages 5 and up)
1377 Bay Street, next to Mo's Restaurant; (541) 997–9691; www.westward-ho.com. Departs 11:00 A.M., 1:00 P.M., 2:00 P.M., and 3:00 P.M. May through September. One-hour trips: $$$ adults, $$ ages 12 and under. Half-hour trips: $$ adults and ages 12 and under.

THE SOUTH COAST

Florence

Winchester Bay • • Reedsport

Charleston • North Bend
Coos Bay

Bandon •

Port Orford •

Gold Beach •

Brookings

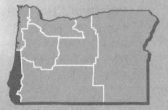

Take the 65-foot *Westward Ho!* sternwheeler for a one-hour or half-hour trip up the Siuslaw River. In the summer kids enjoy sitting on the boat's top level as the frontier sternwheeler chugs upriver. Lunch and dinner cruises are also available by reservation only.

Old Town Gazebo Park (all ages)

Located on Bay Street at the end of Laurel Street; (541) 997–3128. Always open. Free.

This small public park has a boat dock that's fenced to keep kids from falling into the Siuslaw River. Take the opportunity to throw a fishing line or a crab ring in here.

Siuslaw Pioneer Museum (ages 5 and up)

85294 US 101 South, just south of the Florence bridge in an old barn-shaped church; (541) 997–7884. Open Tuesday through Sunday noon–4:00 P.M. in summer, 10:00 A.M.–2:00 P.M. October through February; closed Thanksgiving through January. $ adults, children under 16 free.

The museum displays trace the area's past, including exhibits on home life, a general store, and the fishing, farming, logging, and shipbuilding industries. A large dugout canoe found at the mouth of the river is a central feature in the museum's collection. The Siuslaw and Siletz trading baskets are beautiful in their simplicity and utility.

Dolly Wares Doll Museum (ages 5 and up)

3620 US 101; (541) 997–3391. Usually open Tuesday through Sunday 10:00 A.M.–5:00 P.M. $ adults and children 5–12, under 5 free.

You'll be amazed at the variety within the collection. From a pre-Columbian clay figure to high-fired porcelain from China, the dolls attest to a common human need to play at parenting. If your child has a broken doll, you can bring it here for repair and restoration.

Siltcoos Lake (all ages)

Located 6 miles south of Florence on the east side of US 101; (541) 997–3128. Always open. Free.

The largest lake in Florence, it covers more than 3,000 acres. You can rent watercraft from pedal boats to motorboats, canoes to jet skis.

Super Shopping

Old Town Florence, located at the waterfront below the Siuslaw River Bridge (US 101), is a charming, quiet spot to explore antiques stores, art galleries, and gift and specialty shops.

Fun Fact

Florence marks the exact north–south center of the Oregon coast. It is also the start of the largest expanse of sand dunes in the United States, stretching 50 miles south to Coos Bay.

Woahink Lake (all ages)

Located just north of Siltcoos Lake; (541) 997–3128. Always open. **Free.**

Woahink is the first lake south of town and offers swimming, waterskiing, and fishing.

Jessie L. Honeyman State Park (all ages)

Located 3 miles south of Florence; (541) 997–3641 or (800) 551–6949 for information; (800) 452–5687 for campground reservations; www.oregonstateparks.org. $ day-use fee.

This park spans a diverse natural landscape, from ocean and sand dunes to lake and forest. On the east side it's bordered by 350-acre Woahink Lake. Cleawox Lake, which covers a mere 87 acres, is the perfect size for paddling around in; you can rent boats at the lodge. The west side of the lake is a big sand dune that's ideal for kids to run down and into the water. Six miles of hiking trails wind through the 522-acre park.

Honeyman Park Lodge (ages 5 and up)

(541) 997–2118 or (541) 997-3641. Open daily in summer; call for hours and prices.

Rent canoes, rowboats, kayaks, or pedal boats for Cleawox Lake and purchase snacks here.

Fun Fact

Dave Barry made Florence famous with his report of an actual—he was not making this up—exploding whale. When confronted with what to do about a 45-foot-long, eight-ton beached whale, the Oregon Highway Department decided the situation called for a half ton of dynamite. Pieces of whale carcass landed everywhere—including on the many spectators who'd gathered to watch!

Sea Lion Caves (ages 5 and up)

Located 11 miles north of Florence at 91560 US 101 North; (541) 547–3111; www.sea lioncaves.com. Open daily 9:00 A.M., 8:00 A.M. July and August; closing hours vary. $$ ages 16 and older, $ ages 6–15, under 5 free.

After walking down stairs and a ramp to the elevator, you'll descend nearly 200 feet to the largest sea cave in North America, with a two-acre base and a 125-foot vaulted ceiling. Depending on the time of year, you might see a hundred or more Steller (northern) sea lions in the cave—or just a few. Find out what to expect at the gift shop.

Oregon Dunes National Recreation Area (ages 5 and up)

Begins in Florence and continues south on the coast to Coos Bay Visitor Center at the junction of US 101 and State Highway 38; (541) 271–3611; www.fs.fed.us/r6/siuslaw/odnra.htm. Visitor center open 8:00 A.M.–4:30 P.M. daily in summer. The $ day-use fee also covers the Cape Perpetua National Scenic Area.

Oregon Dunes National Recreation Area (ODNRA) will make your kids gape with wonder at this seemingly endless sandbox containing thirty lakes, thirteen campgrounds, and more than 10,000 acres of sand. ODNRA stretches from Florence to Coos Bay, with a number of dune access roads, campgrounds, and day-use picnic areas along the way. Ten miles south of Florence is the **Oregon Dunes Overlook,** a nicely constructed series of viewpoints overlooking the dunes. In summer guided tours are offered. The area is crisscrossed by fourteen hiking trails; maps are available at the visitor center.

Family Favorites on the South Coast

1. Oregon Dunes National Recreation Area, Florence to Coos Bay
2. Jessie L. Honeyman State Park, near Florence
3. Dean Creek Elk Viewing Area, Reedsport
4. South Slough National Estuarine Research Reserve, Charleston
5. Shore Acres State Park, near Charleston
6. Coquille River Museum, Bandon
7. Umpqua Discovery Center, Reedsport
8. Bandon State Park–Face Rock Wayside
9. Cape Blanco State Park, near Port Orford
10. Samuel H. Boardman State Scenic Corridor, Brookings

C & M Stables (ages 8 and up)

Located 8 miles north of Florence at 90241 US 101 North; (541) 997–7540. (Call ahead for reservations.) Open daily year-round 10:00 A.M.–dusk in summer, 10:00 A.M.–4:00 P.M. in winter. $$$$; $$ for a ten-minute corral ride for children 5 and under.

Rent a horse for any skill level and ride on the beach or dune trails. You can keep the horses out until dusk, which allows time for enjoying the ocean sunset on horseback.

Hiking/Cycling around Florence

You can enjoy miles of off-road hiking or cycling trails around Florence. Here are four trails that you can explore by foot or on wheels.

- **Threemile Lake Trail.** 14 miles south of Florence on the west side of US 101. This 7-mile round-trip trail offers great scenery with some hills to climb on the way.

- **Siltcoos Lake Trail.** 7 miles south of Florence on the highway's east side. The trail takes you 2.25 miles through a sixty-year-old forest to the lake.

- **Sutton Creek Trail.** 3 miles north of Florence on the west side of the highway. You'll find at least 5 miles of assorted, mostly flat trails.

- **Valley/China Creek Trail.** 13.5 miles north of Florence on the east side of the highway. This area offers great photo opportunities on about 2 miles of flat trail with a picnic area about 1 mile in at the site of an old homestead.

Darlingtonia State Natural Site (ages 5 and up) 🚻 🚷

Located 5 miles north of Florence, 0.25 mile off US 101 on Mercer Lake Road; (541) 997–3128 or (800) 551–6949; www.oregonstateparks.org/park_115.php. Call for hours. Free.

Here's something to delight the gore-loving imagination of many a youth. A loop trail overlooks thousands of carnivorous plants that flourish in the marshy area of this eighteen-acre park. *Darlingtonia californica,* better known as the cobra lily or pitcher plant, lures insects with a sticky, sweet-smelling nectar, then traps and eats them.

Crosswind Air Tours (ages 8 and up)

Located at the Florence Airport, 2000 Airport Way; (541) 991–6822. Operates sunrise to sunset, weather permitting. Half-hour and fifteen-minute tours $$$$ for up to three people.

The pilot can take up to three passengers at a time on flights overlooking the lakes, coastal forests, and ocean. You might even spot migrating whales.

Sandland Adventures Family Fun Center (ages 8 and up) 🚷

85366 US 101, located less than 1 mile south of Florence; (541) 997–8087; www .sandland.com. Open daily 9:00 A.M.; closing hours vary according to season. Dune-buggy tours $$–$$$$; self-driven rentals $$$$ per hour.

While the older members of the family hit the beach in a mini-rail buggy, parents can take turns staying behind with younger ones to play miniature golf or ride in bumper boats or go-carts. The whole family can take a tour in open-air dune buggies that seat a driver and four to five passengers or in the giant dune buggy for large groups.

Top Florence **Events**

May

Rhododendron Festival. Florence's yearly event draws thousands who enjoy arts and crafts, floral displays, 5K and 10K runs, parades, and more. (541) 997–3128; www.florencechamber.com.

September

Chowder Blues and Brews Festival. This event welcomes fall with a chowder cook-off, live music, arts and crafts, and microbrew tasting. A carnival in Old Town is just the ticket for the kids. (541) 997–3128 or (541) 997–1994.

Reedsport

Home to the Oregon Dunes National Recreation Area headquarters, Reedsport is close to several freshwater lakes and often-overlooked campgrounds that are filled with wax myrtle and huckleberry bushes. It might be one of the few areas along the coast that offer a measure of outdoor privacy in the summer.

Umpqua Discovery Center (ages 5 and up)

409 Riverfront Way, off US 101; (541) 271–4816; www.umpquadiscoverycenter.com; e-mail: umpquadiscoverycenter@charterinternet.net. Open daily 9:00 A.M.–5:00 P.M. in summer, 10:00 A.M.–4:00 P.M. rest of year. $ adults and children ages 6–15, under 6 free. Family ticket $$ for two adults and up to three children.

The center opened in 1993 and has developed an impressive exhibit area designed to educate visitors about the local geography, geology, and relationships between people and the environment. Kids love the periscope and computerized information stations. A new interactive exhibit wing explores the unique cultural history of tidewater towns, where life revolved around whether the tide was coming in or going out. The natural-history wing features area geology and the changing landscape. A working weather station helps kids learn about maritime climates.

Loon Lake Recreation Area (all ages)

Located east on State Highway 38, about 20 miles east of Reedsport; (541) 599–2254 for information; (888) 242–4256 for campground reservations. Call for hours and fees. Always open. $ day-use fee per vehicle or walk-in; $ boat launch.

Created by a major landslide about 1,400 years ago, the area is now a popular summertime spot for swimming, camping, waterskiing, and fishing. When it's foggy on the coast in the summer, locals often head here to find the sun. Throughout the summer park rangers offer interpretive programs and nature walks. **Loon Lake Lodge** (541–599–2244) offers boat rentals, cabin and room rentals, and a boat dock.

Umpqua Lighthouse State Park (ages 5 and up)

Located 6 miles south of Reedsport, less than 1 mile off US 101; (541) 271–4631 or (800) 551–6949; (800) 452–5687 for campground reservations; (541) 271–4118 for yurt or cabin reservations; www.oregonstateparks.org. $, children under 12 free.

Here's a gem tucked in a rolling coastal hillside covered with fir, Sitka spruce, and hemlock, with huckleberry and rhododendron creating a lush understory. At the center of the park is tiny **Lake Marie,** with a sandy beach near a picnic area. Hiking trails circle the lake and lead to the beach, passing a viewpoint overlooking the large Punch Bowl area of the Oregon Dunes. Yurts and log cabins are available to rent, in addition to RV and tent camping spaces.

Top Reedsport **Events**

June through September
Riverfront Rhythm Summer Concerts. Held on the grounds of the Umpqua Discovery Center most Friday evenings from mid-June through mid-September, starting at 6:30 P.M.

July
Reedsport Ocean Festival. Kite-flying contests, old-time games, arts and crafts booths, and live music in a beer garden are all part of this oceanside community's summer celebration. A parade on Saturday and a salmon dinner Sunday evening at Winchester Bay round out the festivities.

August
Dune Fest. Dune-buggy races and all kinds of fun in the sand.

September
Tsalila Education Days and Umpqua River Festival. Pronounced "sa-lee-la," this cross-cultural event features entertaining and educational activities that are free and open to the public. Visitors can walk through the salmon maze, enjoy Native American drumming and dancing performances, listen to top musical acts and storytelling by Pacific Northwest entertainers, or participate in hands-on watershed education programs. Held at the Umpqua Discovery Center in Reedsport.

For more information on Reedsport events, visit www.reedsportcc.org/events.html or call (800) 247–2155 or (541) 271–3495.

Umpqua River Lighthouse (ages 5 and up) 🏛
Located 6 miles south of Reedsport, less than 1 mile off US 101; (800) 247–2155 or (541) 271–4631; www.oregonstateparks.org or www.umpqualighthouse.org. Open daily except Tuesday for tours, May through September, 9:00–11:30 A.M. and 1:00–3:30 P.M., Sunday 1:00–4:00 P.M.; off-season tours by appointment. $, children under 12 free.

Inside is a museum that tells the story of this 1894 lighthouse and of Fort Umpqua, built to protect the lighthouse and settlers from the Umpqua Indians, who didn't welcome either intrusion. The 67-foot tower contains the light, which still shines out on the sea.

The Great Oregon **Beach Cleanup**

SOLV is a nonprofit organization that brings together government agencies, businesses, and individual volunteers to enhance the livability of Oregon. Twice a year, in spring and fall, SOLV sponsors the Great Oregon Beach Cleanup. Thousands of people go to their favorite spots on the coastline to pick up litter and debris that have washed ashore. It's like an upside-down treasure hunt, searching for trash instead of treasure, but who knows what you'll find along the way—and it's a great feeling to help contribute to the beauty of the Oregon coast. For more information, call (541) 844–9571 or visit www.solv.org.

Dean Creek Elk Viewing Area (ages 5 and up)
Located 3 miles upriver on State Highway 38; (541) 756–0100; e-mail: coosbay@or.blm .gov. Always open. Free.

The excellent interpretive panels at the O.H. Hinsdale Interpretive Center describe the resident herd of more than a hundred elk and some of the other wildlife you might see. If you don't find any elk here, drive on a bit. They're often sighted next to the road in the early morning or evening hours. Bring your binoculars.

Winchester Bay

This small town at the mouth of Winchester Bay provides the nearest access to the Oregon Dunes National Recreation Area. Restless children will appreciate the chance to walk along the docks that moor mammoth fishing boats. A cannery offers information about local oyster farming and oysters to eat fresh on the premises or to take home.

Dune buggies are a fun way to explore the area. Rentals are available from a variety of sources, including:

Winchester Bay Dune Buggy Adventures. 881 US 101, Winchester Bay; (541) 271–6972; www.dunebuggyadventure.com. Sandboard, ATV rentals, and tours.

Dune Country ATV. Located on Salmon Harbor Boulevard, Winchester Bay; (541) 271–9357.

Great Adventures: Oregon Dune Rides Plus. By appointment only. (877) 271–0369. Guided dune-buggy tours for groups from one to a hundred, as well as bicycle and walking tours. Small company that gives individual attention.

William M. Tugman State Park (all ages) (♿) (≋) (🏛) (⛺)

Located next to Eel Lake, 9 miles south of Reedsport; (800) 551–6949 for information; (800) 452–5687 for reservations; www.oregonstateparks.org. Open year-round. Day-use area free.

On the land side of the highway, the lake has a campground where privacy is protected with wax myrtle and huckleberry bushes. It's closed in winter, but the day-use area remains open year-round. Yurt camping as well as walk-in campsites are available. Kids will appreciate the playground and designated swimming area.

Oregon's Bay Area

Welcome to Oregon's Bay Area. That's how signs greet you as you enter this region of three towns—Coos Bay, Charleston, and North Bend—bordering Oregon's largest natural deepwater port.

North Bend

This community marks the southern edge of the Oregon Dunes National Recreation Area, that giant sandbox stretching 45 miles north to Florence. There are a variety of options for exploring this popular recreation area, including cars, boats, dune buggies, and hiking trails.

Pacific Coast Recreation (ages 8 and up) (🚜)

68512 US 101; (541) 756–7183. Open daily 9:00 A.M.–6:00 P.M. Four-wheeler rental $$$$ per hour; sand dune tour $$$ adults, $$ ages 14 and under.

You and your kids will enjoy these sand dune tours, which include World War II military transports.. You can also rent your own four-wheel ATVs, depending on your children's size and ability.

Super Shopping

The Real Oregon Gift Myrtlewood Factory Tour. This is a good stop if you're looking for unique gifts to bring home to friends and family. Located in North Bend, 68794 Hauser Depot Road. (541) 756–2220 or (877) 755–2220; www.realoregongift.com. Open daily 10:00 A.M.–3:00 P.M.; shop open until 5:00 P.M. Call first to book a five- to ten-minute tour (summer only). Free.

Top Bay Area **Events**

July

Oregon Coast Music Festival. These concerts, which are held in Shore Acres State Park in Coos Bay, run the gamut from classical to jazz and folk. A number of events during the festival weeks are geared to introducing children to classical music. (877) 897–9350 or (541) 267–0938; www.oregoncoastmusic.com.

August

Blackberry Arts Festival. This annual fair in Coos Bay features handmade arts and crafts along with food booths and live entertainment. (541) 751–9663.

September

Bay Area Fun Festival. Held in downtown Coos Bay, this midmonth weekend starts with a parade and includes live entertainment and family-oriented activities. (541) 269–0215; www.oregonsbayareachamber.com.

Spinreel Dunebuggy Rentals (ages 8 and up)

67045 Spinreel Road, 10 miles north on US 101; (541) 759–3313; www.ridetheoregon dunes.com. Open daily 9:00 A.M.–sunset year-round; call ahead in winter. Four-wheeler rental $$$$ per hour; dune-buggy tour $$$ per hour. Three-person minimum. Children can take out four-wheelers with parental supervision.

Coos County Historical and Maritime Museum (ages 5 and up)

1220 Sherman Avenue (US 101); (541) 756–6320; www.cooshistory.org. Open Tuesday through Saturday 10:00 A.M.–4:00 P.M. $, children under 5 free.

Old Locomotive 104 from the Coos Bay Lumber Company rests outside. Inside your kids will appreciate the miniature boat model and learn about several area shipwrecks. Efforts are underway to renovate and move to the Old Mansfield Historic District and integrate the museum and the waterfront boardwalk.

Money-Saving **Travel Tip**

Check museums for special children's programs that are offered during the summer months. Some schedule half-day programs that provide a nice respite for families with preschoolers.

An Adventure to Remember

South Slough National Estuarine Research Reserve (5 and up). P.O. Box 5417, Charleston, OR 97420; located on Seven Devils Road, south of Charleston; (541) 888–5558; www.southsloughestuary.org. Open daily 10:00 A.M.–4:30 P.M. in summer; Monday through Saturday 10:00 A.M.–4:30 P.M. in winter. Free.

This slightly out-of-the-way oasis provides a wonderful environmental learning adventure for the entire family. The 4,400-acre South Slough, reserved for the study of estuarine life and ecosystems, is one of only a few remaining sloughs in the United States that do not have a city or town built on their shores. An estuary marks the junction where the river meets the sea, mixing fresh and salt water to create a complex environment that supports a unique variety of plants and animals. This South Slough is the southwestern arm of the larger Coos estuary. There's a dramatic shift in temperature as you begin your hike to the marshes. At the trailhead are deciduous trees, which suddenly give way to fragrant, moist ferns and a much cooler terrain—an instant lesson for children about the ways flora and fauna impact climate. At the end of the trail, you're rewarded with a viewing deck from which to marvel at the expanse of fresh- and saltwater marshes and mudflats. Be sure to stop by the Interpretive Center at the top of the hill above the estuary, where you will find detailed trail maps and can view exhibits on the wildlife found in the estuary. An informational video is available at the center for those unable to walk the trail. Write or call ahead for a list of summer educational programs or visit the Web site.

Simpson Park (all ages) 👥

On Sherman Avenue, adjacent to North Bend Visitors Center and Coos County Historical County Museum; (541) 756–2656. Always open. Free.

The park has picnic tables and a Frisbee golf course that will have your whole family stepping up to the "tee" to meet the challenge of landing the Frisbee in basket "holes" atop bright poles. Pick up a free scorecard from the Visitor Center next to the museum. If you left your Frisbee at home, **Moe's Bike Shop** (1397 Sherman Avenue; 541–756–7536) across the street has several varieties for sale.

Coos Bay

Bayfront Boardwalk and Interpretive Structures (ages 5 and up)

Located at the Coos Bay waterfront; (541) 269–8918. Always open. Free.

The new Coos Bay waterfront project and paved trail is an easy 0.3-mile walk where the kids can view a tiny tug and colorful flag display. Huge ships from all over the world dock here. Several cafes and eateries line nearby avenues.

Egyptian Theatre (ages 5 and up)

229 South Broadway; (541) 269–8650; www.egyptian-theatre.com. Call for prices and times.

If the weather turns foul, you can warm up inside this old theater. It's a classic remnant of the elegant 1920s era.

Coos Art Museum (ages 8 and up)

235 Anderson Avenue; (541) 267–3901; www.coosart.org. Open Tuesday through Friday 10:00 A.M.–4:00 P.M., Saturday 1:00–4:00 P.M. Free, but donations accepted.

Here you'll find an impressive collection of both contemporary and historic art. Call ahead to find out about the many children's educational programs offered throughout the year.

Other Things to See and Do
in the Bay Area

Rockhounding (all ages). Best spot is 8 miles south of Charleston at Seven Devils Wayside State Park and Whiskey Run Beach. Day-use area. Free. Agates, agatized myrtle, jasper, and other woods can be gathered here. (800) 551–6949.

Clamming (ages 5 and up). Best locations are the tiny seafront community of Charleston and the Coos Bay estuary. Always open. Free when you bring your own buckets and digging tools. Abundant in this area are mussels and soft-shell, bay, butter, littleneck, cockle, and gaper clams. All local waters are open for clamming. Although clams may be removed without a license, it's unlawful to remove them from their shells before leaving the clamming area.

For more information, call the Bay Area Chamber of Commerce at (541) 269–0215; www.oregonsbayareachamber.com.

Fun Facts

The Doerner Fir in Coos Bay is the largest-known Douglas fir in the world. You can reach it by driving south on US 101, then heading east on State Highway 42. The kids will be awestruck by the 329-foot-tall, 11.5-foot-wide tree. A self-guided tour map is available from the local Bureau of Land Management office (541–756–0100). Take advantage of the **free** working forest tour offered by Menasha Forest Products Corp. (Call 800–824–8486 for reservations.)

Coos Bay sits at the midpoint between Seattle, Washington, and San Francisco, California.

Mingus Park (ages 5 and up)

725 North Tenth Avenue; arboretum at 500 Central Avenue; skate park at Tenth and Commercial; (541) 267–1360. Always open. **Free.**

The community swimming pool, open during summer months, will occupy the kids while you walk the trails in the adjacent arboretum and rhododendron gardens. A playground sits next to a pond where ducks and geese clamor for crumbs. The skateboard park is a destination spot for older kids, and the park also offers an eighteen-hole Frisbee golf course (on East Park Roadway behind Milner Crest School).

Empire Lakes at John Topits Park (ages 5 and up)

Located on Hull Street next to Southwest Oregon Community College, north of Newmark Avenue; (541) 269–8918. Always open. **Free.**

Two lakes reserved for nonmotorized boating and rimmed with 5.5 miles of walking and cycling trails make this a nice retreat for the day. A paved walking and biking path circles Lower Empire Lake, which also boasts a swimming beach.

Millicoma Marsh Interpretive Trail (ages 5 and up)

Located on Blossom Gulch, near Blossom Gulch School in Coos Bay; (541) 269–0215. Always open. **Free.**

This self-guided 1-mile trail at Coos Bay leads to an estuary and freshwater marshes and offers a great spot for bird-watching.

Cranberry Sweets Candy Factory (all ages) 🔘 🍴

1005 Newmark Avenue; (541) 888–9824; www.cranberrysweetsandmore.com. Open Monday through Saturday 9:00 A.M.–5:00 P.M.

Your children will enjoy this factory and store where scrumptious chocolate and cranberry confections are made and sold.

Charleston Area

Shore Acres State Park (ages 5 and up) 🔘 🔘 🔘

Located on Cape Arago Highway 4 miles southwest of Charleston; (800) 551–6949 or (541) 888–3732; www.oregonstateparks.org. Open daily 8:00 A.M.–dusk. $ day-use fee.

The dramatic tilt of the layered rock formations, with waves crashing over them, lures artists and photographers to the cliff tops. The botanical and Japanese gardens are not, perhaps, your child's idea of a great time, but there are plenty of places for kids to run while the grown-ups appreciate the beauty of the exquisitely landscaped gardens. Once the home of lumber baron Louis J. Simpson, the park is open throughout the year. Part of the Oregon Coast Trail winds through the park. During the winter, storm watching is awe-inspiring from the large, glass-enclosed gazebo above the cliffs. In December visit the park just before dusk, when the garden is transformed with thousands of colored lights.

Cape Arago State Park and Lighthouse (ages 5 and up) 🔘 🏛 🔘

Located 5 miles southwest of Charleston off US 101; (541) 888–3778, ext.26; www.oregonstate parks.org. Call for hours. Free.

The victim of erosion and harsh weather, the lighthouse is not open to the public, but tremendous views are available just south of it. For tide-pooling, head down the steep trail to South Cove, where the rocky shoreline is bursting with sea life. Watch out for slippery rocks.

Bandon

Bandon-by-the-Sea is such a popular spot, you'll want to make plans well in advance, particularly now that it's home to three world-class golf courses. The local beach, renowned for its majestic rock formations, is also the perfect spot for bird-watching and sand castle building. Rock hounds often find agate, jasper, and petrified wood here.

Coquille River Museum, Bandon Historical Society (ages 5 and up)

270 Fillmore Street and US 101; (541) 347–2164. Open Monday through Saturday 10:00 A.M.–4:00 P.M.; Sunday afternoon late May through September (hours vary). $ adults, children 12 and under free.

A nice array of exhibits that includes local history, pioneer and maritime life, Native American culture, the Bandon fire, and cranberry-industry memorabilia.

Bandon's Old Town District (ages 5 and up)

Located between US 101 and the Bandon Boat Basin; (541) 347–9616. Most shops are open daily year-round 9:00 A.M.–6:00 P.M.

Take your time strolling in and out of this colorful blend of curio, book, and arts and crafts shops.

Big Wheel General Store (ages 5 and up)

Baltimore between First and Second Streets; (541) 347–3719. Open 9:00 A.M.–5:30 P.M. daily, 10:00 A.M.–5:00 P.M. on Sunday.

After your fresh shrimp or crab salad, buy a sweet treat at the store's fudge factory. Check out the free "driftwood museum" while you're there.

Cranberry Sweets (all ages)

Chicago Avenue and First Street; (541) 347–9475. Monday through Saturday 10:00 A.M.–6:00 P.M.

If the fudge wasn't quite enough, satisfy your sweet tooth at this sweet shop.

Free Thing to Do in Bandon

Tide Pools (ages 5 and up)

Face Rock Wayside. Located in Bandon State Natural Area, along Beach Loop Road just south of Bandon; (800) 551–6949; www.oregonstateparks .org. Day use only. Call for hours. Free. The sea stacks along this stretch of beach all have names. **Face Rock,** the most distinctive of these, is named for Ewauna, the beautiful daughter of Chief Siskiyou. She swam alone in the sea and was caught by the evil ocean spirit Seatka, who threw Ewauna's cat and kittens into the sea with her and turned them all to stone. Ewauna's chin points toward **Cat and Kittens Rocks** to the north.

Top Bandon **Events**

May

Sand Castle and Sand Sculpture Contest. Build a sand castle or sculpture by yourself or team up with other beach artisans.

July

Old-fashioned July Fourth Celebration. Join the residents of this charming coastal community in their Independence Day celebration, complete with a parade, old-fashioned fireworks, annual fish fry, and crafts fair.

September

Cranberry Festival. This lively local event features a street fair, parade, food booths, dances, and, of course, cranberries.

Winter

Bandon Storm Watchers. For years this lively group has gathered in winter to watch nature's own drama play out in the sea. Members serve as interpretive guides to visitors. (541) 347–4721; www.bandon.com/storms.

For information on Bandon events, call (541) 347–9616; www.bandon .com; e-mail: bandoncc@harborside.com.

The Boat Basin (all ages) 🐟

Located on First Street at the Old Town dock; (541) 347–2437 or (541) 347–9616. Free.

This is a great place to watch the boats or head out on the pier for fishing or crabbing.

Port o' Call (ages 5 and up) 🐟 ⚠

On the dock in Old Town at 155 First Street; (541) 347–2875. Open daily 6:00 A.M.–5:00 P.M. Clamming and crabbing $; fishing $$ (includes bait, rod, and hooks).

Rent crab rings, fishing rods, and boats here. They'll tell you the best spots for jetty fishing or clamming, and they'll even cook your crabs. If you don't feel like catching your own, they sell freshly caught seafood.

Adventure Kayak (ages 10 and up) �“

315 First Street; (541) 347–3480; www.adventurekayak.com. Open daily in summer 8:00 A.M.–5:00 P.M.; call for winter hours. $$$$ single or double kayak for two hours; tours $$$$ per person. Reservations required.

Learn about the natural wildlife and estuaries in the area from professional kayak guides. There's no white water to worry about, only gorgeous scenery to watch from water level. Tours run for two hours and depart twice daily. Special tours are scheduled as needed.

Bullards Beach State Park and Coquille River Lighthouse (all ages)
🚻 🐾 ⛺ ⚑

Located 2 miles north of Bandon; (541) 347–2209; (800) 452–5687 for campground reservations; www.oregonstateparks.org. Park open daily year-round. Lighthouse tours offered daily May through October 10:00 A.M.–4:00 P.M. Free.

This large park is home to the 1896 Coquille River Lighthouse, a unique octagonal structure situated alongside the river. In the summer, park staffers offer daily interpretive tours leading to the lantern room. Camping among the shore pines is available year-round, with yurts, hiker/biker campsites, RV hookups, and a horse camp. You can hike on a variety of trails (including a 1-mile paved trail from the campground booth to the beach), try your hand at the exceptional fishing or crabbing in the Coquille River, or just wander along 4.5 miles of broad beach.

Oregon Islands National Wildlife Refuge (ages 5 and up) 🐘 🚻

Located on Eleventh Street Southwest; (541) 347–3683. Always open, but best time to view wildlife is early morning or late afternoon. Free.

The "islands" are actually large offshore rocks that provide habitat for a great number of seabirds and mammals. The Coquille Point area presents one of the most spectacular places for viewing puffins, murres, oystercatchers, seals, and other animals that congregate on these offshore rocks. A group called Shoreline Education for Awareness (SEA) often has volunteers here and elsewhere along the coast with spotting scopes to enhance your viewing.

Money-Saving **Travel Tip**

Consider having your main meal at noon, when restaurants sometimes offer the same menu items at half the cost of dinner entrees.

Bandon Marsh National Wildlife Refuge (ages 5 and up)

Located at the mouth of the Coquille River off Riverside Drive; (541) 867–4550; oregon coast.fws.gov/bandonmarsh; e-mail: oregoncoast@fws.gov. Day-use area. Always open. **Free.**

This estuary at the river mouth contains nearly 300 acres of salt marsh. Some 115 species of migratory birds, 8 species of mammals, 45 species of fish, and other forms of sea life can be found within the refuge. Bring your binoculars for a closer look. SEA (Shoreline Education for Awareness) volunteers are often here with spotting scopes and to show visitors the legal access routes.

Free Flight (ages 5 and up)

1185 Portland Avenue; (541) 347–3882. Call for reservations. **Free,** but donations welcome.

Bandon's bird and mammal rescue and rehabilitation volunteers are happy to talk to visitors about local efforts to return wildlife to their natural habitats. Tours are available by appointment.

Bandon Beach Riding Stables (ages 5 and up)

Along Beach Loop Road; (541) 347–3423. Rides depart every two hours beginning at 10:00 A.M. year-round. Call for reservations. $$$$.

Guided horse rides with gentle horses are available for all ages, but children under five must ride double. Especially unusual are 1.5- to-2-hour-long sunset rides.

West Coast Game Park (all ages)

Located 7 miles south of Bandon on US 101; (541) 347–3106; www.gameparksafari.com. Open daily in summer, weather permitting, 9:00 A.M.–7:00 P.M.; check for closing times. $$$ ages 13 and older; $$ ages 7–12, $ ages 2–6; under 2 **free.**

If your kids are fond of animals, this will be a sure winner. A walk-through safari covering ten acres of the twenty-one-acre preserve brings you up close and personal with seventy-five different species of wildlife. Children might pet bear cubs, tiger cubs, or baby leopards. The many hoofed animals—deer, goats, caribou, and others—swarm around you as you feed them from ice-cream cones filled with animal ambrosia.

Faber Farms Bog Tour & The Oregon Cranberry Company

54980 Morrison Road; (541) 347–1166 or (866) 347–1166; www.faberfarms.com. Open daily 10:00 A.M.–4:00 P.M.; extended hours during October, which is harvest time. **Free.**

Take a tour of this working cranberry farm, which welcomes private parties and large groups.

Fun Fact

Oregon is one of the five states in the country where tart and tangy cranberries are grown. Buy them in candy form in several of the local shops, celebrate them at the community's fall festival, or view them along the highway in late September and October.

Port Orford

The westernmost town in the lower forty-eight states, Port Orford is perched on the headland in the shadow of Humbug Mountain. The picturesque commercial harbor is unique in that it opens directly to the sea, without a river bar.

Battle Rock City Park (all ages)

Located on the shore adjacent to US 101 at the south end of Port Orford. Visitor center next to park is open daily; (541) 332–8055. Free.

This is a good place for picnicking or letting the kids play in the sand. After lunch take advantage of an obliging hiking trail. It was the scene of a fierce Native American battle in 1851. For an in-depth account of the battle, click on "Battle Rock" under the "Visiting" menu at www.portorford.org.

Buffington Park (ages 5 and up)

Located off Fourteenth Street and Lakeshore Drive; Dreamland Skate Park at Thirteenth and Arizona; (541) 332–8055 or (541) 332–3681. Always open. Free.

Sit in the shade while your kids run off energy, swing from the playground equipment, or try out the curves at Dreamland Skate Park. The park provides picnic facilities, tennis and handball courts, basketball courts, and a nature jogging trail.

Berry Interesting

In late September and throughout October, you will see farmers harvesting cranberries along US 101 in Port Orford. Watch them gathering these round, red berries with a "beater" that churns the bog water and loosens them from their vines.

Top Port Orford **Events**

September
Port Orford Arts & Seafood Festival. You'll find junk art, beach games, dock walks, and music here, plus a scrumptious albacore barbecue.

December
Hughes House Christmas Tours. The whole community gets involved in decorating this resplendent 1898 Victorian house, which is nestled in Cape Blanco State Park.

For more information on Port Orford events, call (541) 332–8055 or visit www.portorfordoregon.com or www.discoverportorford.com.

Cape Blanco State Park and Lighthouse (ages 5 and up)

Located 9 miles north off US 101; (541) 756–0100; www.oregonstateparks.org. Lighthouse open April 1 through October 31 Thursday through Monday 10:00 A.M.–3:30 P.M. Park open year-round. $.

The renovated 1870 Cape Blanco Lighthouse, the oldest continuously operating lighthouse in Oregon, is located on the westernmost point of the forty-eight contiguous states. The campground, on a bluff adjacent to the lighthouse area, provides electrical sites with picnic tables, fire rings, and water. Bushes of huckleberry, salal, salmonberry, and thimbleberry lend privacy to the individual campsites. Several trails take off from the campground. Within the park is the 1898 **Hughes House** (www .hugheshouse.org), which visitors can explore April 1 through October 31, except Mondays 10:00 A.M.–3:30 P.M.

Fun Fact

Port Orford's port is the only natural open-water port for 600 miles, and it's one of only a half-dozen "dolly" ports left in the world. A dolly, or giant hoist, is used to lift boats into and out of the water. Rough seas prevent boats from mooring in the ocean, so they must be kept on land.

Humbug Mountain State Park (ages 5 and up) (icons)

Six miles south of Port Orford on US 101; (541) 332–6774 or (800) 551–6949; www.oregon stateparks.org. Open daily year-round. Free.

From the campground, a fairly strenuous trail leads 3 miles to the summit of Humbug Mountain where, if the weather is clear, you'll enjoy an amazing 360-degree view. If the children are not up for climbing, try the lesser-known 2.6-mile hike north from the campground along the old coast highway. The trail ends at the highway just south of Rocky Point, which is a terrific spot for exploring tide pools.

Port Orford Lifeboat Station (ages 8 and up) (icons)

92331 Coast Guard Hill Road; head west on Ninth Street (at mile marker 301) and up Coast Guard Hill to the park; (541) 332–0521; www.portorfordlifeboatstation.org. Open April through October 10:00 A.M.–3:30 P.M. Thursday through Monday; by appointment other times of the year. Free.

The 1934 lifeboat station is located on what is known as "the Heads" or "Coast Guard Hill" and now houses a museum in the main barracks building. Listed on the National Register of Historic Places, the site also features the original officers' quarters as well as other outbuildings. Museum exhibits include a Lyle gun (line-throwing cannon), information on the Japanese attacks on Curry County during World War II, the Dog Tag Maker, local shipwrecks and rescues, and signaling systems (semaphore flags and flares). Hiking trails surround the station, providing spectacular ocean views, and lead to the lookout and Nellie's Cove, where lifeboats were once launched for rescues.

Prehistoric Gardens (ages 5 and up) (icon)

About 12 miles south of Port Orford; (541) 332–4463 or (877) 332–4463; ; www.the prehistoricgardens.com; e-mail: info@prehistoricgardens.com. Open in summer 8:00 A.M.–dusk; call for winter hours. $$ adults and children ages 11–18; $ ages 3–10; 2 and under free.

Wander through a dense coastal rain forest where life-size models of prehistoric dinosaurs and other creatures lurk. Jurassic Park? Well, no, but young children will be captivated by the huge, brightly colored creatures they've read about. Parents will appreciate the luxuriant foliage of ferns and mosses that keep the forest looking green and lush year-round. The giant *Tyrannosaurus rex* standing alongside the highway lets you know you've arrived. Some visitors say winter is the best time to visit the gardens because Oregon's misty weather provides just the right prehistoric ambience.

Elk River Fish Hatchery (ages 3 and up) 🐘 🐟 😌

Three miles north of Port Orford and 8 miles east of US 101 on Elk River Road; (541) 332–7025. Call for hours. Free.

Interpretive signs describe how the Oregon Department of Fish and Wildlife hatchery raises salmon and steelhead smolts that are released to return as spawning adults. The hatchery produces 475,000 fall chinook salmon smolts for the Elk and Chetco Rivers and other area waterways and some 50,000 winter steelhead smolts. About 700 rainbow trout are raised for the "lunkers" program, a special project to release large trout (three to six pounds each) into Floras Lake, Garrison Lake, and Libby Pond. Each spring the hatchery sponsors a free fishing day for children. Staff and volunteers teach kids about fishing and let them fish in a rearing pond stocked with trout—some of which have been fed all year by visitors and have become enormous—until they have caught their limit of three fish. There's also swimming at the Elk River boat launch for older children.

Gold Beach

Nestled on the shores of the Rogue River is Gold Beach, where early prospectors literally scooped up gold off the beaches. Later the area attracted sport fishermen. It was here that Zane Grey wrote his novel *The Rogue River Feud*. Now Gold Beach is the launching spot for a variety of jet boat tours.

Rogue Wilderness Whitewater Trips (ages 8 and up) 🔺

P.O. Box 1110, 325 Galice Road, Merlin, OR 97532; (800) 336–1647 or (541) 479–9554; www.wildrogue.com/water.htm; e-mail: rwi@wildrogue.com. Operates May through September; trips begin at 9:00 A.M. and noon. Advance reservations required. $$$$.

Rafting presents another way for the family to take in river sites. This company offers four-hour white-water rides and a wide variety of fly-fishing, wilderness lodge, and hiking trips.

Fun Fact

Gold was discovered in the sands of Curry County in the 1850s, and hundreds of placer miners set up operations near the mouth of the Rogue River. The settlement here was originally called Ellensburg after the daughter of Captain William Tichenor, an early area explorer, but was later renamed Gold Beach to avoid confusion with a town in Washington Territory.

Hawk's Rest Ranch Stables and Trail Rides (ages 8 and up) 🐎

94667 North Bank Pistol River Road; located 11 miles south of Gold Beach at the Siskiyou West Day Lodge, east at Pistol River junction; (541) 247–6423; www.siskiyou west.com/hawk's_rest_ranch.htm. Open daily year-round 8:00 A.M.–6:00 P.M. $$–$$$$ for fifteen- to ninety-minute rides.

Experience the old-fashioned way of exploration, beginning your day with a ride up an alder-lined creek or ending it with a sunset ride on the beach. They'll also take you on a half-hour surrey ride. Free petting zoo in summer.

Jerry's Rogue River Museum (ages 6 and up) 🏛️

Port of Gold Beach off Port Drive Mail; (541) 247–4571 or (800) 451–3645. Open daily year-round. Free.

This family-run jet boat tour company has collected river memorabilia and geological exhibits that follow the formation of the Rogue River Canyon.

Jet Boating the Rogue River

One of the most popular experiences in Gold Beach is a jet boat trip up the wild and scenic Rogue River. Several tour companies operate full- and half-day trips on the river, stopping for lunch at one of several resort lodges upriver. Tours start the first of May and usually end in late October. There's no age limit for either of the following trips.

Jerry's Jet Boats. Port of Gold Beach off Port Drive Mail; (800) 451–3645 or (541) 247–4571; www.jerrysroguejets.com. Open May 1 through October 15. Tours depart daily at 8:00 A.M. May through October and 8:30 A.M., noon, and 2:30 P.M. July through Labor Day. $$$$ adults, $$$ ages 4–11, under 4 free for 64-mile "short trip"; prices vary for longer trips.

Mail Boat Hydro Jets. Take Rogue River Road east from US 101 at the Wedderburn Store, just north of Gold Beach; (800) 458–3511 for reservations; (541) 247–7033 for brochure or information; e-mail: info@mailboat .com; www.mailboat.com. Open May 1 to October 15. Tours depart 8:30 A.M. except July 1 through Labor Day when trips are offered at 8:30 A.M. and 2:30 P.M. $$$$ adults, $$$ ages 4–11, under 4 free. Take the 64-mile Original Postman's Run and learn how the area's first postmen delivered mail to the remote community of Agness. Expect to get splashed a bit on the longer trips (84-mile and 104-mile), which surge through river rapids.

Top Gold Beach **Event**

July

Curry County Fair. One of Oregon's largest flower shows plus a parade, rodeo, and lamb barbecue are featured at this annual county-sponsored event. (541) 247–4541; e-mail: curryfair@harborside.com.

Curry County Historical Museum (ages 5 and up)
Located at the Curry County Fairgrounds, 29419 Ellensburg Avenue; (541) 247–6396; www.curryhistory.com. Open Tuesday through Saturday 10:00 A.M.–4:00 P.M. June through September, Saturday noon–4:00 P.M. rest of year; closed in January. $.

You'll see exhibits of old-time logging equipment and Native American arrowheads, petroglyphs, baskets, and other artifacts, including a canoe. A maritime display shows old photographs of shipwrecks that occurred along the Pacific coast. Call to find out about the free monthly programs offered September through May.

Brookings

Brookings is known as Oregon's "Banana Belt," where the weather is warm and sunny more often than anywhere else on the Oregon coast—and sometimes in the entire state! Coming into Brookings from Gold Beach, you'll cross Thomas Creek Bridge, which, at 345 feet high, is the highest bridge in Oregon. Less than ten minutes from the California border, Brookings is within easy reach of northern California's majestic redwoods.

Fun Fact

Named for the lumber baron John E. Brookings, president of the Brookings Lumber & Box Company, Brookings was founded as a company town in 1908. A cousin, Robert S. Brookings, provided financial support and hired a San Francisco architect to design the town site— the only early plat in Oregon to receive such professional attention, according to *Oregon Geographic Names* by Lewis L. McArthur.

Tidewind Sportfishing (ages 8 and up)

16368 Lower Harbor Road, Brookings-Harbor; (541) 469–0337 or (800) 799–0337; www .tidewindsportfishing.com; e-mail: tidewinds@harborside.com. Open daily 6:00 A.M.– 5:00 P.M. Fishing charter $$$$; scenic tour $$$ adults, $$ children.

Tidewind offers fishing and scenic tour charters as well as whale-watching trips. Costs include tackle and gear. Just bring a lunch.

Bud Cross Park (all ages)

Third Street and Ransom Avenue; (541) 469–2163; www.brookings.or.us. Open daily sunrise to sunset year-round. Free. Swimming pool open in summer; call (541) 469– 4711 for days and hours. $, children under 48 inches tall free (must be accompanied by an adult at all times).

Bud Cross Park was named for a longtime chief of police and is the major recreational park in Brookings. It offers baseball fields, tennis and basketball courts, and the municipal swimming pool. The **Skate Park,** located within the park at Third and Has-sett Streets, was designed and built by Dreamland Team and has a huge doughnut shape, a triple bowl in the middle, and walls 4 to 10 feet high.

Kidtown in Azalea Park (all ages)

Follow the signs at the north end of Harbor Bridge; park entrance is on the right on North Bank Chetco River Road. (541) 469–3181, (541) 469–2021, or (800) 535–9469. Day use only. Free.

Younger children love it here. It's a child-size fortress, complete with turrets and tow-ers, slides and tunnels. Parents will enjoy wandering among the park's many azalea bushes—some 300 years old—when the spring bloom is on.

Samuel H. Boardman State Scenic Corridor (all ages)

Located 4 miles north on US 101; (800) 551–6949; www.oregonstateparks.org. Closes at dusk; open year-round. Free.

Named for the state's first parks superintendent, who believed Oregon's shining coastline should be saved for the public, the park covers 12 miles of coastline, beginning 4 miles north of Brookings. All along this stretch are fascinat-ing and picturesque rock formations and tide pools to explore. You can gain access to the beach at both Whale-head Cove Viewpoint, overlooking Whalehead Island, and at Indian Sands Wayside. At the south end of Indian Sands beach, look for the Indian midden, an area with huge piles of shells and bones left behind after many feasts. This is a look-but-don't-touch situation—disturbing the midden is against federal law. The park offers several interpretive events and nature programs in the summer.

Fun Fact

Sam Boardman is known for planting trees along treeless areas of the Old Oregon Trail and the Columbia River Highway. Later his plantings were taken over by the state highway department.

Natural Bridge Viewpoint (ages 5 and up)

Located about 9 miles north of Brookings near the beach access point at Miner Creek; (800) 535–9469. Always open. Free.

From the parking area, walk south along the trail to a viewing platform to see the remains of ancient sea caves that collapsed eons ago. It's a short but often steep walk to the beach. For trail maps, write to the Trails Coordinator, Oregon State Parks, 1115 Commercial Street NE, Salem 97310. The 27-mile Oregon Coast Trail winds through the park.

Alfred A. Loeb State Park (all ages)

North Chetco River Road, 8 miles northeast of Brookings; (541) 469–2021 or (800) 551–6949; www.oregonstateparks.org. Open daily year-round. Free.

Loeb State Park sits in a grove of old-growth myrtlewood. You can camp and picnic here, take a swim in the Chetco River, throw a fishing line into one of the best salmon

Top Brookings **Events**

May

Azalea Festival. This week of special events celebrates the glories of springtime on the coast. (800) 877–9741 or (541) 469–3181.

May through September

American Music Festival. Concerts are held in Azalea Park every other Sunday from the end of May through mid-September. (541) 469–4580.

July

Southern Oregon Kite Festival. Fly your own kite or watch others launch theirs at the Port of Brookings-Harbor. (541) 469–2218.

December

Nature's Coastal Holiday. Programs offered in Azalea Park from 5:00 to 9:00 P.M. nightly. (541) 469–3181.

Fun Fact

The name Chetco comes from the Indians who were the original inhabitants of this area. The last member of the tribe, a woman who went by the name Lucky Dick, died in the 1940s.

streams in the area (Emily Creek), or walk a 1.25-mile nature loop trail through a redwood forest. Yes, redwoods in Oregon! The most impressive of the trees you'll pass are between 300 and 800 years old. A self-guiding brochure with a map is available at the trailhead in the day-use area of the park along the Chetco River. In addition to campsites, log cabins are available to rent.

Chetco Valley Historical Society Museum (ages 6 and up)

15461 Museum Road; (541) 469–6651. Open Thursday through Sunday, noon–4:00 P.M. mid-March through October; extended days and hours in the summer. Free, but donations welcome.

This pioneer museum is housed in the historic Blacke House. The largest Monterey cypress tree in the United States is on the grounds.

Where to Eat

IN BANDON

Bandon Baking Co. & Deli. 160 Second Street; (541) 347–9440. An Old Town favorite with a delicious selection of cookies, pastries, croissants, and breads, plus breakfast and, for lunch, homemade soup and sandwiches. $–$$

The Station Restaurant. US 101, just east of Old Town; (541) 347–9615. In the gift shop next door, kids enjoy watching the German-made LGB model trains and the glass hive full of live honeybees. Breakfast, lunch, and dinner. $$–$$$

IN BROOKINGS

Slugs and Stones and Ice Cream Cones. 97950 Holly Lane, Port of Brookings-Harbor; (541) 469–7584. You can bribe your children to let you peacefully enjoy the stunning viewpoints along the way with a promise of an ice-cream cone. The "For Kids Only" menu offers Slyme Sundae and Baby Pickles Gummy Worm Sundae. $

Wharfside Seafood Restaurant. 16362 Lower Harbor Road; (541) 469–7316. Kids enjoy the old boat incorporated into the restaurant's structure. In addition to indoor seating, there's also window service for the covered picnic tables outside. Seafood and vegetarian entrees. $$

IN COOS BAY

Benetti's Italian Restaurant. 260 South Broadway; (541) 267–6066. Home-style Italian food with a downstairs area for family dining. $–$$

Blue Heron Bistro. 100 Commercial Street; (541) 267–3933. It has a European feel and serves somewhat upscale food with all fresh ingredients, but the atmosphere is definitely casual. $$–$$$

IN FLORENCE

Bridgewater Restaurant. 1297 Bay Street; (541) 997–9405; www.bridgewater .oldtownflorence.com. Seafood entrees are offered in a tropical-like setting that supplies crayons and colorable children's menus. $$–$$$

Cackleberries Restaurant. 1675 US 101; (541) 997–9670; www.bluehencafe.com. The whole family will enjoy the extensive breakfast menu. Huge portions at all meals make this a best buy. Oregon's People's Choice and *Oregon Coast* magazine winner for best chowders. $–$$

Clawson's Windward Inn Restaurant. 3787 North US 101 in the north end of town; (541) 997–8243. Local seafood, steaks, and homemade bread and pastries are served. It also offers bistro dinners for the budget-conscious. $$–$$$

Mo's Restaurant. 1436 Bay Street; (541) 997–2185; www.moschowder.com. Here's another chance to stop by the state's legendary chowder chain for a bowl of hearty clam chowder. The kids will have fun watching the boats go by. $–$$

IN GOLD BEACH

Chives Ocean Front Dining. 29212 Ellensburg Avenue (US 101); (541) 247–4121 or (866) 4–CHIVES. Fresh seafood, steaks, pasta, and salads; only unobstructed ocean-view dining for 50 miles. $$–$$$

Playa del Sol. 29455 Ellensburg Avenue (US 101); (541) 247–0314. Family-run Mexican restaurant offering specialty shrimp and crab enchiladas. $–$$

Savory Natural Foods. 29441 Ellensburg Avenue (US 101); (541) 247–0297. This natural grocery deli has organic produce, bulk foods, a juice bar, and a small cafe. $

Spada's Family Restaurant. 29374 Ellensburg Avenue (US 101); (541) 247–7732. Seafood, steaks, Italian dinners, sandwiches, and New York pizza round out an extensive menu. Breakfast, lunch, dinner, and Sunday buffet. $$–$$$

IN REEDSPORT

Don's Main Street Family Restaurant. 2115 Winchester Avenue; (541) 271–2032. Here's a casual dining establishment for breakfast, lunch, or dinner, with ice-cream treats for the kids. $–$$

Where to Stay

IN BANDON

Bullards Beach State Park. Located 2 miles north of Bandon; (800) 452–5687 for reservations; www.oregonstateparks.org. Campsites and yurt camping are available here year-round. Beach access. In the summer state rangers provide educational activities for children. $

Sunset Oceanfront Lodging. 1865 Beach Loop Drive; (800) 842–2407 or (541) 347–2453; www.sunsetmotel.com. Kitchenettes, pets allowed, spa pool, and easy access to Bandon's famous beach. $$–$$$

Table Rock Motel. 840 Beach Loop Drive; (541) 347–2700 or (800) 457–9141; www .tablerockmotel.com; e-mail: tablerock@ harborside.com. Simple but clean rooms. Kitchenettes; pets allowed. Just behind the building is the Oregon Island Bird Sanctuary. Vacation rentals also available. $–$$$

IN THE BAY AREA

Best Western Holiday Motel. 411 North Bayshore Drive, Coos Bay; (541) 269–5111 or (800) 228–8655; e-mail: 0063@hotel .bestwestern.com. Complimentary continental breakfast, kitchenettes, spa, pool, fitness center. Pets allowed; kids under 12 stay free. $$–$$$

Red Lion Hotel. 1313 North Bayshore Drive, Coos Bay; (541) 267–4141 or (800) 733–5466. Dining room, swimming pool, spa, and large rooms make this a favorite central spot for families. $$–$$$

Sunset Bay State Park. Located 3 miles south of Charleston on Cape Arago Highway; (800) 452–5687; www.oregonstate parks.org. One of the most beautiful state parks in Oregon, nestled in a snug cove at the base of coastal hills with easy access to the beach and hiking trails. $

IN BROOKINGS

Best Western Beachfront Inn. 16008 Boat Basin Road; (800) 468–4081 or (541) 469–7779. Many of the guest rooms are within 50 feet of the ocean. Kitchenettes, heated pool, spa. All rooms have an ocean view with microwave, fridge, and coffeemaker. Easy beach access. Small pets allowed. $$–$$$$

Harris Beach State Park. 1655 US 101 North, 2 miles north of Brookings; (541) 469–2021; (800) 452–5687 for reservations; www.oregonstateparks.org. Tent and yurt camping. Five RV spaces. $

Westward Inn. 1026 Chetco Avenue; (541) 469–7471 or (888) 521–6020. Small pets OK, downtown location, walking distance to shops. $–$$

IN FLORENCE

Driftwood Shores Resort. 88416 First Avenue; (800) 422–5091 or (541) 997–8263; www.driftwoodshores.com. Restaurant, indoor pool, spa. All rooms have ocean views. $$–$$$

Fish Mill Lodge and RV Park. Located 5.5 miles south of Florence off US 101 at 4484 Fish Mill Way; (541) 997–2511; www .members.tripod.com/~fishmill/homepage .html. Fully-equipped kitchen rooms overlooking Siltcoos Lake. $$

Holiday Inn Express. 2475 US 101; (541) 997–7797 or (800)–HOLIDAY; www.ichotels group.com/h/d/EX/hd/flcex; e-mail: holiday inn@florenceininc.com. Continental breakfast, spa and exercise room, laundry facilities. $$–$$$

Lighthouse Inn. 155 US 101; (541) 997–3221; www.lighthouseinn.tripod.com; e-mail: lighthouse@winfinity.com. A traditional motel with recently refurbished family units and a large suite that accommodates families of six, it sits a block off the river near Old Town. Pets allowed. $$–$$$

IN GOLD BEACH

Azalea Lodge. 29481 Ellensburg Avenue (US 101); (800) 381–6635 or (541) 247–6635. Small and centrally located. Free limited breakfast; in-room coffeemaker, fridge; cable TV; laundry facilities. $$

Gold Beach Resort and Condominiums. 29232 South Ellensburg Avenue (US 101); (541) 247–7066 or (800) 541–0947; www.gbresort.com. One of the only beachfront accommodations in the area, offering rooms and condos. Indoor swimming pool, hot tub. Microwave, refrigerator, coffeemaker in each room. All rooms have ocean view. Restaurant just across the parking lot. $$–$$$$

Inn of the Beachcomber. 29266 Ellensburg Avenue (US 101); (800) 690–2378 or (541) 247–6691. Ocean views, beach access, fireplaces, kitchenettes, pool, and spa. $$–$$$$

Ireland's Rustic Lodges. 1220 South Ellensburg Avenue (US 101); (541) 247–7718; www.irelandsrusticlodges.com. Log cabins and lodge rooms, some with kitchens and fireplaces. Shaded parklike setting. $–$$

IN REEDSPORT

Anchor Bay Inn. 1821 Winchester; (541) 271–2149 or (800) 767–1821; www.ohwy .com/or/a/anchobin.htm; e-mail: anchorbay @presys.com. One, two, or three beds; family suite; and kitchenettes. Outdoor pool, guest laundry, continental breakfast. Microwave, fridge available for small fee. Pets OK (extra fee). $–$$

Winchester Bay Inn. 390 Broadway, Winchester Bay; (541) 271–4871 or (800) 246–1462; www.winbayinn.com. Free continental breakfast, cable TV, and HBO. Some harbor-view rooms, kitchens, kitchenettes, in-room spas, suites. Kids under eighteen stay **free.**

For More Information

Bandon Chamber of Commerce. P.O. Box 1515, 300 Southeast Second Street, Bandon, OR 97411; (541) 347–9616; www.bandon.com.

Bay Area Chamber of Commerce. 50 East Central Avenue, Coos Bay, OR 97420; (800) 824–8486 or (541) 269–0215; www .oregonsbayareachamber.com; e-mail: bacc@oregonsbayareachamber.com.

Brookings-Harbor Chamber of Commerce. P.O. Box 940, 16330 Lower Harbor Road, Brookings, OR 97415; (800) 535–9469 or (541) 469–3181; www.brookings or.com; e-mail: chamber@wave.net.

Charleston Information Center. P.O. Box 5735, Charleston, OR 97420; (800) 824–8486 or (541) 888–2311 (May through September).

Coquille Chamber of Commerce. 119 North Birch Street, Coquille, OR 97423; (541) 396–3414; www.coquillechamber .com; e-mail: chamber2000@harborside .com.

Florence Area Chamber of Commerce. 290 US 101, Florence, OR 97439; (541) 997–3128 or (800) 524–4864; www .florencechamber.com; e-mail: florence@ oregonfast.net.

Gold Beach Chamber of Commerce Visitor Center. 29692 Ellensburg Avenue, #6, Gold Beach, OR 97444; (800) 525–2334 or (541) 247–0923; www.goldbeachchamber.com; e-mail: info@goldbeachchamber.com. See also: www.goldbeach.org.

Oregon Dunes National Recreation Area Visitor Center. 855 Highway Avenue, Reedsport, OR 97467; (541) 271–3611; www.fs.fed.us/r6/siuslaw/ odnra.htm.

Port Orford Chamber of Commerce. P.O. Box 637, Battle Rock Park, US 101 South, Port Orford, OR 97465; (541) 332–8055; www.portorfordoregon.com; e-mail: chamber@portorfordoregon.com. See also: www.discoverportorford.com.

Reedsport-Winchester Bay Chamber of Commerce. 855 Highway Avenue, Reedsport, OR 97467; (800) 247–2155 or (541) 271–3495; e-mail: info@reedsport.com.

Portland
and the
Columbia
Gorge

The confluence of the Willamette River and the mighty Columbia seemed a natural place to establish a port city that would serve as a shipping center for getting goods to settlers along both rivers. Portland, named after Portland, Maine, on the toss of a coin, has a population of more than 450,000 in the city and 1.5 million in the larger metropolitan area.

Now known as the City of Roses, Portland grew from the pioneer spirit that brought hundreds of thousands of settlers along the Oregon Trail despite often heartbreaking hardships. The Columbia River was perhaps the most formidable challenge they faced, and many decided to take the longer, more strenuous overland route rather than risk all on the churning waters of the river. To look at it today, with its wide, calm waters tamed by a series of dams, you'd think no river could be more placid. For many pioneers it wasn't until the river stretched wide beyond the Columbia River Gorge that it calmed enough for them to think of settling along its banks.

Portland

Central

Growing up on the outskirts of Portland meant easy access to the big city—Downtown, with a capital D. I'd take the bus after high school to my favorite parks, bookshops, and coffee shops and just hang out until my mother's workday ended and we drove home together. The bookstores and restaurants have changed dramatically, but Portland's central core is still one of my favorite places to wander, window-shop, and, especially, dine. Public transit still makes Portland both accessible and easy to get around, and most of downtown is part of "Fareless Square," meaning you can hop on and off buses and the light-rail system for free (see page 80 for more information).

PORTLAND AND THE COLUMBIA GORGE

Pioneer Courthouse Square (all ages)

Located in the block between Broadway and Fifth, and Southwest Morrison and Yamhill; (800) 962–3700, (503) 823–2223, or (503) 275–8355; www.travelportland.com or www.parks.ci.portland.or.us. Open 5:00 A.M.–midnight. Free.

Kids enjoy splashing in the fountain or trying to get a smile from the "umbrella man"—a lifelike bronze sculpture. The **Weather Machine** is another kid favorite. At noon each day the machine plays a musical fanfare and sprays mist, out of which comes the symbol for the day's weather—a stylized sun, a dragon for storms, or a great blue heron for Oregon's perennial drizzle. In summertime the square comes alive with concerts, some planned and some impromptu, from sometimes very talented buskers (street musicians). The square is also home to the Portland Visitors Association and the Tri-Met offices, where you can get information on bus and light-rail services in the city.

Portland Art Museum (ages 5 and up) 🏛

1219 Southwest Park Avenue; (503) 226–2811; www.pam.org. Open Tuesday through Saturday 10:00 A.M.–5:00 P.M.; Thursday and Friday until 8:00 P.M.; Sunday noon–5:00 P.M.; $$, children under 5 free.

The kids will love seeing one of the premier collections of Northwest Indian art in the country, especially the ceremonial masks used in dances and potlatch celebrations. The museum also hosts many distinguished traveling exhibits that have included such artists as M.C. Escher, Gauguin, and Monet.

Oregon Historical Society (ages 5 and up) 🏛

1200 Southwest Park Avenue; (503) 222–1741; www.ohs.org. Call or check the Web site for new opening hours and days. $$ adults; $ seniors, students 19 and older, and children ages 6–18; 5 and under free.

Many kid-centered exhibits and programs are shown in this recently renovated museum. Children also enjoy the larger-than-life-size murals outside, bordering the Portland Park Blocks.

Ticket Central

Like several of the world's major cities, Portland now has a central location for purchasing day-of-show discount theater tickets. Located in the Pioneer Courthouse Square at 701 Southwest Sixth Avenue, Ticket Central lets you book all your tickets in advance or take advantage of last-minute deals. For information, call (503) 275–8352; for day-of-show offerings, call (503) 275–8358.

Fun Fact

The *Portlandia* statue on the Portland Building (Southwest Fifth Avenue between Main and Madison Streets) is the world's second-largest hammered copper sculpture, smaller only than the Statue of Liberty.

Portland Classical Chinese Garden (ages 3 and up)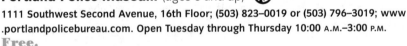

Northwest Third Avenue and Everett Street; (503) 228–8131; www.portlandchinese garden.org. Open daily November through March 10:00 A.M.–5:00 P.M., April through October 9:00 A.M.–6:00 P.M. Tours offered daily at noon and 1:00 P.M. $$ adults, $ students, children under 5 free.

Created to mimic a Ming dynasty garden, Portland's authentic Suzhou-style garden was designed by architects and artisans from China to convey artistic beauty and symbolic meaning, embodying the balance and harmony of nature. The 40,000-square-foot walled garden encloses a full city block and includes an 8,000-square-foot lake, a teahouse, nine restful pavilions, and nearly one hundred specimen trees, water plants, bamboo, and orchids. The standing Taihu rocks were mined from Lake Tai, a freshwater lake near Suzhou in China. More than 500 tons of rocks were shipped to Portland along with the fir, gingko, and nanmu woods used for columns and beams in the pavilions. This is an amazing oasis of tranquility in the heart of Portland's bustling downtown.

Portland Police Museum (ages 6 and up)

1111 Southwest Second Avenue, 16th Floor; (503) 823–0019 or (503) 796–3019; www .portlandpolicebureau.com. Open Tuesday through Thursday 10:00 A.M.–3:00 P.M. Free.

Get a look at police uniforms, handcuffs, and weapons from a century of policing in Portland.

Lloyd Center Mall and Ice Rink (all ages)

2201 Lloyd Center; (503) 288–6073; www.lloydcenter.com. Call for hours.

The completely refurbished mall is a favorite teen spot, but kids of all ages love the **Lloyd Center Ice Rink** (503–288–6073), which has been entertaining families for nearly forty years. Lloyd Center was one of the first large shopping malls in the country. There's also a movie theater in the center, near the food court.

Swimming in the City

Sometimes kids just need to get wet! When the water beckons, here are several choices in the Portland area for taking a dip.

Indoor Pools

- **Buckman Pool.** 320 Southeast Sixteenth Avenue; (503) 823–3668. Twenty-yard swimming pool, eighty-three degrees. Program offerings include swimming lessons, lap swims, water exercise classes, and recreational play swims.

- **Columbia Pool.** 7701 North Chautauqua Boulevard; (503) 823–3669. Twenty-five-yard swimming pool, heated year-round, eighty-four to eighty-six degrees. Water depths range from 1.5 feet to 8 feet. Programs include swimming lessons, lap swims, water exercise classes, and recreational play swims.

- **Dishman Pool.** 77 Northeast Knott; (503) 823–3673. Twenty-five-yard, L-shaped heated pool (84 degrees) with whirlpool spa (102 degrees) and diving boards. Water depths are 2 feet to 12 feet. Programs include swimming lessons, lap swims, water exercise classes, and recreational play swims.

- **Mt. Scott Pool.** 5530 Southeast Seventy-second Avenue at Harold; (503) 823–3183. Leisure pool with slide, current channel, and interactive toys. Lap pool with water basketball and rope swing.

- **Southwest Community Center Pool.** 6820 Southwest Forty-fifth Avenue; (503) 823–2840. Leisure pool with slide, rope swing, and four lanes for lap swimming.

Outdoor Pools

- **Creston Pool.** Southeast Forty-fourth Avenue and Powell Boulevard; (503) 823–3672. Heated.

- **Grant Pool.** 2300 Northeast Thirty-third Avenue; (503) 823–3674. Heated.

- **Montavilla Pool.** 8219 Northeast Glisan; (503) 823–3675. Heated.

- **Peninsula Pool.** 700 North Portland Boulevard; (503) 823–3677.

- **Pier Pool.** North Seneca and St. Johns; (503) 823–3678.

- **Sellwood Pool.** 7951 Southeast Seventh Avenue; (503) 823–3679. Heated.

Getting around Portland

Portland's public transit system is easy to use, inexpensive, and extensive. The **MAX Light Rail** travels east and west from downtown. Eastbound from Pioneer Courthouse Square takes you through Old Town before crossing the Willamette River and heading for Lloyd Center and on to Gresham or the Portland airport. Westbound travels through the deepest underground railway tunnel in North America and stops at the Oregon Zoo and the World Forestry Center before continuing to Beaverton and Hillsboro. Trains run every seven minutes during high-traffic times and every fifteen minutes at other times.

Fareless Square is a 300-block downtown area in which passengers on buses and the MAX ride free. See downtown kiosks for boundaries. Basic fares outside Fareless Square are $1.10, 85 cents for children, kids under seven free; seniors ride anywhere for 50 cents. Day passes cost $3.50.

Vintage trolleys operate from 10:00 A.M.–6:00 P.M. weekends and 9:30 A.M.–3:00 P.M. weekdays on the MAX line every half hour from May through December; weekends only in March and April. The forty-minute round-trip on the trolleys from Lloyd Center to downtown is free.

Nike Town (all ages)

930 Southwest Sixth at Sixth Avenue and Salmon Street; (503) 221–6453. Open Monday through Thursday and Saturday 10:00 A.M.–7:00 P.M., Friday 10:00 A.M.–8:00 P.M., Sunday, 11:30 A.M.–6:30 P.M.

For sports enthusiasts, this is a must. Enter through sliding doors reminiscent of *Star Trek*, and tour the two-story museum and gallery that contains memorabilia from some of the greatest professional sports stars. Of course, the retail store is here, too, but you can enjoy the museum without buying anything.

Powell's City of Books (all ages) 🅐

1005 West Burnside; (800) 878–7323 or (503) 228–4651; www.powells.com. Open daily 9:00 A.M.–11:00 P.M.

Here's a bookstore that's very close to being a city within a city—it takes a map to find your way through the stacks and stacks of books in room after room. Families will want to head to the "rose" room for children's books. Both new and used books are available. There's a coffeehouse-style cafe upstairs that serves espresso drinks for weary moms and dads and cookies and pastries for kids. Powell's is the largest new and used bookstore in the world, with more than a million books.

Oregon Zoo (all ages)

4001 Southwest Canyon Road, 2 miles west of Portland off US 26; (503) 226–1561; www.oregonzoo.org. Open daily 9:00 A.M.–6:00 P.M. (last entry at 4:00 P.M.) April 15 through September 15, 9:00 A.M.–4:00 P.M. September 16 through April 14. $$ adults, $ children ages 3–11, ages 2 and under free. Free **Zoo Day the second Tuesday of every month after 1:00 P.M.**

From a thunder-and-lightning storm in the West African rain forest to the underwater viewing areas in the Penguinarium and the Arctic tundra where the polar bears roam, the zoo takes your family into strange and wonderful new worlds. Visit Packy, the "baby" elephant that made international headlines on April 14, 1962, as the first elephant born in captivity. Every year there's a birthday celebration for the now ponderous pachyderm. Have a snack or lunch in the Africafe while you watch exotic birds flying in the aviary. The Amazon Flooded Forest exhibit opened recently, offering above- and below-water viewing. You'll feel as if you're exploring a remote South American jungle.

International Rose Test Gardens (ages 5 and up)

400 Southwest Kingston Avenue; (503) 823–3636. Open daily 7:00 A.M.–10:00 P.M. Free.

Roses begin blooming in late May and continue through September in this 4.5-acre sanctuary. The many rhododendrons and azaleas start the blazing show off early in March or April. In the summer free concerts are held in the amphitheater, and you can spread out a picnic lunch just about anywhere. This is one of the largest and oldest rose test gardens in the United States. The **Zoo Train** skirts the zoo perimeter and travels through the arboretum. Proceeds from the gift shop support the gardens.

Hoyt Arboretum (ages 5 and up)

4000 Fairview Boulevard, adjacent to the Oregon Zoo and International Rose Test Gardens; (503) 865–8733; www.hoytarboretum.org; e-mail: info@hoytarboretum.org. Open 9:00 A.M.–4:00 P.M. Monday through Friday, 9:00 A.M.–3:00 P.M. Saturday. Free.

Laced with 10 miles of trails that wind through the largest selection of conifer species in the United States, as well as a huge variety of deciduous trees and shrubs, the arboretum is a quiet respite from the lively zoo. Markers identify the various species. In the fall take a self-guided "autumn color" walk through 1.5 miles of vibrant maple, persimmon, dogwood, and photinia. New plantings include a bamboo garden, a magnolia area that blooms April through June, and a holly area with hollies from all over the world.

Japanese Garden (ages 5 and up)

Just up the hill from the International Rose Test Gardens; (503) 223–1321; www .japanesegarden.com. Open Tuesday through Sunday 10:00 A.M.–7:00 P.M., Monday noon–7:00 P.M. Last entry one-half hour before closing. $$ adults, $ students, children 5 and under free.

Take a breather from the busier pace at the zoo and stroll through these soothing and peaceful gardens. In May there's a special Children's Day.

World Forestry Center (ages 5 and up)

4033 Southwest Canyon Road, across the large parking lot from the zoo; (503) 228–1367; www.worldforestry.org. Open daily 10:00 A.M.–5:00 P.M. in winter, 9:00 A.M.–5:00 P.M. rest of year. $, children 2 and under free.

Families have a chance to see petrified wood, view exhibits on old-growth and rain forests, and participate in a wide range of activities directed at both children and adults.

Tryon Creek State Natural Area (ages 5 and up)

11321 Southwest Terwilliger Boulevard; (503) 636–4398, (503) 636–9886, or (800) 551–6949; www.oregonstateparks.org. Open dawn to dusk. Free.

More than a dozen miles of walking and cycling trails are available here, including the **Trillium Trail,** which is fully accessible. The **Nature Center** presents exhibits and programs for kids and adults throughout the year.

Recommended **Reading**

Wild in the City is a comprehensive guide to Portland's natural areas. Published by the Oregon Historical Society Press in collaboration with the Audubon Society's Urban Naturalist program, *Wild in the City* guides you to nearly a hundred sites and provides detailed maps to natural spaces, trails, waterways, parks, golf courses, and even cemeteries, where wildlife habitat or natural-history features can be viewed. It also includes "must see" nature events throughout the year, such as the return of bald eagles to their winter roost, the gathering of Vaux's swifts in the fall, and spring wildflowers. The $21.95 book is available at the Audubon Society Nature Store, the Oregon History Center, and bookstores throughout Portland.

Forest Park (ages 5 and up)

Stretches 8 miles through the hills of northwest Portland; (800) 962–3700 or (503) 823–2223; www.parks.ci.portland.or.us. Open daily dawn to dusk. Free.

With nearly 5,000 acres, this is the largest forested municipal park in the nation. Its amazing network of more than 70 miles of hiking and biking trails through tall timber allows city dwellers to escape into a wilderness experience right in their backyard. Elk, black bears, and deer live in this virtually untouched municipal park. For a map of **Wildwood Trail** and others in Forest Park, stop at Hoyt Arboretum Visitor Center, 4000 Fairview Boulevard.

Audubon House (ages 5 and up)

Located next to Forest Park, 5151 Northwest Cornell Road; (503) 292–9453 or (503) 292–6855; www.audubonportland.org. Park open dawn to dusk; house open 10:00 A.M.– 6:00 P.M. Monday through Saturday, 10:00 A.M.–5:00 P.M. Sunday. No dogs allowed. Free.

Audubon House rests at the edge of its own extensive park. Your kids can stroll in search of the many bird species attracted by the nesting and feeding stations. The Audubon Society frequently offers nature walks, birdhouse-building workshops, and other events to entertain and educate your youngsters.

Portland's Pittock Mansion (ages 8 and up)

3229 Northwest Pittock Drive; (503) 823–3623; www.pittockmansion.com. House open daily noon–4:00 P.M., 11:00 A.M.–4:00 P.M. in summer; park open 7:00 A.M.–9:00 P.M. year-round. Closed major holidays and the month of January. $, children 5 and under free.

Take a guided tour of this 1914 mansion and grounds, which are open to the public. You can picnic on the lawn of this forty-six-acre park, which connects with Forest Park and its many walking trails.

CM2: Children's Museum–Second Generation (ages 6 months and up)

4015 Southwest Canyon Road; (503) 223–6500; www.pdxchildrensmuseum.org. Open Monday through Saturday 9:00 A.M.–5:00 P.M., Sunday 11:00 A.M.–5:00 P.M. $, children under 1 free.

Plan on spending an afternoon in this wonderland for kids, which has three floors of exploratory hands-on exhibits, art activities, and fun centers. The Clay Shop gives budding sculptors a chance to create, and the carpeted Baby Room challenges little ones from infancy to two years with all kinds of visual and physical stimuli. The latest area, Kid City Medical Center, gives kids a chance to play doctor with parental supervision in a realistic setting.

The Rose Sternwheeler (all ages) ⚠

6211 North Ensign Street, docks at RiverPlace Marina; (503) 286–7673; www.stern wheelerrose.com. Call for hours, prices, and reservations.

The 130-passenger sternwheeler offers lunch and dinner cruises that let you experience the Willamette River from the water.

Willamette Shore Trolley (all ages)

North terminal at RiverPlace, off Southwest Clay; south terminal at 311 North State Street in Lake Oswego; (503) 697–7436; www.oregonelectricrailway.org. Call for hours, fares, and departure times.

This antique trolley line operates May through September between Portland's River-Place and Lake Oswego, passing through a warehouse district to the river's shore, then past Willamette Park and through the 1,400-foot S-shaped Elk Rock Tunnel. At Lake Oswego the **Tillamook Ice-Creamery,** about a block from the train stop at 37 Southwest A Street, sells the delectable ice-cream cones usually found only at the coastal factory in Tillamook.

Gov. Tom McCall Waterfront Park (all ages) 🏕 🚲 🍴

Located in downtown Portland, stretching 2 miles along the Willamette River; (800) 962–3700 or (503) 823–2223; www.parks.ci.portland.or.us. Always open. **Free.**

This is a terrific place for walking, jogging, cycling, and roller-skating. From the Saturday Market under the Burnside Bridge, you can stroll through the park, hang out around the Salmon Street Springs fountain, then head south along the river to the **RiverPlace Promenade,** where you can get ice-cream cones or espresso from sidewalk vendors or grab a curbside cafe table for a bite of lunch. Horse-drawn carriages take off from RiverPlace and are fun to watch even if you don't want to splurge for your own ride.

Oregon Maritime Museum (ages 5 and up) 🚢

Located aboard the steamer *Portland,* moored at Waterfront Park at the foot of Pine Street; (503) 224–7724. Open Friday, Saturday, and Sunday 11:00 A.M.–4:00 P.M. $, children under 6 **free.**

Young and old alike are intrigued by the many scale-model ships and nautical artifacts on display. The most fascinating part of the museum is listening to the "watch-standers," volunteer docents who provide living-history programs—each one an "old salt" with many years at sea. You'll also tour the historic steam sternwheeler *Portland.*

Oregon Museum of Science and Industry (OMSI) (ages 5 and up) 🔵

1945 Southeast Water Avenue; (800) 955–6674 or (503) 797–4000; www.omsi.edu. Summer hours 9:30 A.M.–7:00 P.M., winter hours 9:30 A.M.–5:30 P.M., closed Mondays. $$, children 2 and under free. OMNIMAX shows $$, submarine tours, planetarium, and laser shows $ each. Combination tickets $$$ and include museum entrance plus one OMNIMAX show and either the planetarium show or submarine tour.

Let your kids experience interactive exhibits that teach as well as entertain. Hands-on fun ranges from computer games to earthquake and tornado simulations. The **OMNIMAX Theater** here is the first of its kind in Oregon, with a five-story domed screen and complete surround sound, light, and motion that let you experience changing exhibitions, from earthquakes to volcanic eruptions, or journeys, such as exploring the Grand Canyon from top to bottom. The **Murdock Sky Theater** presents amazing laser-light and astronomy shows. The OMNIMAX shows change periodically, and hours vary, so call first.

An Adventure to Remember

We've been to the Oregon Museum of Science and Industry (OMSI) a number of times, both as a family and with out-of-town visitors. Situated in a gorgeous waterfront location, the museum is a bit out of the main traffic stream now but well worth a visit. There's an extensive gift shop, restaurant, OMNIMAX Theater, and numerous hands-on exhibit rooms; you will find that several hours pass with nary a "When are we leaving?" inquiry from the little ones. Send away for a brochure, because the museum schedules well in advance classes and exhibits that not only educate but intrigue. You can spend hours looking at hands-on exhibits that explore human body systems; dioramas that depict the evolution of man; and look-and-touch displays that examine, through superheroes such as Superman, Wonder Woman, and Batman, the marvels of movement, speed, and space. The OMNIMAX Theater blends the wonders of nature and technology with explorations of the most intrepid human adventures, such as a climb up Mt. Everest, a river-rafting trip along the Colorado, and an airplane ride over the Grand Canyon. The images on the massive screen quite literally envelop the viewer and force the squeamish of stomach to hold onto their seats.

Willamette Jet Boat Excursions (ages 6 and up)

1945 Southeast Water Avenue, adjacent to the Oregon Museum of Science and Industry (OMSI); (800) 538–2628 or (503) 231–1532; www.willamettejet.com. Reservations recommended; arrive at least fifteen minutes before departure. Daily departures for two-hour city and falls tour are April through mid-October at 10:45 A.M. and 2:45 P.M.; July and August at 10:45 A.M., 1:45 P.M., and 5:45 P.M. July and August one-hour harbor tour departs at 4:15 P.M.; $$$, children 3 and under free. Regular tours $$$$ adults, $ ages 4–11, 3 and under free.

This is an exciting way to view the Portland skyline, waterfront activity, and bird life on a 37-mile round-trip excursion from the docks next to OMSI to the base of Willamette Falls in Oregon City.

Eastbank Esplanade (all ages)

Stretches from the Steel Bridge to the Hawthorne Bridge on the east side of the Willamette River; (503) 823–2223; Open daily year-round. Free.

The mile-long esplanade features a 1,200-foot floating walkway—the longest in the United States—public boat docks, river overlooks and cantilevered walkways, plazas, urban markers and interpretive panels, public art, and access to the **Steel Bridge Walkway,** built for bicyclists and pedestrians on the lower deck of the Steel Bridge. Fully accessible, the walkway gives pedestrians a safe connection to the Convention Center, Lloyd District, and Old Town/Downtown. The Steel Bridge is on the National Register of Historic Places and is the only telescoping vertical lift span truss bridge in operation in America.

Samtrak Excursion Train (all ages)

(503) 659–5452 or (503) 653–2380. Operates weekends May and June, daily except Monday and Tuesday in July and August. $, children under 2 free.

At OMSI, hop on this open-air train that travels along the banks of the Willamette River to **Oaks Amusement Park,** a 3-mile route that runs through the **Oaks Bottom Wildlife Refuge.** The round-trip takes an hour, but you can stop off at either end of the line to enjoy the OMSI or the park.

Oaks Amusement Park (ages 5 and up)

Located alongside the Willamette River, just east of the Sellwood Bridge; (503) 233–5777; www.oakspark.com. Open Memorial Day through Labor Day; call for times. Free entry; charge for individual rides.

Considered the oldest continuously running amusement park in the country, this park has been delighting kids of all ages since 1904. The fun includes a year-round roller-skating rink complete with 1923 Wurlitzer organ, amusement rides that range from toddler swings and an antique carousel to the Looping Thunder roller coaster and the Screaming Eagle ride. There's also a beautiful shady picnic area and a sandy beach.

Ladybug Theater (ages 3 and up)

Located at Smile Station, 8210 Southeast Thirteenth, at the foot of Southeast Spokane Street; (503) 232–2346. Call for show schedule, hours, and prices.

Oregon's premier children's theater offers a wonderful introduction to live performing arts for kids two and a half and older.

Mt. Tabor Park (ages 5 and up)

Southeast Salmon and Sixtieth; (800) 962–3700 or (503) 823–7529; www.parks.ci .portland.or.us. Call for hours. Free.

This 195-acre park frames the only extinct volcano within the limits of any U.S. metropolitan area. The park contains a permanent exhibit of the volcanic cone. Hiking trails take you to the top, where the view of Portland is terrific. A new exhibit displays volcanic cinders found in the park and outlines its geologic history.

The Grotto (all ages)

Sandy Boulevard at Eighty-fifth Street; (503) 245–7371; www.thegrotto.org. Gardens and gift shop are open daily year-round. Call for hours and admission price.

You will find respite at this sixty-two-acre garden that includes a natural stone grotto in the side of a cliff. The lands of this meditative setting are owned by the Roman Catholic Church, but people of all faiths are welcome. Regular church services are held outdoors at the Grotto during spring and summer, weather permitting. Two annual events, the Christmas Festival of Lights and Gallery in the Woods, are held here in December and June, respectively.

Portland Saturday Market (all ages)

Second Avenue and Burnside under the Burnside Bridge; (503) 222–6072; www .portland saturdaymarket.com. Rain or shine, open Saturday 10:00 A.M.–5:00 P.M., Sunday 11:00 A.M.– 4:30 P.M., March through December 24. Free entry.

About 450 crafts and food booths transform this asphalt area from April through December every Saturday and Sunday. Most weekends there's nonstop entertainment that aims to please the whole family. Clowns with balloons and vendors who paint faces attract kids like magnets.

Laurelhurst Park (all ages)

Southeast Thirty-ninth and Stark; (503) 823–2223; www.parks.ci.portland.or.us; e-mail: pkweb@ci.portland.us. Open daily dawn to dusk. Free.

When I was a child, this was my favorite Portland park. Its natural beauty, towering trees, lush rhododendrons, and noisy ducks who clamored for crumbs on Laurelhurst Lake all reside vividly in my memory. Therefore, it's truly enchanting to return here and find little changed, except for the addition of lighted tennis courts, volleyball courts, and a bigger playground.

Art for Kids (all ages)

Located along the Transit Mall, easily identified by the brick streets and wide sidewalks at Southwest Fifth and Sixth Avenues; (800) 962–3700 or (503) 275–8355. Always open. Free.

Look for the animals—large bronze, cement, or marble structures that invite climbing and touching (it's OK; that was the artists' intent). In the park blocks between Park and Ninth, stretching from Burnside to Portland State University, you'll also find a variety of sculptures, ranging from traditional to contemporary.

Ira Keller Fountain (all ages)

At Third Avenue between Clay and Market Streets, across from the Civic Auditorium; (503) 823–7529.

You'll see this fountain alive with kids and families cooling off in the summer or just enjoying the sound of cascading water in this city-block-size water park.

North Side

Sauvie Island (all ages)

18330 Northwest Sauvie Island Road (for trail maps), about 10 miles north of downtown Portland off US 30; (503) 621–3488. Call for hours. Parking $ per day, $$$ annually.

If you are looking for a wonderful retreat, whether it be a beach picnic and swim in August, a trip to island farms to select jack-o'-lanterns, or bird-watching for sandhill cranes in March, Sauvie Island has it all. It's home to farmers as well as to the **Sauvie Island Wildlife Area,** which is open daily. However, during waterfowl season much of the area is closed to protect migrating geese, ducks, and swans. Hiking trails wind through the 12,000-acre wildlife area, which covers half of the island. Wheelchair-accessible fishing docks are available at the Big Eddy and Gilbert River boat ramps in the wildlife area. **Walton Beach,** located about 10 miles north of the Sauvie Island Wildlife Office off Reeder Road, is a 3-mile stretch of sandy beach along the Columbia River. It's a favorite spot for swimming, fishing, and picnicking (no tables, but you can spread your blanket on the sand). Stop by the **Cracker Barrel Grocery Store** for provisions on the way.

Bybee Howell House (ages 5 and up)

13901 Northwest Howell Road on Sauvie Island; (503) 797–1850; www.ohs.org. Open Saturday and Sunday noon–5:00 P.M. Memorial Day through Labor Day. Recommended donation $.

This museum is located in an old colonial-style farmhouse operated by the Oregon Historical

Society. Next door, stop in to view farm tools from the 1840s to the turn of the twentieth century, before the introduction of gasoline-powered farm equipment. Kids will also enjoy looking at the old farm photographs. They can climb on some of the larger pieces of equipment.

West Side

Portland's western hills are a popular spot in the summer and fall for appreciating the bounty of the harvest. U-pick farms abound, for everything from Oregon's own marionberries (grown in very few places in the country), delicious peaches, and tasty hazelnuts to bright orange pumpkins and juicy wine grapes. For a display of fall colors, take a drive from Beaverton along Farmington Road.

Jenkins Estate (all ages)

Grabhorn Road, off Farmington and 209th; continue along Grabhorn to its junction with Scholls Ferry Road, then return on the loop to Beaverton; (503) 642–3855; www.thprd.org. Grounds open daily 8:00 A.M.–8:00 P.M. in summer, 8:00 A.M.–5:00 P.M. October through May. Call for information about touring building. Free.

Once a private residence and now a public park, the estate has lovely gardens for a walk or a picnic. You'll pass a number of farms before you get there, many of which produce, in September and October, the most spicily refreshing apple cider you've ever tasted. You will also find U-pick walnut and hazelnut farms. For adults, a stop at one of several wineries along the way is especially fun.

Malibu Grand Prix (see height requirement below)

9405 Southwest Cascade Avenue; (503) 641–8122. Open Monday through Saturday 11:00 A.M.–11:00 P.M., Sunday 11:00 A.M.–9:00 P.M. Call for prices. To arrange birthday parties, call (503) 641–0772.

For fast-paced family fun, primarily for families with kids who are at least 4 feet, 6 inches tall, you'll find adult- and kid-size "Indy-500" cars to put to the test on the racetrack.

Jackson Bottom Wetlands (all ages)

Trailhead is located off State Highway 219 south of Hillsboro; (503) 681–6206; www.jackson bottom.org. Open dawn to dusk. Education Center hours are 10:00 A.M.–4:00 P.M. daily. No dogs or bicycles. Free.

The preserve has developed a number of educational programs that you and your kids can appreciate together. One of the simplest ways to get a sense of the wetlands environment is to walk the **Kingfisher Marsh Interpretive Trail,** which takes you on a 3-mile-long walk along the Tualatin River and into the Kingfisher Marsh.

East Side

Troutdale is the home of a large factory outlet shopping center and **Lewis & Clark State Park** on the Sandy River, just south of where it empties into the Columbia. Just before you leave the main area of town, you'll see the small but fascinating rail museum.

Troutdale Rail Museum (ages 5 and up)

473 East Historic Columbia River Highway, located at the edge of town toward the Sandy River; (503) 661-2164. Open May through September Monday through Friday 10:00 A.M.– 4:00 P.M.; call for weekend hours. $, children under 12 free.

It's an original 1882 rail depot and one of the earliest stations along the Columbia.

Blue Lake Park (ages 5 and up)

Located on Marine Drive, off 205th Avenue; (800) 962-3700; www.travelportland.com. Call for hours. Free entry; $ swimming fee; $–$$ boat rentals.

Concrete-bordered swimming areas line the sandy north shore. The inventive dragon slide and other playground equipment keep kids busy between stops at the snack bar. You can rent paddleboats, canoes, and rowboats.

Family Favorites
in Portland and the Columbia Gorge

1. Saturday Market
2. Oregon Zoo
3. Japanese Garden
4. Oregon Museum of Science and Industry
5. CM2: Children's Museum
6. Oaks Amusement Park
7. Powell's City of Books
8. Columbia River Gorge National Scenic Area
9. Scenic Mt. Hood Railroad
10. Ramona Falls, near Sandy

Fun Facts

- Matt Groening, creator of the popular TV show *The Simpsons*, got his start in Portland.

- Portland's Mt. Tabor is the only extinct volcano located within a city's limits in the United States.

- Mill Ends Park is 24 inches in diameter and the world's smallest dedicated park. Portland also has Forest Park, the largest forested municipal park in the nation.

- Powell's City of Books is the largest new and used bookstore in the world, with more than one million books in a store that takes up a full city block.

Candy Basket (ages 5 and up) 🔘

1924 Northeast 181st; (800) 864–1924 or (503) 666–2000. Open 9:00 A.M.–6:00 P.M. Monday through Saturday, 11:00 A.M.– 5:00 P.M. Sunday.

A stream of warm, luscious chocolate cascades over 20 feet, 3 inches of sculpted marble and bronze in this will-bending store. The fountain circulates 2,700 pounds of chocolate, and the aroma is scrumptious. The one-of-a-kind cascade is part of a tour through the candy factory.

South Side

Oregon City was founded by the Hudson's Bay Company, which had been launched by the fur trade and had its western headquarters at Fort Vancouver, Washington, just across the Columbia River. This community is considered by many to be the end of the Oregon Trail.

Oregon Trail Interpretive Center (ages 5 and up) 🏛 🔘

Take I–205 to exit 10; turn right at the first light—you can't miss the center's enormous covered wagons; (503) 557–1151; www.endoftheoregontrail.org. Open Monday through Saturday 9:30 A.M.–5:30 P.M., Sunday 10:30 A.M.–5:30 P.M. $$ adults, $ ages 5–12, under 5 **free.**

The center consists of a complex of three 50-foot-tall Conestoga wagon–shaped buildings commemorating the importance of the trail to our nation's growth. One building contains living-history programs and an audiovisual presentation to acquaint

Top Portland **Events**

May

Cinco de Mayo. Sample authentic award-winning food, from tortas to tamales to the latest in southwestern and Mexican cuisine. Dance to merengue, cumbias, and the modern rhythms of Tejano music or simply enjoy peaceful music from the Andes. You can take home your own clay pot, watch a bilingual puppet show, or buy some folk arts and crafts hand-made by visiting artisans from Portland's sister city, Guadalajara. Held in Gov. Tom McCall Waterfront Park; (503) 222–9807.

Summer

Your Zoo and All That Jazz concerts are held on the lawn outside the Africafe at the Oregon Zoo every Wednesday night in summer; Thursdays bring **Rhythm and Blues Zoo Concerts.** Pack a picnic lunch and wind down here for the day. (800) 962–3700.

June

Hot Air Balloon Classic. Head for Beaverton to see the sky filled with colorful hot-air balloons during three days of festivities. (800) 962–3700.
Junior Rose Festival Parade. The largest children's parade in the world, which takes places at Gov. Tom McCall Waterfront Park, usually involves more than 10,000 kids. (503) 227–2681.
Portland Rose Festival. This yearly megaevent includes parades, carnivals, concerts, boat and Indy-car races, an air show, and fireworks. (503) 227–2681.

July

Portland Highland Games. For more than fifty years, this event has brought bagpipers, drummers, Highland dancers, Scottish food and wares, clan tents, and an evening *ceilidh* (traditional Highland music party) to the city. (503) 293–8501.

August

Homowo Festival. Originating in Ghana, the two-day festival features music, dance, African and Caribbean food, arts and crafts, and storytelling for the kids. (503) 288–3025.
Wilsonville Celebration Days. This family event features continuous main-stage entertainment, a kids' stage, inflatables, roving entertainers, a

carnival, and a Pied Piper costume booth, where kids pick a costume and go on parade with a clown through the park. (503) 620–6791.

Summer Festival. A free festival of music, hands-on art booths for kids, food, and fun. Entertainment accompanies the Interstate Avenue Fair & Garage Sale. Held at the Interstate Firehouse Cultural Center. (503) 823–4322.

India Festival. The India Cultural Association hosts a celebration of Indian culture and authentic food and dancing. Held in Pioneer Courthouse Square. (503) 223–1613.

September

Oregon Polish Festival. The swirling colors of Eastern European folk dancers and the savory scents of rich ethnic foods entice crowds to the St. Stanislaus Polish Catholic Church. (503) 281–7532.

October

Haunted Caves. The Washington County Fairplex annually houses this long-time event that benefits local charities. (800) 537–3149 or (503) 644–5555.

visitors with the history of the Oregon Trail. Another is designed in the style of a Missouri provisioner's store—sort of a mid-nineteenth-century superstore, according to one of the organizers. The third building offers exhibits, living-history demonstration areas, and a gift shop.

Clackamas County History Museum (ages 5 and up)

211 Tumwater Drive, located on the bluff above the river; (503) 655–5574; www.orcity.com/ museum. Open daily 11:00 A.M.–4:00 P.M. $, family admission (up to five persons) $$, children under 5 free.

One of the treasures among small-town history museums, the exhibits cover the course of local history, from Native American life and culture to the fur-trading days of the Hudson's Bay Company and the settlement of early pioneers.

Family Fun Center and Bullwinkle's Restaurant (ages 1–12)

29111 Southwest Town Center Loop, Wilsonville; located off I–5 at exit 283, 20 miles south of Portland; (503) 685–5000; www.fun-center.com. Open Sunday through Thursday 10:00 A.M.–10:00 P.M., Friday and Saturday 10:00 A.M.–11:00 P.M. Call for prices.

A variety of play areas for kids twelve months to twelve years old makes this a welcome stop for the whole family. Socks are required, and shoes are left behind when you venture into the "soft" playgrounds. There are forty events covering three levels, including a cafeteria, a video-game room, go-carts, bumper cars, a climbing wall, and a miniature-golf course.

McLoughlin House (ages 5 and up)
713 Center Street; (503) 656–5146; www.mcloughlinhouse.org. Open Wednesday through Saturday 10:00 A.M.–4:00 P.M., Sunday 1:00–4:00 P.M., closed Monday, Tuesday, holidays, and the month of January. $, children under 6 free.

Take a guided tour of the home in which Dr. John McLoughlin of the Hudson's Bay Company retired in 1846. The furnishings have been fully restored and are authentic to the mid-nineteenth century. More developments may be expected once the National Park Service takes over operation of the house.

Oregon City Tower (ages 5 and up)
Located near the McLoughlin House; (800) 962–3700 or (503) 275–8355. Call for hours. Free.

Take the elevator or stairs from the top of the bluff down to river level; from the observation deck at the top you have a great view of the Oregon City Falls.

George Rogers Park (ages 5 and up)
Located at the south end of State Street in Lake Oswego; (503) 266–4600. Call for hours. Free.

One of the most complete family-fun parks in the metro area, George Rogers Park offers swimming areas, sandy beaches, a wading stream for kids to splash around in, a waterfall that adds a lilting cascade of sound, great playground structures, and a walking trail that connects with **Mary Young State Park,** about 5 miles upriver. More trails take you to Oswego Creek, and there's even a bit of intriguing local history left in the park—a large chimney that's the last remnant of Oregon's first iron smelter.

Molalla

To reach Molalla, take State Highway 213 south from Oregon City. Signs in town point to Feyrer Park and Shady Dell; both are highly recommended locations.

Feyrer Park (all ages)
Located on the Molalla River; (503) 829–6941 or (503) 353–4422. Open 6:00 A.M.–10:00 P.M. May through September, 6:00 A.M.– 6:00 P.M. October through April. $ day-use fee on weekends and holidays; weekdays free.

Swimming holes, picnic tables, and playground equipment make a summertime visit worthwhile for families with energetic kids who have been in the car all day. Camping is available May through September for a fee.

Shady Dell Pacific Northwest Live Steamers (all ages)
Follow signs in town toward Feyrer Park; turn onto Shady Dell Drive; (503) 829–6866. Open Sunday noon–5:00 P.M. May through October, weather permitting.

Train rides are **free,** although donations are gratefully received. The kids will love the electric, steam, and diesel trains this group runs on small-scale tracks along a placid stream, around a pond, over trestles, and through the forest in the Molalla Train Park.

Canby Ferry (all ages) ⓐ
To reach the ferry, drive along the Willamette River on State Highway 99E; (503) 650–3030. Call for hours and rates.

The ferry has operated since 1914. The ride across the river takes only five minutes, and you can either continue your journey on the opposite side or just ride the ferry back across the river.

Molalla River State Park (all ages) 🚶🏕
Located downriver from the Canby Ferry; (800) 551–6949; www.oregonstateparks.org. Day-use area. Free.

A gem of a park, this beautiful spot has paved walking trails; lots of ducks, frogs, great blue herons, and other marsh-loving critters; and two picnic areas. In summer locals often bring radio-controlled planes to fly in the open field between the two picnic areas.

Top Molalla **Event**

October
Apple Festival. Enjoy entertainment, apple pie, and homemade ice cream while celebrating Molalla's pioneering heritage with tours of the historic Dibble and Von der Ahe houses. (503) 829–5521.

Sandy

A quiet community in the foothills, Sandy is the gateway to Mt. Hood from the west. Here you'll find a variety of restaurants and lodging options, often less expensive than those on the mountain.

Rainbow Trout Farm (all ages)

Located 7.5 miles east of Sandy off Sylvan Drive; (503) 622–5223. Open daily 8:00 A.M.–dusk March 1 through October 15. Price based on size of fish caught.

Kids will have fun reeling in their very own fish at this U-catch pond.

Oregon Candy Farm (all ages)

48620 US 26, 5.5 miles east of Sandy; (503) 668–5066; www.theoregoncandyfarm.com. Open Monday through Friday 9:00 A.M.–5:00 P.M., Saturday and Sunday noon–5:00 P.M. Closed all major holidays.

A viewing window lets your kids watch the candy-making process in the factory, and you can purchase some of the more than one hundred chocolate and nonchocolate confections in the "candy room" shop to take home for gifts or munch on in the car.

Lost Lake (all ages)

Located 40 miles northeast of Sandy, 20 miles southwest of Hood River on Lost Lake Road; (541) 352–6002 (Forest Service) or (541) 386–6366 (resort); www.lostlakeresort .org. Call for hours and campground fees.

This is one of the most photographed lakes in the nation because of the snowcapped peak of Mt. Hood, which rises above and often casts its reflection upon the lake's pristine waters. Rent a rowboat, drop a line in the water to catch one of the brown or rainbow trout lurking beneath the surface of this 231-acre lake, or hike the trail surrounding the lake. Native Americans called the lake E-e-kwahl-a-mat-yan-ishkt, which means "heart of the mountains." It was a favored camping ground, and according to legend, during a pot-latch wolves pursued a snow-white doe that jumped into the lake, swam to the middle, and disappeared. Medicine men called this a bad omen, and the Native Americans left the camp immediately and never returned.

Ramona Falls (all ages)

65000 US 26 in Welches, located off Lolo Pass Road and Forest Road 1825; (503) 622–7674 or (800) 622–4822; www.fs.fed.us/r6. Call for hours and fees.

During the summer take the 4.5-mile loop trail (Trail #797) leading to the falls. It's one of the most popular day hikes on the mountain, both because it's easy enough for young children and because of the stunningly beautiful falls awaiting you.

Top Sandy **Event**

July

Music Fair & Feast. The four-day festival starts with a parade and continues with live music, a talent show, food, microbrews and wine from the local winery, and arts and crafts to make this a fun event for the whole family. (503) 668–4006; www.sandyoregonchamber.org.

Columbia Gorge

This area is so intensely beautiful it's been designated a National Scenic Area. You can explore its westernmost gateway from the old road, U.S. Highway 30, leading out of Troutdale past a score of waterfalls and stunning viewpoints. Or take Interstate 84 east from Portland for a water-level view of highlights such as Multnomah Falls and Bonneville Dam. In the east the gorge extends to Hood River and The Dalles.

Historic Columbia River Scenic Highway (all ages) 🏛 👥

Crossing the bridge from Troutdale over the Sandy River leads you along the Columbia River Scenic Highway (US 30); (888) 275–6368 or (541) 386–2333; www.odot.state .or.us/hcrh or www.fs.fed.us/r6/columbia. Always open. Free.

An engineering feat when it was built between 1913 and 1922, this 55-mile highway winds through rich agricultural land and deep forests and cuts through the sides of steep basalt cliffs to a series of waterfalls that pour over the edge on their way to the Columbia. Designated a National Historic Landmark, it was the first modern highway in the Northwest. Several waterfalls here are worth driving many miles to see. Hiking trails take you between falls or to the points where the falls cascade over the cliff tops. Paths at Latourel Falls, Bridal Veil Falls, Wahkeena Falls, Multnomah Falls, Oneonta Gorge, Horsetail Falls, and Elowah Falls are all under a mile.

Crown Point Vista House (ages 5 and up) 🏛

Located 5 miles east of Troutdale on the Columbia River Scenic Highway; (503) 695–2230; www.vistahouse.com. Open daily to the public mid-April through mid-October 8:30 A.M.–6:00 P.M. Free, but donations welcome.

One of the first stops along the way on the Columbia River Scenic Highway, the recently renovated 1917 house gives you a perfect viewpoint from which to see the rugged gorge and the river that carved it. A small gallery and interpretive center, open mid-April through mid-October, offer information on the area. On Saturdays during the summer months, the whole family can enjoy folk-art demonstrations or historical and cultural programs.

Multnomah Falls (ages 8 and up)

Located in the Columbia Gorge on I–84; (503) 695–2372 (visitor center); www.fs.fed.us/ r6/columbia. Visitor center open daily year-round 9:00 A.M.–5:00 P.M., until 7:00 P.M. in summer. Free.

At 620 feet high, Multnomah Falls is the second-highest waterfall in the United States. If you have the time and your kids have the energy, walk the trail to the top of the upper falls, about 1 mile of fairly steep climbing on a paved path. At the top, follow the creek upstream to some beautiful shaded dells where children can dabble their feet in the water or search for crawdads.

Oneonta Falls (ages 10 and up) ⊗

Located on the Columbia River Scenic Highway (US 30) east of Multnomah Falls; (541) 386–2333; www.fs.fed.us/r6/columbia. Free.

Oneonta Falls isn't the tallest or most beautiful of the falls, but it is a favorite because it's the most fun to get to. Not appropriate for very young children, Oneonta Falls is at the end of a tall, narrow slit carved by Oneonta Creek. The walls rise a sheer 150 feet above the creek bed. The most kid-satisfying and most direct route to the falls is 0.25 mile and gives the kids a chance to hop rocks in the creek and get delightfully damp in the process. Oneonta means "place of peace," and that sense of peace pervades this gorge.

Benson State Recreation Area (all ages) ⊜ ⊛ ⊛ ⊛ ⊛

On the Columbia River 30 miles east of Portland off I–84 (eastbound access only); (800) 551–6949; www.oregonstateparks.org. Open year-round. $ day-use fee.

Benson Lake is a non-motorboat lake, making it a great spot for swimming. There's even a Frisbee golf course. The first weekend in June brings kids out for a free fishing day on the lake.

Rooster Rock State Park (all ages) ⊛ ⊜ ⊛

Accessible only from I–84; (800) 551–6949 or (503) 695–2261. Open daily 7:00 A.M.– dusk. $ day-use fee.

You won't have a hard time finding this park because the large basalt "rooster tail" rock that rises above it makes the site easy to spot. The park has shaded picnic groves, a protected moorage area, and sandy beaches. You may want to be fore- warned that at the far east end of the park, a stairway leads to secluded beaches where nude sunbathing is allowed beyond a point 100 yards farther east.

Bonneville Locks and Dam and Fish Hatchery (ages 5 and up)
🐘 🚗 🏛

From Portland take I–84 east to exit 40; (541) 374–8442; http://corpslakes.army.mil/visitors/project2. Call for hours. Free.

The visitor center at the dam has some very impressive educational exhibits on river history, the production of electricity, and a Native American sacred burial ground. The viewing windows looking into the fish ladder in the Underwater Observatory give you an up-close look at fish that are bigger than some children. The sturgeon pond, where these ancient giants cruise through water rimmed with lily pads, always was my favorite part of the fish hatchery. These prehistoric fish, which thrive in the Columbia River, have been around for 200 million years and grow to lengths of 10 feet and more. Your kids get the whole picture of the salmon life cycle in several areas of the hatchery, and depending on the time of year, they can view fish culturists removing eggs from spawning females, the incubation room where millions of bright red eggs in trays become tiny salmon fry, or the outdoor pools where the fry grow big enough to be released into Tanner Creek.

Grounds at the hatchery. (541) 374–8393. Open daily 7:30 A.M.–dusk. Enjoy a picnic dinner on the attractive grounds while your kids enjoy feeding the brooder rainbow trout or climbing on the playground equipment.

Eagle Creek (ages 10 and up) 🧗 🌊 🚗

Just east of Bonneville Dam on the north side of I–84 off exit 41. (503) 695–2261 or (541) 386–2333; www.fs.fed.us/r6/columbia. Open year-round. $ day-use fee (Northwest Forest Pass).

At **Eagle Creek Park** you'll find a picnic area, walking trails, and some nice swimming holes on the creek. **Eagle Creek Scenic Trail,** Number 440, takes you past Metlako, Punchbowl, Loowit, and Tunnel Falls in just 6 miles on the way into the **Columbia Wilderness Area.** With kids you'll probably want to walk only the 2 miles to **Punchbowl Falls,** truly one of the most impressive around. Because there are some sheer cliffs with no guardrails, this hike may not be suitable for some children.

Hood River

The Hood River Valley is Oregon's largest producer of fruit, yielding apples and pears that are valued across the United States. A loop drive, best in late August and early September, takes you past a number of fruit stands where you can buy direct from the growers.

Fun Fact

Viento is Spanish for "wind," but although the state park with this name sits in one of Oregon's windiest places, it was actually named for the three railroad tycoons who built the first railroad in the area: Villard, Endicott, and Tollman.

Scenic Mt. Hood Railroad (all ages) 🏛

110 Railroad Avenue; (800) 872–4661 or (541) 386–3556; www.mthoodrr.com. Morning excursions weekdays, morning and afternoon excursions weekends; dinner train. Call for hours and fees.

The 1906 train, which departs from the Mt. Hood Railroad Depot, is a link between the Columbia River Gorge and the foothills of this area's other natural wonder, Mt. Hood, the state's highest peak. The Timberline car has snacks and beverages to enjoy along the way.

Hood River Water Play (ages 10 and up)

(541) 386–9463 or (800) 963–7873; www.hoodriverwaterplay.com. Open daily; call for hours and fees.

Want to test your might against the famous Columbia Gorge winds? This is one of many surf shops in town, but it offers special kids' programs and rental equipment.

Jackson Park (all ages) 🚻

Thirteenth and May Streets; (800) 366–3530. Open dawn to dusk. **Free.**

Families are the center of the fun every Thursday evening in August, with the Families in the Park entertainment series. Bring a picnic and enjoy the program.

Saturday Farmer's Market (all ages)

Parking lot between Fifth and Seventh, and Cascade and Columbia; (800) 366–3530; www.hoodriverchamber.org. Open Saturday 9:00 A.M.–3:00 P.M. mid-May through mid-October. **Free.**

Pick up luscious fruit for snacks from local growers at this open-air market.

Fun Fact

Hood River is the windsurfing capital of the world.

Top Hood River **Events**

April

Hood River Blossom Festival. Blossoming pear and apple orchards create an exquisite backdrop for Hood River's springtime festival. (800) 366–3530 or (541) 386–2000.

July

Hood River Cherry Days. Fresh-picked cherries and all kinds of specialty products are part of the Hood River Fruit Loop's annual Cherry Days, which features cherry tasting, cherry picking, farm tours, kids' activities, and a variety of other events located throughout the valley. (541) 386–7697; www.hoodriverfruitloop.com.

August

Gravenstein Apple Days. With—you guessed it—plenty of apples and apple-inspired goodies to sample, this might be just the pick for a lunch stop. (541) 386–7697.

October through November

Hood River Valley Harvest Fest. An annual celebration that expresses appreciation for the bounty of fall harvest with food booths, arts and crafts, and pumpkin carving. (800) 366–3530 or (541) 386–2000.

Mt. Hood Holiday Spook Train. Ghosts, goblins, witches, and warlocks will be among your fellow passengers on this train. (800) 872–4661; www.mthoodrr.com.

Rasmussen Farms Pumpkin Funland. Sometimes beginning as early as September, the farm's Pumpkin Funland usually runs through mid-November and includes a Halloween hunt and corn-husk maze. (541) 386–4622 or (800) 548–2243; www.rasmussenfarms.com.

December

Mt. Hood Railroad Christmas Tree Train. If you're traveling through here during the winter, this magical train ride will make your holiday special with carolers, a country-style holiday meal, and, if you're not far from home, the chance to pick up a Christmas tree. (800) 872–4661; www.mthoodrr.com.

For more information on Hood River events, call (800) 366–3530 or (541) 386–2000 or visit www.hoodriver.org.

Viento State Park (all ages)

Located about 8 miles west of Hood River; (541) 374–8811 or (800) 551–6949; www .oregon stateparks.org. $ day-use fee.

Viento is one of several state parks that sit alongside the Columbia River. A mix of maple, fir, willow, and pine nestle with tent and trailer sites, making this a pretty place to plunk down for a night's rest. There's a 0.25-mile nature trail to **Viento Lake,** where the wetlands surrounding it provide a good spot for bird-watching. The **Starvation Creek Trail** takes you 1 mile along a section of the Historic Columbia River Highway.

Cascade Locks and Cascade Locks Historical Museum (ages 5 and up)

Located in Cascade Locks Marine Park, west of Hood River; (541) 374–8619. Open daily noon–5:00 P.M. May through September. Free, but donations welcome.

"Cascade" refers not to the mountain range to the east but to the cascading waters once in this part of the Columbia's journey to the sea. Located in the park are displays that describe the river's history. An outdoor barn contains a variety of wagons, and a small building houses the first steam locomotive in the Northwest.

Columbia Gorge Sternwheeler (ages 6 and up)

Board from Marine Park in Cascade Locks, 20 minutes west of Hood River on I–84 at exit 44; (503) 224–3900 or (800) 224–3901; www.sternwheeler.com; e-mail: sales@ sternwheeler.com. Daily cruises Memorial Day through Labor Day, Saturday and Sunday only through September; $$$ adults, $$ children for two-hour narrated cruises, departing at noon and 3:00 P.M. (noon cruise is a champagne brunch on weekends, $$$$); $$$$ for two-hour sunset dinner cruises, departing 7:00 P.M. Friday, 6:30 P.M. Saturday. In December the sternwheeler departs from the seawall in Gov. Tom McCall Waterfront Park in Portland for special holiday cruises. Call for other specialty cruises and off-season schedules.

When you board the sternwheeler *Columbia Gorge,* you combine a history lesson with a step back in time. Riverboats took Lewis and Clark on the first stage of their journey that eventually brought them to the wild waters of the Columbia River. Considerably tamed since the days of their expedition, the river now reflects the history as well as the natural beauty of the Columbia Gorge. The riverboat captain provides a

narrative about the Lewis and Clark expedition, travelers along the Oregon Trail, and the traditions of local Native Americans, who still fish from platforms, as has been done for centuries.

Marine Park (all ages) 👫

355 Wanapa, Cascade Locks; follow Main Street to the park; (541) 374–8619. Open daily dawn–10:00 P.M. Free.

The story of Lewis and Clark's trip with Sacajawea and her papoose and how they navigated the treacherous Columbia with its many chutes comes alive here. Now several dams have tamed the once-wild river. Native Americans sometimes fish here in the traditional manner. A marina is also available in the park.

Hood River Fruit Loop (ages 5 and up) 🍁 🏠

A 35-mile loop drive; (541) 386–7697; www.hoodriverfruitloop.com. Hours vary at farm stands and farms along the route. See printable map and list of vendors on the Web site or call for brochure. Free.

During harvest season there's no richer place for tasting the fruits of nature than the Hood River valley. Thousands of acres of lush orchards and rich farmland form the foreground, with Mt. Hood in the background—it's definitely an opportunity for photographs! A wide variety of vendors are open along the route for produce and delicious products made from local fruits and berries. The produce changes through the seasons: strawberries and raspberries in June; cherries, apricots, and blueberries in July; peaches in August; apples and pears in August and September. October brings chestnuts for roasting and sunny orange pumpkins.

Mountain View Cycle (all ages) 🚲

411 Oak Street; (541) 386–2453; www.mtviewcycles.com. Open Monday through Saturday 9:00 A.M.–6:00 P.M., Sunday 9:00 A.M.–5:00 P.M. Mountain bikes and road bikes $$ per hour, $$$$ per day; kids' bikes and bike trailers $ per hour, $$$$ per day.

Located in historic downtown Hood River, Mountain View Cycle & Fitness rents mountain, road, and children's bikes as well as trailers for towing toddlers.

Hood River County Historical Museum (ages 5 and up) 🏛

Located in Port Marina Park; (541) 386–6772; www.co.hood-river.or.us/museum; e-mail: hrchm@gorge.net. April through August, open Monday through Saturday 10:00 A.M.–4:00 P.M., Sunday noon–4:00 P.M.; September and October, open daily noon–4:00 P.M. Closed November through March. Free, but donations welcome.

Native American artifacts and pioneer relics, as well as displays on the development of the lumber and fruit-growing industries in the region, make this museum a worthwhile stop.

International Museum of Carousel Art (ages 3 and up)
304 Oak Street; (541) 387–4622; www.carouselmuseum.com; e-mail: mail@carousel museum.com. Open Monday through Saturday 11:00 A.M.–3:00 P.M., Sunday noon– 4:00 P.M. $, children under 5 free.

Billed as having "the world's largest collection of antique carousel art," this museum includes around 140 carousel animals and chariots, an antique steam engine, and a fully operational 1917 Wurlitzer band organ.

Phoenix Pharms U-catch Trout Farm (ages 3 and up)
4349 Baldwin Creek Road, 12 miles south of Hood River off U.S. Highway 35; (541) 352–6090; summer hours Wednesday through Saturday 10:00 A.M.–5:30 P.M. Call for off-season hours and prices.

Let your little one get the joy of reeling in a "big one" at this well-stocked pond. There's no license required, and bait and pole are provided. You're also welcome to picnic on the grounds after your angling adventure.

Mt. Hood

Winter isn't the only season for enjoying this majestic mountain, which at 11,235 feet is Oregon's tallest peak. Summer brings hikers, mountain climbers, anglers, boaters, and bird-watchers to the slopes. The winter recreation activities usually extend from late fall through early spring, with year-round skiing available at Timberline Lodge. Several ski resorts on the mountain offer everything from beginner hills to steep, mogul-covered slopes. Night skiing, ski and snowboard rentals, and lessons are available at each site. Sno-park passes are required November 15 through April 30 and are available at the Hood River or Zigzag ranger stations located on US 30 beyond Mt. Hood Meadows or at the Forest Service's information center at Mt. Hood RV Village, 13 miles east of Sandy on US 26. Check road conditions before driving to the mountain (800–977–6368 or 503–588–2941; www.tripcheck.com), and be sure to carry chains.

Mt. Hood Meadows (ages 5 and up)
Located on US 35; (503) 337–2222 or (800) 754–4663; (503) 227–SNOW (snow report); www.skihood.com; e-mail: mhminfo@skihood.com. Call for snow levels, prices, and hours.

With 2,150 skiable acres, this is the largest resort on the mountain. The "Meadows" usually opens after mid-November, depending on snow levels, of course. It is a full-service facility that offers instruction, child care, restaurants, plus parks and pipes for young skiers and snowboarders.

Top Mt. Hood **Events**

September

Autumn Festival. An Oregon celebration of Mt. Hood's cuisine, culture, and forest spread among the villages on the mountain: Government Camp, Rhododendron, and Welches. There's an entertainment stage, living-history village, forest festival, and activities centered around Native American culture, pioneer life, forest and wildlife conservation, and arts and crafts. (503) 622–4822; e-mail: autumnfestival@mthood.info.

Mt. Hood Huckleberry Festival & Barlow Trail Days. Held at Mt. Hood Village, 65000 East US 26, and sponsored by the Cascade Geographic Society, this event focuses on pioneer history and the plentiful huckleberries turning blue all over the mountain. (503) 622–4798.

Cooper Spur Mountain Resort (ages 5 and up)

10755 Cooper Spur Road; (541) 352–7803; (541) 352–6692 (lodging); (541) 352–6037 (restaurant); www.cooperspur.com; e-mail: info@cooperspur.com. Call for snow levels, hours, and fees.

This ski area specializes in presenting affordable winter fun for the whole family, offering ten runs for skiing and snowboarding and a tubing center. A day lodge and restaurant provide a place to warm up, and a newly expanded deck allows guests to soak up sunshine while keeping track of the rest of their party, as almost the entire ski area is viewable from the base lodge. The Nordic Center provides 6.5 kilometers of groomed trails, and separate snowshoe trails are also available. Probably the best deal on the mountain is the $15 lesson, which provides unlimited all-day access to roving skiing and snowboarding instructors.

Mt. Hood Skibowl (ages 5 and up)

87000 East US 26, Government Camp; (503) 272–3206 or (800) 754–2695; (503) 222–2695 (snow report); www.skibowl.com. Open daily in winter; call or check the Web site for summer hours and pricing.

You'll find skiing, snowboarding, and tubing in winter. In summer your kids will be thrilled by the Action Park's 1,000 acres of rides, including a 0.5-mile-long mountain-hugging luge that takes you down S-curves in sleds complete with brake levers that even young children can control—you go as fast or as slow as you like. A racecourse for fancy go-carts, interpretive nature trails, and a "sky chair" that takes hikers and mountain bikers to the top of the lift so they can walk or ride down make this an unforgettable family fun spot in any season.

Summit Ski Area (ages 5 and up)

Located at the east end of Government Camp on US 26; (503) 272–0256. Open weekends and holidays 8:30 A.M.–4:00 P.M. Call for snow levels. $$$$ all-day lift ticket; $$$ tube rental.

You'll find a great slope for kids to slide down on sleds, inner tubes, plastic bags, or cardboard boxes—anything works to bring giggles and squeals on the slippery slope. Inner-tube rentals for snow play on the hill are available here, along with snowboarding and alpine skiing.

Teacup Lake Nordic Center (ages 6 and up)

Located on US 35; e-mail: info@teacupnordic.org. $ day-use donation.

Groomed cross-country trails are available. Ungroomed trails take off from a variety of Sno-Parks (plowed parking areas) on the mountain.

Timberline Lodge and Ski Resort (ages 5 and up)

Off US 26; (503) 622–7979; (503) 222–2211 (snow report); www.timberlinelodge.com; e-mail: information@timberlinelodge.com. Call for snow levels, hours, and prices.

Timberline enjoys the longest ski season in North America, with more than 1,000 acres of skiable terrain. The Magic Carpet lift supports a wide range of children's learning programs. Foot passengers are also allowed on the **Magic Mile Sky Ride** daily, weather and lift lines permitting. Ages six and under **free** of charge when accompanied by parents. If you're just visiting the mountain for the day, summer or winter, stop by the lodge to appreciate the impressive views and equally impressive 1930s construction of this National Historic Landmark. Built as a WPA project, the lodge has the classic rough-hewn, massive scale of the period. Have your kids try to find the various animals carved into wooden structures throughout the building.

The Dalles

The early French *voyageurs* gave the name *Le Dalle,* or "the trough," to the falls at a Native American fishery about 6 miles above the current town site because of the frequency with which they were pulled under by the force of the water at the bottom of the falls. The falls have long since been covered with calm waters pooled behind the Dalles Dam.

Columbia Gorge Discovery Center & Wasco County Historical Museum (ages 5 and up) 🔶 🍴

5000 Discovery Drive; (541) 296–8600; www.gorgediscovery.org. Open daily 9:00 A.M.–5:00 P.M. Tours start at 10:00 A.M. $$ adults; $ ages 6–16, 5 and under free.

You'll want to spend the whole day in this 50,000-square-foot facility, exploring two museums, talking with "pioneers" in the Oregon Trail Living History Park, walking the interpretive trail, or having lunch in the Basalt Rock Cafe. This is the official interpretive center for the Columbia River Gorge National Scenic Area, and its exhibits on geology, wildlife, and ancient cultures will add meaning to your travels in the gorge.

Fort Dalles Museum (ages 5 and up) 🔶

Fifteenth and Garrison Streets; (541) 296–4547; www.wascochs.org/ftdm.htm. Open daily in summer 10:00 A.M.–5:00 P.M.; call for off-season hours. $, children 7 and under free.

Housed in the last remaining building of Fort Dalles, the museum was built in the wake of the Whitman massacre across the river. Originally the surgeon's quarters, the building now aptly serves to tell the story of the early decades of the community. The grounds contain a wide range of horse-drawn vehicles, and across the street you can visit an old homestead, granary, and barn.

Dalles Dam and Tour Train (all ages) 🏛

A half-hour train ride starts from the visitor center, at the end of Bret Cladfelter Way off exit 87 of I–84; (541) 296–9778. Call for seasonal hours. Free.

A train-ride tour of the dam provides a lot of history as well as fun. The pool of water behind the dam covers two Native American sites: a sacred burial ground and the ancient fishing grounds of **Celilo Falls**. Photographs in the **Seufert Visitor Center** show the fishing platforms built over basalt rocks so the Yakima Nation Indians could spear salmon as they jumped the falls on their migration upriver. You'll also see petroglyphs that were recovered before the dam was built. You have the option to get off at the powerhouse and fish ladders or a picnic area and return on a later train. The center's collections and interpretive displays provide background on Lewis and Clark and other local history.

Top Event in The Dalles

April
Northwest Cherry Festival. A parade, live music, health fair, food court, and crafts are all a part of this weeklong celebration of cherry blossoms. (800) 255–3385; www.thedalleschamber.com.

Fun Facts

- The Dalles is one of the oldest inhabited locations in North America, serving as a center of Native American trade for at least 10,000 years.
- The Dalles is one of the oldest incorporated cities in the United States.

Riverfront Park (all ages)
Take I–84 to exit 85; (541) 296–9533. Open dawn to dusk. Free.

Give your teenagers a relatively safe place to try out sailboarding. The offshore islands protect beginners from both the main river current and barge traffic. Equipment rentals and lessons are available through vendors operating at the park in the summer.

Memaloose State Park (all ages)
Eleven miles west of The Dalles; accessible only from the westbound freeway; (541) 478–3008 or (800) 551–6949; (800) 452–5687 for campground reservations; www .oregonstateparks.org. Campground open March through October; day-use area open year-round. Call for hours and campground fees; day-use area free.

You can see the lower and only remaining of two Memaloose Islands, which were sacred Native American burial grounds. *Memaloose* is the Chinook Indian word for "island of the dead." The park provides a cool summer oasis in the hottest part of the gorge.

The Dalles Talking Murals (all ages)
Located on a dozen building walls around historic downtown; keys for activating sound are $ (including a keepsake key ring), good for life, and available from the chamber of commerce (404 West Second), Klindt's Booksellers (315 East Second), and the Art Box (517 East Second).

The Dalles has made history by adding talking narration to its already fascinating murals—a first in the nation. With thirty-five historically accurate murals currently wired for sound and plans for more to be added over the next three years, this is an enchanting way to spend a leisurely afternoon. The underpass linking the downtown area to the river has been renovated recently, so enjoy a stroll to the riverfront after your mural tour.

Deschutes River State Recreation Area (all ages)

Located east of The Dalles on State Highway 206; (800) 551–6949 or (503) 228–9561; (800) 452–5687 for campground reservations; www.oregonstateparks.org. $ day-use fee.

This is where the Deschutes River flows into the Columbia. Recreation options include hiking, cycling, camping, boating, and—most popular—fishing. The Deschutes is one of Oregon's finest fishing rivers, popular among local Native Americans who dip-net fish from platforms along the riverbanks. An exhibit provides information about the pioneers who turned south just beyond here to follow the Barlow Trail spur of the Oregon Trail rather than risk disaster on the Columbia River. You can even rent a covered wagon to camp in! A mountain-bike trail takes off from the park entrance and follows an old railroad bed for 17 miles alongside the Deschutes. For a shady walk, take the **Atiyeh Deschutes River Trail** through white alder and birch forest. Look for oriole nests that resemble hanging baskets. This is rattlesnake country, so be careful!

Mayer State Park (all ages)

Located off I–84 10 miles west of The Dalles; (800) 551–6949 or (503) 228–9561; www.oregonstateparks.org. Day-use area. $ day-use fee.

Call ahead to arrange for a free naturalist-led tour. A swimming area in a small lake on the west side of the park is perfect for little ones. From the park, take the 9-mile scenic drive to Rowena Crest, a viewpoint high above the river that gives access to the Tom McCall Nature Preserve on the Rowena Plateau.

Tom McCall Nature Preserve

Located on the Rowena Plateau, 8 miles west of The Dalles (Mosier or Rowena exits from I–84); (503) 230–1221; www.nature.org. Open daily. Free.

This premier wildflower meadow, preserved by the Nature Conservancy, is best visited between early March and late May, when the blooms reach their peak. Hiking paths weave across the meadow and along the cliffs, but use caution because this is rattlesnake country.

Where to Eat

IN THE DALLES

Cousins' Restaurant. 2116 West Sixth Street; (541) 298–2771; www.cousins restaurant.com. Homestyle breakfast, lunch, and dinner spot well known for its cinnamon rolls, turkey sandwiches, and pot roast. $–$$

IN HOOD RIVER

The Crazy Pepper. 103 Fourth Street; (541) 387–2454. This Mexican restaurant has excellent food, good prices, fast service, and kids' favorites (hamburgers with fries, hot dogs, and grilled cheese). $–$$

Sol Luna. 1302 Thirteenth Street; (541) 386–2022; e-mail: solluna@gorge.net. Good Mediterranean food and moderate prices, but the real plus here is the separate **Kids Cafe.** For a price, your child has dinner and supervised entertainment/play time while you enjoy a nice dinner in an intimate atmosphere. $$–$$$

Wildflower Cafe. 904 Second Avenue, Mosier; (541) 478–0111. Very comfortable family atmosphere with good food and friendly service. The menu is traditional American, with potpies, sandwiches, soups, steak, and great homemade pies and cobblers. $–$$

IN MT. HOOD

Huckleberry Inn. Government Camp Loop Road; (503) 272–3325. Open twenty-four hours a day, it's a great breakfast or lunch stop. $–$$$

Mt. Hood Brewing Company. Government Camp Loop Road; (503) 622–0724; www.mthoodbrewing.com. Families are more than welcome at this mountainside dining establishment. Parents can enjoy the local brew while kids partake of classic pub hamburgers and fries. $–$$$

IN PORTLAND

Alexis Restaurant. 215 West Burnside; (503) 224–8577. This lively place is often crowded, so try to get there early for all your Greek favorites. If Greek food is new for the kids, try the extensive appetizer menu to give them a taste of some tantalizing possibilities. $$

Bread and Ink Cafe. 3610 Southeast Hawthorne; (503) 239–4756. Open for breakfast, lunch, and dinner, this casual neighborhood cafe has been voted one of the best restaurants in Oregon. $$

Tom's Pancake House. 12925 Southwest Canyon Road, Beaverton; (503) 646–2688.

Just as its name suggests, this place specializes in all flavors and types of pancakes, plus waffles and omelettes. Children's menu. $$

IN SANDY

Calamity Jane's Hamburger Parlor. 42015 US 26; (503) 668–7817. You can choose from fifty different burgers, and the milkshakes are made with real ice cream. $$

Where to Stay

IN THE DALLES

Comfort Inn. 351 Lone Pine Drive; (541) 298–2800 or (800) 955–9626; www.gorge hotels.com. This is the only motel in The Dalles with an indoor pool, which makes it especially popular with families during the Northwest Cherry Festival. $$–$$$

Cousins' Country Inn. 2114 West Sixth Street; (800) 848–9378 or (541) 298–5161; www.cousinscountryinn.com. Kids love the Old West exterior, and you'll love the outdoor swimming pool and indoor spa; in-room coffeemaker, microwave, refrigerator, and VCR; gas fireplaces; and access to the fitness center. Some kitchen units. $$$

IN HOOD RIVER

Best Western Hood River Inn. 1108 East Marina Way; (800) 828–7873 or (541) 386– 8905; www.hoodriverinn.com. Air-conditioned riverfront rooms, a restaurant, and a heated outdoor pool and spa are situated right in the heart of the Columbia River Gorge. Dogs OK. $$–$$$$

Columbia Gorge Hotel. 4000 Westcliff Drive; (800) 345–1921 or (541) 386–5566; www.columbiagorgehotel.com; e-mail: cghotel@gorge.net. This historic hotel, with its Spanish-style exterior, is all old-world luxury on the inside. The hotel was built in 1921 by lumber magnate Simon

Benson on the site of an old Native American meeting ground. An inviting lobby and fireside coffee room don't seem geared to children, but little ones are welcome at this stately old hotel. They'll enjoy exploring the grounds outside, where an arched stone footbridge crosses a small stream that meanders through the property. Family suites are available. $$$$

Hood River Hotel. Oak Street and First; (800) 386–1859 or (514) 386–1900; www .hoodriverhotel.com; e-mail: hrhotel@ gorge.net. Built in 1913 and on the National Historic Register, it has been refurbished as an enjoyable hotel with reasonable rates and many rooms overlooking the river. In the comfortable lounge, a basketful of toys helps entertain the kids. $–$$$

IN THE MT. HOOD AREA

Huckleberry Inn. Government Camp Loop Road, off US 26; (503) 272–3325; www.huckleberry-inn.com. A restaurant, kitchenettes, and laundry facilities make this small inn an especially handy place to stay during ski season. $–$$$

Timberline Lodge and Ski Resort. Off US 26 about 60 miles east of Portland; (800) 547–1406 or (503) 272–3311; www.timberlinelodge.com. The oldest resort on the mountain is a convenient place to reserve for a winter ski vacation— or summer outdoor fun. Visitors appreciate the impressive views and the 1930s construction in this National Historic Landmark that was built as a WPA project. $$$–$$$$

Trillium Lake Basin Cabins. P.O. Box 28, Government Camp, OR 97028; (503) 781– 6352 or (503) 232–4099; www.trillium lake.com; e-mail: info@trilliumlake.com. Located at the base of Multorpor (Skibowl East), the cabins are close to the downhill ski centers along a lovely stream. From your cabin door you can walk to the ski

area and ski right onto an extensive system of cross-country trails or hike to Trillium Lake, where you can also camp in the summer. $$–$$$

IN PORTLAND

Days Inn. 1414 Southwest Sixth Avenue; (503) 221–1611 or (800) 329–7466; www .daysinn.com. Right in the heart of downtown Portland, this is an excellent choice for families. Each bright and cheery room has a small library of hardbound books. You'll also find laundry service, an outdoor swimming pool, and complimentary newspapers. $$–$$$

DoubleTree Lloyd Center. 1000 Northeast Multnomah Street; (503) 281–6111 or (800) 996–0510; www.doubletree.com. Glass elevators give you a bird's-eye view of the modern, spacious lobby and the Portland environs. There are two formal restaurants plus a friendly family-style coffee shop. Just across the street is the Lloyd Center mall, with an ice-skating rink, dozens of eateries, and enough shops to provide hours of entertainment for everyone. $$–$$$$

Holiday Inn. 1441 Northeast Second Avenue; (800) HOLIDAY; www.holiday-inn .com. Complimentary newspapers, coffeemakers, continental breakfasts, in-room movies, laundry service, and a heated indoor pool offer something for every family member. Children under nineteen stay free. $$$–$$$$

Hotel deLuxe. 729 Southwest Fifteenth Avenue; (866) 895–2094 or (503) 219– 2094; www.hoteldeluxeportland.com. A spacious lobby with ornate wainscoting and an enormous chandelier creates a warm welcome in this family-oriented facility located on the MAX line. A reasonably priced restaurant, laundry service, and 1:00 P.M. checkout make this place a hidden gem in downtown Portland. Free parking and continental breakfast. Some suites. $$$–$$$$

McMenamin's Edgefield Manor. 2126 Southwest Halsey Street; (503) 669–8610 or (800) 699–8610; www.mcmenamins .com. Once a farm home, this delightful refurbished bed-and-breakfast inn, pub, movie theater, and restaurant is a welcoming place for families to stop for lunch or overnight. $$–$$$

IN SANDY

Best Western Sandy Inn. 37465 US 26; (800) 359–4827 or (503) 668–7100. A spa, indoor pool, suites, continental breakfast, and exercise room await you in this establishment next to Mt. Hood. $–$$$

For More Information

Beaverton Area Chamber of Commerce. 12655 Southwest Center Street, Suite 140, Beaverton, OR 97005; (503) 644–0123; www.beaverton.org; e-mail: info@beaverton.org.

Columbia River Gorge Visitors Association. 2149 West Cascade, #106A, Hood River, OR 97031; (800) 984–6743; www .crgva.org; e-mail: info@crgva.org.

The Dalles Area Chamber of Commerce. 404 West Second Street, The Dalles, OR 97058; (800) 255–3385 or (503) 296–2231; www.thedalleschamber.com or www.tdedc.com; e-mail: info@tdedc.com.

Hood River Chamber of Commerce. 405 Portway Avenue, Hood River, OR 97431; (541) 386–2000 or (800) 366–3530; www.hoodriver.org; e-mail: hrccc@hood river.org.

Molalla Area Chamber of Commerce. P.O. Box 578, 101 North Molalla Avenue, Molalla, OR 97038; (503) 829–6941; www .molallachamber.com; e-mail: macc@ molalla.net.

Mount Hood Information Center. 65000 East US 26, Welches, OR 97067; (503) 622–4822 or (888) 622–4822; www.mthood .info; e-mail: info@mthood.info.

Port of Cascade Locks Visitor Center. P.O. Box 307, Marine Park Drive, Cascade Locks, OR 97014; (503) 374–8619; www .cascadelocks.net.

Portland/Oregon Visitors Association. 1000 Southwest Broadway, Suite 2300, Portland, OR 97205; (800) 678–5263 or (503) 222–2223; (877) 678–5263 (hotel reservations); Walk-in Information Center, 701 Southwest Sixth Avenue, Pioneer Square; (541) 275–8355; www.travelport land.com; e-mail: info@pova.com.

Sandy Area Chamber of Commerce. 38775 Pioneer Boulevard, Sandy, OR 97055; (503) 668–4006; www.sandyoregon chamber.org.

Troutdale Area Chamber of Commerce. P.O. Box 245, 338 East Historic Columbia River Highway, Troutdale, OR 97060; (503) 669–7473; www.troutdalechamber.org; e-mail: troutdale@stateoforegon.com.

Washington County Visitors Association. 5075 Southwest Griffith Drive, Suite 120, Beaverton, OR 97005; (800) 537–3149 or (503) 644–5555; www.wcva.org; e-mail: info@countrysideofportland.com.

Woodburn Area Chamber of Commerce. P.O. Box 194, 2241 Country Club Road, Woodburn, OR 97071; (503) 982–8221; www.woodburnchamber.org; e-mail: info@woodburnchamber.org.

Other Important **Resources**

- **Portland Parks and Recreation.** 1120 Southwest Fifth Avenue, Suite 1302; (503) 823–7529; www.parks.ci.portland.or.us; e-mail: pkweb@ci .portland.or.us.

- **Oregon Tourism Travel Information Line.** (800) 547–7842.

- **State Park Campsite and Reservations.** (800) 452–5687; www.oregon stateparks.org.

- **Welcome to Oregon.** www.el.com/to/portland

the Willamette Valley

O regon's Willamette Valley represented the dream, the inspiration that brought 300,000 people from the middle west of the young nation on a 2,000-mile trek laden with untold hardship. It was the promise of land so rich you could sow corn in the morning and harvest it in the afternoon, of rivers teeming with fish, and of forests running thick with deer and elk. Today the Willamette Valley is still the agricultural heartland of the state. In summer you're never very far from a roadside fruit and vegetable stand, where you can buy produce that was washed on the vine with the morning's dew. U-pick fields abound, too, starting with strawberries in late May or early June, moving through peaches and cherries in July, then raspberries and blueberries in August. In fall, apples, pears, walnuts, and filberts are ready for gathering.

Newberg and McMinnville

Champoeg State Heritage Area (ages 5 and up) 🚶 🚴 🏛

Located 7 miles east of Newberg off U.S. Highway 99 west; take exit 278 west from I-5. (800) 551-6949 for information; (800) 452-5687 for reservations; www.oregonstate parks.org. Park open dawn to dusk. $ park admission fee.

Once a small town site and in 1843 the seat of the first provisional government body on the West Coast, Champoeg (sham-poo-ee) is now a quiet riverside retreat not far from the bustle of the big city. Before it was used by settlers, the site was a Kalapuya Indian village. Much of this area's history is described in the exhibits at the visitor center, near the park entrance. Ten miles of walking and cycling trails are good ways to explore, and a map is available at the visitor center that shows both the paths and the original location of town buildings swept away by an 1860 flood. Tour **Newell House,** the **Pioneer Mothers Log Cabin Museum,** and in summer take a guided walk to tour historic **Manson Farmstead** and old Champoeg town site.

THE WILLAMETTE VALLEY

Top **Events** in Newberg and Mt. Angel

September

Pioneer Farmstead Day. Old-time crafts, entertainment, and covered-wagon rides at Champoeg State Heritage Area. (503) 678–1251.

Oktoberfest. Visit this Bavarian celebration in Mt. Angel on a weekday to avoid the crowds. Although the Biergarten is for adults only, much of the entertainment, such as pony rides, miniature carnival rides, puppet shows, and magicians, is geared to families with young children. For information, visit www.oktoberfest.org or e-mail info@oktoberfest.org.

Flying M Ranch (ages 5 and up) 🌀🚫🔺🐾〰️🍴

23029 Northwest Flying M Road, Yamhill, 10 miles west of McMinnville; (503) 662–3222; www.flying-m-ranch.com; e-mail: flyingm@bigplanet.com. Open year-round; call for hours. Bunkhouse motel rooms and cabins sleeping two to ten $$$$; rustic camping $$$; hourly horseback ride $$$; daylong ride $$$$; kiddie ride $ for fifteen minutes. Call for times and reservations.

Set in the foothills of the Coast Range along the North Yamhill River, the ranch offers a rustic country experience within easy reach of the city. In addition to horseback rides, you can enjoy fishing, swimming, volleyball, and other sports and walking the many trails through forest and meadow. The lodge dining room serves breakfast, lunch, and dinner.

Evergreen Aviation Museum (ages 5 and up) 🔰🏛️

500 Northeast Capt. Michael King Smith Way, 1 mile east of McMinnville off State Highway 18; (503) 434–4180; www.sprucegoose.org. Open daily 9:00 A.M.–5:00 P.M., $$ adults, $ students, children 5 and under free.

Get "up close and personal" with historic, world-famous aircraft—the most famous of which is the Hughes Flying Boat, affectionately called the Spruce Goose. Designed as a cargo vessel to transport men and materials over long distances, it was the biggest airplane ever built. Its history is one of personal sacrifice, determination, and technological development. The museum houses a number of other aircraft and offers hands-on activities for visitors of all ages.

Kid-Friendly **Book**

Best Hikes with Children in Western and Central Oregon. Bonnie Henderson, 1992; paperback.

Aurora

Aurora, a small community northeast of Woodburn, began as a German-American communal society. The followers of religious visionary Wilhelm Keil established the first West Coast religious commune in 1855, and its appearance has changed little since then. In fact, the center of town has been designated a National Historic District. You can reach Aurora by traveling east about 2.5 miles from exit 278 on I–5 or by driving north on State Highway 99E from Woodburn for about 8 miles.

Old Aurora Colony Museum (ages 5 and up)

1508 Second Street; (503) 678–5754; www.auroracolonymuseum.com; email: info@auroracolonymuseum.com. Open March through December Friday and Saturday 10:00 A.M.–4:00 P.M., Sunday noon–4:00 P.M.; also Tuesday through Thursday mid-April through mid-October 11:00 A.M.–4:00 P.M. $.

A guide takes you through the old ox barn and a rough log cabin as well as other original buildings used by commune members. Your kids will appreciate the frontier-life demonstrations that emphasize the amount of work necessary to survive day-to-day. Pick up a self-guided walking-tour brochure at the Historical Society's **William Keil & Co. Store.**

Top Aurora **Events**

June
Strawberry Festival. Hosted by the Old Aurora Colony, the shortcake and ice-cream social helps raise funds for the museum. (503) 678–5754.

August
Aurora Colony Days. Historic town celebration of its pioneer past. Museum entrance is **free** during this event. (503) 678–2288.

Salem

Just twenty years ago Salem was a sleepy town that housed Oregon's capitol, but in recent years the city has metamorphosed into a bustling center of commerce and culture. Renovated historic buildings, coffeehouses, and department stores all add to the fabric of Salem's spirited city blocks.

State Capitol (ages 8 and up)

900 Court Street Northeast; (503) 986–1388; www.oregonlink.com/capitol_tour. Self-guided tours available throughout the year; on weekdays during summer months building tours available every hour, tower tours every half hour. Free.

Salem's most visible and most visited landmark, the capitol building is white marble topped with a 23-foot-high sculpture of the golden Oregon Pioneer. Inside, large murals depict elements of Oregon's history on a grand scale. Give your kids a taste of both history and contemporary state government with a stop at the capitol building.

A. C. Gilbert's Discovery Village (all ages)

116 Marion Street Northeast, under the Marion Street Bridge that crosses the Willamette; (503) 371–3631; www.acgilbert.org. Open Monday through Saturday 10:00 A.M.–5:00 P.M., Sunday noon–5:00 P.M. $, children 1 and under free.

This place is a must on your Salem itinerary. A. C. Gilbert is the man who gave children of the 1940s and 1950s the original Erector sets, chemistry sets, and other fun and educational toys. The two historic houses have become a hands-on exploratorium for children, with innovative exhibits and activities in the sciences, arts, and humanities. Plan to spend several hours here because the kids will want to try everything at least twice.

Mission Mill Museum Village (ages 5 and up)

1314 Mill Street, off Twelfth Street Southeast; (503) 585–7012; www.oregonlink.com/mission_mill/. Open Monday through Saturday 10:00 A.M.–5:00 P.M. $$ adults, $ seniors and ages 6–18, under 6 free.

Hour-long guided tours of the mill and three historic houses that date from the 1840s begin at the ticket booth on the grounds. There's also a charming gift shop with old-fashioned ambience.

Marion County Historical Society Museum (ages 5 and up)

1313 Mill Street Southeast, on the northwest corner of Mission Mill Village; (503) 364–2128; www.open.org/~mchs; e-mail: mchs@open.org. Open Tuesday through Friday, noon–4:00 P.M. $, children 5 and under free.

The exhibits begin with the Kalapuya Indians and cover pioneer life and the development of Salem as the seat of state governance. The prize possession of the museum is a 125-year-old dugout canoe, which especially impresses kids.

Top Salem **Events**

July

Salem Art Fair & Festival. A plethora of Oregon artists and craftspeople fill the park and sell their wares at booths. Performers and children's activities complete the schedule of events. (503) 581–2228; www.salemart .org/fair/.

July through August

Great Oregon Steam-Up. During this event at the **Western Antique Powerland Museum,** kids have a chance to ride on some of their huge examples of antique farm equipment, and there are demonstrations of old-style threshing, flour milling, and blacksmithing. (503) 393–2424; www.antiquepowerland.com.

August through September

Oregon State Fair. Walk through the animal exhibition areas and laugh at the crowing roosters and odd-looking ducks, guess which bunny should get the blue ribbon, and watch the 4-H kids trying to keep their pigs clean before the show. Dozens of food booths offer everything from hot corn on the cob, slathered with butter, to Thai noodles. (503) 947–3247; www .fair.state.or.us.

Enchanted Forest (all ages)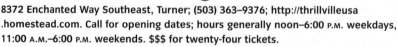

8462 Enchanted Way Southeast, Turner; located between exits 244 and 248 just off I–5 7 miles south of Salem; (503) 371–4242 or (503) 363–3060; www.enchantedforest.com. Open daily May through Labor Day 9:30 A.M.–6:00 P.M., weekends only in April and September. Closed October 1 to March 15. $$, children 2 and under free. Extra fees for large rides.

Some little ones may not be ready for the Haunted House or the Ice Mountain or Timber Log rides, and it may take a while to convince them that walking into the witch's mouth won't mean they will be eaten, but everything else is appropriate for any age. Bring your own picnic basket, or dine at the cafeteria that serves hot dogs and burgers.

Thrillville U.S.A. (ages 5 and up)

8372 Enchanted Way Southeast, Turner; (503) 363–9376; http://thrillvilleusa .homestead.com. Call for opening dates; hours generally noon–6:00 P.M. weekdays, 11:00 A.M.–6:00 P.M. weekends. $$$ for twenty-four tickets.

Attractions for the intrepid include bungee jumping; The Ripper, a giant roller coaster; and the Sky Coaster, which hoists riders 150 feet, then free-falls for 50 feet to swoop through the sky at 50 miles per hour. There are kiddie rides, bumper boats, minigolf, go-carts, games of skill, and giant waterslides.

Western Antique Powerland Museum (ages 5 and up) 🚻

3995 Brooklake Road Northeast, Brooks; (503) 393–2424; www.antiquepowerland .com. Open daily 10:00 A.M.–6:00 P.M. April through October, 10:00 A.M.–4:00 P.M. November through March. Call for special programs. $$, children 12 and under free.

This vast collection of antique farm equipment, from steam engines and kerosene tractors to horse-drawn plows and sowers, is massive enough to grab the attention of kids of all ages.

Bush Pasture Park (all ages) 🚻 🚻 🍂 🚗

Located off Mission Street between High and Twelfth Streets; (503) 363–4714 or (503) 588–6261; www.salemart.org/bush/index.html. Call for hours. Park and art center free. Bush House Museum open Tuesday through Sunday 2:00–5:00 P.M. October through April, noon–5:00 P.M. May through September. $, children under 6 free.

The beautiful **Bush House Museum** and its surrounding gardens, plus the 1882 **Conservatory** and **Bush Barn Art Center,** all provide an agreeable setting for an afternoon family outing. In July the three-day Salem Art Fair draws artists and craftspeople from all over the state who sell their high-quality wares in the park's shady grove.

Silver Falls State Park (all ages) 🚻 🚹 🌊

Located in the Cascade foothills, 26 miles east of Salem by way of State Highway 22 and State Highway 214; (800) 551–6949 or (503) 873–8681, ext. 31 (information); (800) 452–5687 (campground reservations); www.oregonstateparks.org. Call for hours. Camping and $ day-use fees are charged in summer. Campground closes for winter months.

The park includes over 25 miles of trails for hiking, biking, and horseback riding and also has ten waterfalls, half of which cascade more than 100 feet down basalt bluffs. Horse rentals are available from **H.O.R.S.E.S. for the Physically Challenged** (503–873–3890), 10:00 A.M.–5:00 P.M. daily May through September, weather permitting. **The Trail of Ten Falls,** a 9-mile hike along gently sloping trails, takes you through stunning forests, alongside beautiful streams that beckon on hot days, and past waterfalls and geologic wonders that will amaze you. Plan at least five hours for the whole loop, or take shorter hikes from the north and south parking areas. Call for a brochure and maps or download them from the Web site.

Oregon Garden (all ages) 🍁

In Silverton, 15 miles northeast of Salem off I–5; (503) 874–8100 or (877) 674–2733; www.oregongarden.org. Call for special events schedule. Open daily in summer 10:00 A.M.–6:00 P.M.; closes at 3:00 P.M. November through February. $$ adults, $ ages 8–17, $$$ family (two adults and four children), 7 and under free. Gordon House admission $.

Determined to become a rival to the famous Butchart Gardens in British Columbia, the Oregon Garden is growing to become a world-class botanical garden of 240 acres. Currently, 60 acres are open to the public, including the **Children's Garden,** natural meadows and wetlands, an ancient oak grove, and a lovely loop trail through a variety of plant specimens. It will be fun to return every year to watch the garden grow! **The Gordon House,** the only house that architect Frank Lloyd Wright ever designed in Oregon, was moved to the garden in 2001 and is open to the public.

Minto-Brown Island Park and Wildlife Refuge (all ages) 🌲 🐘 🚫

Head south on Commercial Street in central Salem until you reach River Road, looking carefully for the rustic brown sign; (800) 874–7012 or (503) 581–4325. Open 5:00 A.M.–midnight. Free.

More than 20 miles of walking trails, jogging paths, and cycling routes are found in this 900-acre park, plus lots of opportunities for bird-watching, especially blue heron.

Willamette Queen Sternwheeler (ages 8 and up) ⚓

City Dock at Riverfront Park in Salem; (503) 371–1103; www.willamettequeen.com. Call for prices, schedules, and reservations.

The graceful sternwheeler was once an important mode of transportation on the Willamette River, taking people and products to their destinations. Now passengers enjoy leisurely dinner cruises and riverbank sites from the deck.

Independence

Independence marked the end of an arduous covered-wagon trek from Independence, Missouri. The town is now loaded with antiques stores, which probably won't thrill the kids, but you can lure them on with promises of treats at **Taylor's Fountain,** 296 South Main Street, (503) 838–1124, one of the few old-fashioned drugstore soda fountains remaining in the state.

Heritage Museum (ages 5 and up)

112 South Third Street; (503) 838–4989; www.open.org/~herimusm/index.htm; e-mail: herimusm@open.org. Open Wednesday and Saturday 1:00–5:00 P.M., Thursday and Friday, 1:00–4:00 P.M. Tours by appointment. Free.

You'll find all sorts of pioneer paraphernalia in this museum in the heart of the Independence Historic District. It's fun trying to figure out what some of the kitchen gadgets were used for!

Monmouth

Oregon's only "dry" town is located about 15 miles southwest of Salem. It's also home to Western Oregon University, the state's distinguished four-year college for students seeking credentials in education, among other academic disciplines.

Paul Jensen Arctic Museum (ages 5 and up)

Located at Western Oregon University, 590 West Church Street; (503) 838–8468. Open Wednesday through Saturday 10:00 A.M.–4:00 P.M. Admission is free, but donations are appreciated.

Your kids will enjoy seeing the more than 3,000 artifacts gathered by Jensen, who was once president of the college and who traveled to the Arctic on several expeditions. Children shiver at the diorama of wolves snarling at a massive caribou. Special attractions are a sod house and a 27-foot walrus-skin boat, which were given to Dr. Jensen by inhabitants of St. Lawrence Island.

Albany

Historians credit Albany with having the most varied historic buildings in the state. Many, built between 1875 and 1915, are in three districts, all of which are on the National Register of Historic Places. On Sundays in the summer, you can take a horse-drawn carriage tour led by costumed guides who describe the houses and their history.

Monteith House Museum (ages 5 and up)

518 Second Avenue Southwest; (800) 526–2256 or (541) 928–0911. Open Wednesday through Sunday noon–4:00 P.M. mid-June through September, other times by appointment. Free, but donations appreciated.

Visit this home for a closer look at one of the most authentic restored buildings in Oregon and the first frame structure constructed in Albany in 1849.

Top Albany Area **Events**

Summer

River Rhythms Summer Music Series. Located in Albany's beautiful Monteith Park, this Thursday-night program brings in nationally known entertainers. Arrive early to stake out seating with blankets or lawn chairs. Bring your picnic basket or select from a variety of food vendors. **Mondays at Monteith.** Local musicians and groups take the stage for free concerts every Monday night in summer.

For more information on these events, visit ww.riverrythms.org.

June

Linn County Pioneer Picnic. Held every year since 1887, this is the oldest annual celebration in Oregon. Participate in horseshoe tournaments, watch the kiddie parade, and enjoy the logger's jamboree and a flower show. Held in Brownsville's Pioneer Park. (541) 466–5709.

August

Wah Chang Northwest Art & Air Festival. This three-day festival held at Timber Linn Park, Albany Municipal Airport, and West Albany High School combines two Albany events—the Great Balloon Escape and Albany Airport Days—with a juried art show and sale, children's hands-on art, displays of vintage aircraft, airplane and hot-air-balloon rides, food, and live music. More than fifty hot-air-balloons from around the western United States launch each morning, weather permitting, from West Albany High School. Many balloons stage a "Night Glow" at Timber Linn Park at dusk on Friday.

For information on these Albany events, call (800) 526–2256 or (541) 928–0911; www.ci.albany.or.us/parks/nwaaf.

Wavery Lake Park (ages 3 and up)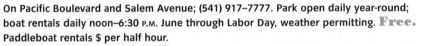

On Pacific Boulevard and Salem Avenue; (541) 917-7777. Park open daily year-round; boat rentals daily noon–6:30 P.M. June through Labor Day, weather permitting. Free. Paddleboat rentals $ per half hour.

Once a log-holding pond, this little lake has become a roadside gem. Feed the resident ducks, have a picnic, walk around the lake, or rent a paddleboat for fun.

Albany Regional Museum (all ages) 🏛️

136 Lyon Street Southwest; (541) 967–7122; www.albanyvisitors.com/pages/historic/ albregional.html; e-mail: armuseum@peak.org. **Open Monday through Saturday noon–4:00 P.M., other times by appointment. Free.**

Old Albany memorabilia, photos, and artifacts fill this regional museum. Peer into a turn-of-the-twentieth-century doctor's office and sit in a chair from a shoe-shine stand that was popular in Albany for decades.

Bryant and Monteith Parks (all ages) 🔺 🚶

Located along the Willamette River, near Northwest Water Street; (541) 917–7777 or (800) 526–2256; www.ci.albany.or.us. Open daily dawn to dusk. Free.

The Willamette River is one of the few rivers in the United States that flow north. Boating and waterskiing are popular along the river. Bluegills, crappies, smallmouth bass, and catfish can be caught where the Willamette and Calapooia Rivers join at Bryant Park in town. You can also fish for trout, steelhead, and salmon in season. Fishing licenses are not required for children under fourteen; licenses are available at most sporting-goods stores.

Foster Lake (all ages) 🏊 🚶 🏛️ 🔺 🚗

Located 29 miles east of Albany off U.S. Highway 20; (541) 367–5127; www.co.linn.or .us/parks. Open April through October. Free day use.

Sunnyside Park on Foster Lake offers a boat ramp, moorage, swimming, waterski- ing, fishing, picnic areas, volleyball courts, and access to the lake for a full day of recreation for your family. The park has 162 tent/trailer sites, 104 with water and elec- tric hookups, and restrooms, showers, and a group camping site.

Linn County Historical Museum (ages 5 and up) 🏛️

101 Park Avenue, Brownsville, 16 miles south of Albany; (541) 466–3390; www.co.linn.or.us/museum. **Open Monday through Saturday 11:00 A.M.–4:00 P.M., Sunday 1:00–5:00 P.M. Free, but donations appreciated.**

Relics of pioneer life are displayed in settings much as they would have appeared during Oregon's early days. Seven old railroad cars have been incorporated into the museum, as well as a covered wagon that arrived in 1865 by way of the Oregon Trail and a col- lection of miniature sleighs and horse-drawn vehicles. An exhibit on the Calapooia (or Kalapuya) Indians doc- uments some of the history of this culture, which was decimated by smallpox brought by missionaries.

Fun Fact

Albany is home to Oregon's broadest range of historic architectural styles.

Corvallis

Corvallis, home to Oregon's oldest state university, is the quintessential college town. It's also a good central location from which to explore the coast, wildlife refuges, and charming rural communities.

Oregon State University (ages 5 and up) 🏛 🎵

LaSells Stewart Center (conference and performing arts center) Twenty-fifth Street across from Reser Stadium; (541) 737–2402; oregonstate.edu/dept/lasells. Call for hours, event schedules, and fees. Gallery viewing and some events free.

Take a walk along the many campus walkways and enjoy the abundant landscaping, public artwork, and varied architecture. The conference center, situated on campus, sponsors a wide variety of events throughout the year and stages performances designed for family entertainment.

Corvallis Bike Paths (ages 5 and up) 🚲

(800) 334–8118 or (541) 757–1544. Always open. Free.

In all, there are more than 25 miles of bike paths and bike lanes in Corvallis. The city is fringed with several sections of paths set off from the roadways to offer safe cycling for families with children. A favorite route is the wide former roadway that connects Oregon State University with the **Benton County Fairgrounds** at Fifty-third. The mile-long section runs through fields where cows, horses, and llamas graze and past the **Irish Bend Covered Bridge.**

Another favorite cycling spot is along the Willamette in **Riverfront Park.** From the parking area near the boat ramp at the end of Tyler Avenue and First Street, you can cycle south to a small loop where the Mary's River flows into the Willamette. You can also continue out to **Avery Park,** along the Mary's River, and on to **Bruce Starker Arts Park,** where you can feed ducks on the ponds or let the kids explore the play structure. In summer, concerts are often held in the grassy amphitheater. Rent bikes for adults and kids at least 5 feet tall at **Peak Sports,** 129 Northwest Second, (541) 754–6444. Call for prices and hours.

Majestic Theatre (all ages) 🎵

115 Southwest Second Avenue; (541) 738–7469 or (541) 766–6976; www.majestic.org; e-mail: mail@majestic.org. Call for hours, prices, and schedules.

This completely renovated 1913 vaudeville house features a wide range of concerts, plays, and productions for families year-round. You're likely to find puppet shows, storytellers, and plays such as Roald Dahl's *Charlie and the Chocolate Factory* on the playbill. In summer, special children's theater camps culminate with lively performances open to the public.

Marys Peak (ages 5 and up) 🚻 ⛺ 🏄

From Corvallis take State Highway 34 west about 18 miles to Marys Peak Road (Forest Road 30); (541) 750–7000. Open dawn to dusk. $ day-use fee.

The most recognizable landmark to the west of Corvallis, Mary's Peak offers prime family recreation. In spring and summer wildflowers blaze on the hillsides near the peak of the 4,097-foot mountain, and in wintertime the hillsides ring with children's shrieks as they hurtle down snowy slopes on inner tubes and sleds. Two trails serve both hikers and cross-country skiers, depending on the season, and the 360-degree view from the summit is something you won't want to miss. Camping is available between late May and October at six sites near the summit.

Family Favorites in the Willamette Valley

1. Champoeg State Heritage Area, Newberg
2. Bush Pasture Park, Salem
3. Silver Falls State Park, near Salem
4. Marys Peak, near Corvallis
5. Alsea Falls, near Corvallis
6. Oregon Garden, Silverton
7. A. C. Gilbert's Discovery Village, Salem
8. Lane County Historical Museum, Eugene
9. Eugene Saturday Market
10. SPLASH! Lively Park Swim Center, Springfield

Alsea Falls (ages 5 and up) 👫🚐🏕️

Farther west on State Highway 34, turn south at the small town of Alsea toward Monroe; you can also reach the falls from State Highway 99W south of Corvallis, off the Benton County Scenic Loop Drive through Alpine; (800) 334–8118 or (541) 757–1544; (503) 375–5646 for campground information. Call for hours. Free day use.

Just driving to Alsea Falls is a wonderful adventure. From Highway 99W you pass through the quaint little hamlets of Alsea and Alpine that are tucked away in Oregon's forested coastal range. From Highway 34 you'll travel several miles of gravel road winding through dense forest. A small campground, a well-maintained picnic area, and an easy 1.9-mile loop await you at Alsea Falls. Take the easy hiking path at the trail sign and enjoy a walk among second-growth hemlock and Douglas fir.

Sheep Barns, Oregon State University (all ages) 🐘

7565 Northwest Oak Creek Drive; (541) 737–4854. Open 9:00 A.M.–2:00 P.M. daily. Free, but donations welcome.

If you're lucky, you'll witness the birth of a baby lamb or watch a mother tenderly washing her newborn. Lambing time varies annually but is usually between February and April. Call for peak viewing times.

Avery Park (ages 5 and up) 👫⛺🏛️

Located along the Marys River south of US 20 at the foot of Southwest Fifteenth Street; (541) 766–6918; www.ci.corvallis.or.us. Open dawn to dusk. Free.

The park delights children with its unusual playground equipment. "Dinosaur bones" and a full-size retired train engine get the kids' vote for the park's favorites. They're located to the left of the park entrance, beyond the small community rose garden. To the right of the entrance, there's another play structure accessible to children of all physical abilities. Trails lead through the woods to the Mary's River for wading.

An Adventure to Remember

There's nothing more exhilarating than a drive in northwestern forests on a fall afternoon. When you travel south from Corvallis and drive west on winding State Highway 34, you will come upon Alsea Falls, one of the most scenic waterfalls west of the Cascade Mountains. The falls, which are an easy walk from the parking lot for people of all ages, slither over monstrous black basalt boulders and continue meandering to a shallow stream. Picnic tables line this fragrant forest and invite you to tarry near the water's gentle sounds.

Top Corvallis **Events**

July

Da Vinci Days. Named for that famous Renaissance artist, scientist, and inventor Leonardo da Vinci, this event attracts thousands for three days of art, science, and fun. The Campo di Kids provides youngsters with activities that change annually, such as fish printing—taking a scaly flounder or rockfish, dipping it in ink, and rolling it on paper to create an indelible impression—or a long, 4-foot-high wooden easel that snakes about 40 feet through the park with buckets of chalk provided. Music on three stages sets the background sound. (541) 757–6363; www.davinci-days.org.

September

Fall Festival. Arts and crafts booths, food booths, live music, and entertainment focus on creativity. Kids get a chance for some hands-on creativity of their own. (541) 752–9655; www.corvallisfallfestival .com; e-mail: director@corvallisfallfestival.com.

McDonald-Dunn Forest (ages 5 and up)
Trail begins at the Forestry Club Cabin in Peavy Arboretum, about 5 miles north of Corvallis off State Highway 99W; (541) 737–4452; www.cof.orst.edu. Open dawn to dusk. Free.

Oregon State University owns this research forest, which offers several walking, mountain-biking, and horse trails. A trail map and brochure, which points out fifteen stops that demonstrate forest-management practices, are usually available at the trailhead.

Finley Wildlife Refuge (ages 5 and up)
26208 Finley Refuge Road, off State Highway 99W, 10 miles south of Corvallis; (541) 757–7236; www.fws.gov/refuges/profiles/index.cfm?id=13589. Open dawn to dusk; office hours 7:00 A.M.– 4:30 P.M. Monday through Friday. Free.

Hundreds of thousands of migrating waterfowl winter along the Willamette Valley and find a safe haven at this 5,325-acre refuge, where you and your children can enjoy walks throughout the year. Even very young children can manage the **Woodpecker Loop Trail,** which winds over 1.25 miles of gentle terrain through forest, meadow, and wetland environments. Have your kids approach the pond slowly and watch and listen for the squeaks of the frogs as they leap into the water. A brochure, usually available at the trailhead (at a small parking lot about 3.6 miles west of Highway 99W on Refuge Road) identifies the woodpeckers you might see as well as plant and other animal species along the trail.

Benton County Historical Museum (ages 5 and up)

1101 Main Street, located in Philomath, 7 miles west of Corvallis; (541) 929–6230; www.bentoncountymuseum.org. Open Tuesday through Saturday 10:30 A.M.–4:30 P.M. Research library open 1:00–4:00 P.M. Tuesday through Saturday or by appointment. Free.

The museum is housed in what was the first college in the territory. Its interpretive exhibits provide insights into the region's pioneer and early industrial life. A rotating art exhibit and a portion of the Horner Collection—consisting of natural-history and archaeological artifacts—are other interesting dimensions of the museum.

Osborn Aquatic Center (all ages) 🏊

1940 Northwest Highland Drive; (541) 766–7946. Call for hours and swim times. $.

The recent addition of Otter Beach—an outdoor area with water cannons, floor geysers, a play structure, pools and falls, and a 22-foot slide—makes this a place for year-round water fun for everyone in the family.

Eugene

Eugene, Oregon's second-largest city, is located at the confluence of the Willamette and McKenzie Rivers in the midst of farmland and forests that stretch to the foothills of the Cascade Mountains to the east and the Oregon Coast Range to the west. The University of Oregon is housed here on a beautiful campus crisscrossed with walking paths. Several lush Eugene parks invite outdoor enthusiasts to jog, cycle, and walk.

Hendricks Park (all ages) 🏕️ 🚶 🌱

Located at the foot of Summit Avenue, off Agate Street; (541) 682–4800; www .eugene-or.gov/portal/server.pt. Always open. Free.

A blur of glorious color peaks in the springtime with more than 6,000 rhododendrons—both native and hybrid. May is the best month for a visit to this twelve-acre garden, but at any time of year you can enjoy a walk through this lush wooded park. **Free** guided tours are offered each spring.

Science Factory (all ages) 🔵

2300 Leo Harris Parkway, off Centennial; (541) 682–7888; www.sciencefactory.org; e-mail: info@sciencefactory.org. Open Friday and Saturday noon–4:00 P.M.; planetarium show Saturday and Sunday 1:00 and 2:00 P.M. Call to confirm hours. $ exhibit or planetarium, $$ for both, children 3 and under free.

Science Factory is a hands-on, user-friendly environment in which kids can explore natural wonders, all the while learning about physics and science concepts. They can shout into an echo tube, experiment with the force of pendulums, or watch what happens when they electrify a bubble. The planetarium is one of the largest facilities of its kind between San Francisco, California, and Vancouver, British Columbia. It offers year-round Saturday programs on touring the solar system, exploring the night sky across the seasons, or learning about cosmic phenomena.

University of Oregon Museum of Natural History (ages 5 and up) 🔵

1680 East Fifteenth Avenue; (541) 346–3024; http://natural-history.uoregon.edu. Open Wednesday through Sunday noon–5:00 P.M. $, children 2 and under free.

Kids get a strong sense of Oregon's very early history through the museum's displays of Native American artifacts, including a pair of 9,000-year-old sagebrush sandals. Changing exhibits explore other cultures throughout the world.

Rafting the McKenzie River (ages 10 and up)

Explore the river with a variety of white-water guide services:

- **River Runner Supply.** 78G Centennial Loop; (541) 343–6883. Call for hours and fees. Kayak and raft rentals and guided tours.

- **Oregon Whitewater Adventures.** 39620 Deerhorn Road, Springfield; (800) 820–7238 or (541) 746–5422; www.oregonwhitewater.com; e-mail: info@oregonwhitewater.com. Guided raft trips $$$$.

- **Oregon River Sports.** 3400 Franklin Boulevard; (541) 334–0696 or (888) 790–7235, www.oregonriversports.com; e-mail: ors@oregonriversports .com. Open daily in summer 9:00 A.M.–6:00 P.M.; call for off-season hours. Raft rentals and guided trips $$$$. Also canoe and kayak rentals for use on the canal in **Alton Baker Park** daily in summer noon–8:00 P.M., 11:00 A.M.–8:00 P.M. Friday and Saturday; weekends only mid-May to mid-June. $$ per hour.

Top Eugene **Events**

June through July

Oregon Bach Festival. The critically acclaimed festival features a series of children's performances as well as **free** noon concerts. Most performances are located at the **Hult Center for the Performing Arts.** (800) 457–1486 or (541) 682–5000; www.oregonbachfestival.com.

July

Oregon Country Fair. Every summer it's as if the clock had stopped somewhere in the late '60s. The Oregon Country Fair draws an amazing crowd of old hippies and new yuppies and their families for what one coordinator called "a walking Whole Earth catalog." The event offers an amazing variety of food booths to satisfy carnivores, vegetarians, and vegans alike. Entertainment ranges from vaudeville and mime to folk and rock 'n' roll. The Energy Park demonstrates alternative energy sources, and the Community Village offers exhibits on political, social, cultural, spiritual, and environmental concerns. (Note: some fairgoers may dispense with clothing.) (541) 343–4298; www.oregoncountryfair.org.

Children's Celebration. This annual event celebrates being a child—no matter what age you are! Island Park in Springfield is transformed into a child's world. (541) 736–4544; www.willamalane.org.

August

Oregon Festival of American Music. Performances by renowned musicians ranging from gospel to jazz and blues are the heart of this program, which is located at the Hult Center for the Performing Arts and the outdoor Cuthbert Amphitheater. (541) 687–6526 or (800) 248–1615; www .ofam.org; e-mail: info@ofam.net.

September

Eugene Celebration. The annual downtown Eugene Celebration held in mid-September has activities such as face painting and miniature golf in the Kid Zone, dozens of food booths, and continuous live entertainment. Don't miss the largest three-day street party in the state. (541) 681–4108; www.eugenecelebration.com.

Fiesta Latina. Annual Latin-American cultural celebration featuring food, local art, music, and dancing. (541) 344–5070.

Jordan Schnitzer Museum of Art (ages 8 and up) 🔈

Located on campus at 1430 Johnson Lane; (541) 346–3027; http://uoma.uoregon.edu. Call for hours and fees.

Visiting exhibits bring a variety of subjects to the campus, from photography to wall-size contemporary oils. The permanent displays include first-rate collections of Asian art, American contemporary art, and photography.

Lane County Historical Museum (ages 5 and up) 🔈

740 West Thirteenth Avenue; (541) 682–4242 or (541) 682–4239; www.lcog.org/admin/ museum.html. Open Wednesday through Friday 10:00 A.M.–4:00 P.M., Saturday and Sunday noon–4:00 P.M. $, children under 2 free.

With collections dating from the 1840s, your kids will imagine themselves along the Oregon Trail, getting dressed up for a flapper's party in the 1920s or riding an early child's bicycle with odd-sized wheels. Inquire about the numerous educational programs the museum offers. You can request a guided tour from one of the museum's docents.

Oregon Air and Space Museum (ages 5 and up) 🔈

90377 Boeing Drive, off Airport Road; (541) 461–1101. Open Wednesday through Sunday noon–4:00 P.M. Call about special events. $, children 5 and under free.

The growing museum now includes an F-4 Phantom jet, a forty-year-old Cessna L-19 that flew in the Korean War, and the oddly shaped Bullet, a home-built plane that never made it off the ground as a commercial venture. Exhibits trace the development of the space industry, and a gift shop sells model planes, T-shirts, and books.

Paul's Bicycle Way of Life (ages 5 and up) 🚲

7:00 P.M., weekends 10:00 A.M.–5:00 P.M. Rentals $$$ per day.

Eugene is a town that reveres cycling. You can tell because of the extensive bike paths and lanes throughout the town and the investment in sophisticated cycling bridges that cross the Willamette and McKenzie Rivers.

Fifth Street Public Market (all ages) 🛍 🍴

Located at 296 East Fifth Street; (541) 484–0383; www.5stmarket.com. Open 10:00 A.M.– 8:00 P.M. Monday through Saturday, 10:00 A.M.–6:00 P.M. Sunday.

Seventy-five shops and numerous restaurants and ethnic-flavored eateries capture Eugene's eclectic essence. French and Middle Eastern cafes nestle with a Thai restaurant and fabulous bakeries. Artisan booths with wood-framed photographs stand near boutiques with handblown glass objects and earthen pottery. There's a Nike store next door, and the kids will enjoy the mini-museum depicting the lives of renowned track-and-field heroes.

Eugene Saturday Market (all ages) 🔵

In downtown park blocks; (541) 686–8885; www.eugenesaturdaymarket.org. Open Saturday 10:00 A.M.–4:00 P.M. April through November; Holiday Market held in Lane County Fairgrounds Exhibit Hall, Thirteenth and Jefferson; call for dates and hours.

Here's another venue that's uniquely Eugene but with even more unusual entrepreneurial enterprises—from farmers selling fresh-cut flowers and garden-grown fruits and vegetables to artisans with quilts, tie-dyed kids' clothing, jewelry, and wonderful wooden handcrafted toys. It's billed as Oregon's oldest weekly open-air crafts festival. The international food court lets you experience tastes of the world.

Lane Ice Center (ages 6 and up) 🔵

796 West Thirteenth; (541) 682–3615 or (541) 682–4292; www.laneicecenter.org. Call for regular hours; Family Night, Tuesday and Thursday 7:00–8:30 P.M. Admission $, skate rental $.

The University of Oregon hockey team plays here, with games held throughout the winter months. When the team isn't on the ice, it's your family's turn.

SPLASH! Lively Park Swim Center (all ages) 🔵

6100 Thurston Road, Springfield; (541) 747–9283 or (541) 736–4244; www.willamalane .org. Monday and Wednesday 6:30–8:30 P.M., Friday 3:30–5:00 P.M. and 6:30–9:00 P.M., Saturday 1:00–5:00 P.M. and 6:30–9:00 P.M., Sunday 1:00–5:00 P.M. $. Discounts for local residents.

The first indoor wave pool on the West Coast opened its doors in Springfield in 1989 and has been drawing hordes of families ever since. The huge pool contains not only the wave pool but a larger-than-usual children's wading pool (complete with floating rubber duckies), a Jacuzzi, a lap pool, and a 136-foot waterslide. You can bring your cooler and eat at one of the many tables. Family changing rooms are equipped with private showers, potties, and sinks, so your little ones don't have to go into the larger dressing room alone. The noise level seems overwhelming sometimes, but that helps contribute to the "lively" atmosphere. You can bring your own masks, goggles, snorkels, and fins.

Willamalane Park (ages 8 and up) 🔵 🔵 🔵

1276 G Street; Swim Center at the corner of Fourteenth and G; (541) 736–4104; www .willamalane.org. Park open daily 6:00 A.M.–10:00 P.M. Free. Call Swim Center for hours and special play swim times; $.

This fourteen-acre park includes a swim center, basketball court, football/soccer field, horseshoe pit, playground, softball field, tennis court, and a very popular skate park. More like an enhanced street scene than the more typical collection of sloping bowls and half-pipes, the skate park features chunky, abrupt shapes with definite corners and a "picnic table" in the middle, a set of "stairs," and a very real fire hydrant.

Springfield Museum (ages 5 and up)

590 Main Street; (541) 726–2300; www.springfieldmuseum.com. Open Tuesday through Friday 10:00 A.M.–5:00 P.M., Saturday noon–4:00 P.M. $, children 18 and under free.

A variety of changing exhibits and a permanent collection of objects ranging from pioneer toys to men's ties invites even locals to visit more than once.

Dorris Ranch Living History Filbert Farm (ages 5 and up)

At the intersection of South Second and Dorris Streets; (541) 736–4544; www .willamalane. org. Open daily 6:00 A.M.–10:00 P.M. Free.

Experience Oregon's history with a visit to Dorris Ranch. Now a living-history farm, it welcomes families to walk among the seventy-five acres of lush orchards, seventy-five acres of riverfront forest, and forty acres of pasture and wetlands. A one-and-a-half-hour self-guided walking tour takes you through each of these environments along a level 2-mile trail. The educational programs offered March through December are well worth joining.

Mt. Pisgah (ages 8 and up)

34901 Frank Parrish Road; to reach the trailhead, take I–5 south of Eugene to the Thir-tieth Avenue exit, then follow signs to Mt. Pisgah Arboretum. Cross the bridge over the Coast Fork of the Willamette River, then turn right and take the trailhead from the parking lot at the end of the road; (541) 747–3817 or (541) 747–1504; www.efn.org/~ mtpisgah; e-mail: mtpisgah@efn.org. $ day-use fee.

It's fairly steep in places, but the views from the top make the climb worth it. The sighting pedestal on the mountaintop will tantalize your kids. Local outdoors author Bonnie Henderson suggests bringing lots of paper and crayons so kids can create rubbings of the bas-relief fish, birds, leaves, and shells that decorate the 40-inch-tall bronze pedestal. The relief map on top identifies visible landmarks. Watch for poison oak along the trail and "cow pies" underfoot. Most of the 7 miles of hiking paths crisscrossing the 208-acre park are now all-weather trails. The arboretum has created several self-guiding brochures for children to learn from on walks through the area.

Fun Fact

Dorris Ranch in Springfield was the first commercial filbert orchard in the United States, beginning in 1892.

Fern Ridge Lake (ages 5 and up) ⊕ ⊜ ⊕ ⊕ ⊕ ⊛

Located 12 miles from downtown Eugene by way of Clear Lake Road off State Highway 99W; (541) 688–8147. Open dawn to dusk. Minimal parking and day-use fee.

Here's another spot that's popular with the locals for camping, picnicking, swimming, waterskiing, sailing, and sailboarding. **Perkins Peninsula Park** offers a swim area, playing field, boardwalk, and interpretive nature trail.

Fall Creek State Recreation Area (ages 5 and up) ⊜ ⊕ ⊕

Located off State Highway 58 about 15 miles southeast of Eugene; (541) 937–1173 or (800) 551–6949; (800) 452–5687 for campground reservations; www.oregonstateparks .org. Always open. $ day-use fee.

When the summer heat starts to get to you, take the family to one of the many nearby swimming holes. Fall Creek has four campgrounds, and a picnic area borders the stream that flows into the reservoir. A few swimming holes beyond the **Puma Creek Campground** offer a little more privacy.

Fall Creek National Recreation Trail (ages 5 and up) ⊛ ⊕

Located about 15 miles west of Eugene on State Highway 58; take the turnoff at Jasper-Lowell through the town of Lowell, turn right at North Shore Road, and continue for about 11 miles. The 14-mile trail begins opposite the Dolly Varden Campground on the creek's south bank. For maps and information, visit the Willamette National Forest office at 211 East Seventh Avenue in Eugene; (541) 465–6521; www .fs.fed.us/r6/willamette.

An old-growth forest and paths lush with maiden and sword ferns give hikers a true sense of getting away from it all without a long or tedious drive.

Aufderheide National Scenic Byway in Willamette National Forest (ages 5 and up) ⊛

Located east of Eugene; follow State Highway 58 to State Highway 126 and turn at Forest Road 19. The drive follows the South Fork of the McKenzie River and the North Fork of the Middle Fork of the Willamette River from Oakridge (30 miles southeast of Eugene) to the small community of McKenzie Bridge. (541) 782–2283 or (541) 822–3381. Open dawn to dusk. $ day-use fee at some parking areas (Northwest Forest Pass).

Willamette National Forest is a beautiful drive, along which there are many places to stop so the kids can run and explore in old-growth forests and woodland streams and waterfalls. Of particular interest to children is the **Delta Nature Trail,** a 0.5-mile loop through towering old-growth trees, some of which are up to 500 years old.

Salt Creek Falls (ages 5 and up) (icon)

Located an hour southwest of Eugene; turnoff located off State Highway 58; look for Salt Creek Falls sign. (541) 465–6521; www.fs.fed.us/r6/willamette. $ day-use fee (Northwest Forest Pass).

Oregon's second-highest waterfall, which tumbles over tall basalt cliffs, presents a blend of history and natural beauty as well as outdoor recreation. Interpretive panels tell of the ladies and gentlemen who rode the train to this spot for a day's picnic outing in the 1920s and of the 7,000-year-old evidence of Molalla and Kalapuya Indian activity in these canyons. Walking trails lead to shaded picnic spots and an observation platform that gives you a bird's-eye view of the 286-foot falls. A 2.5-mile loop hike to Diamond Creek Falls takes about two hours.

Waldo Lake (ages 5 and up) (icons)

Located in the high Oregon Cascades southeast of Eugene; (541) 937–2129; www.fs .fed.us/r6/centraloregon. $ day-use fee (Northwest Forest Pass).

Waldo Lake is one of the purest, clearest lakes in the world, according to water specialists. At an elevation of 5,414 feet, the lake's summer recreation period is fairly short. Three Forest Service campgrounds provide a few amenities (like flush toilets) that make camping less rustic. Hiking trails connect to other lakes, such as tiny **Betty Lake,** which is shallow enough to warm for swimming in the summer. Mountain bikers frequently use the 22-mile **Waldo Lake Trail,** which circles the lake. Trail information is available from the Oakridge Ranger Station on State Highway 58 near Oakridge.

Odell Lake and Crescent Lake (all ages) (icons)

Located on West Odell Road off State Highway 58, approximately 70 miles east of Eugene; (541) 433–3200; www.fs.fed.us/r6/centraloregon. Always open. $ day-use fee.

Boat rentals, swimming beaches, hiking trails, picnic areas, and campgrounds make these lakes easy to enjoy with the family. In winter the lodges are open for cross-country skiers or for downhill enthusiasts skiing at nearby Willamette Pass. Three resorts offer cabins and lodge rooms, boat rentals, and restaurants. Odell Lake Lodge offers cross-country ski rentals, and Crescent Lake Resort rents snowmobiles. All are open year-round; call for hours and rates.

- **Odell Lake Lodge.** East end of Odell Lake; (541) 433–2540; www.odelllake resort.com.
- **Shelter Cove Resort.** On west end of Odell Lake; (541) 433–2548; www.shelter coveresort.com.
- **Crescent Lake Resort.** (541) 433–2505; www.crescentlakeresort.com.

Willamette Pass (ages 5 and up) 🎿🍴

Southwest of Eugene on State Highway 58; (541) 345–7669; www.willamettepass.com. Generally open by mid-November 9:00 A.M.–4:00 P.M.; twilight skiing 12:30– 9:00 P.M. Friday and Saturday. Adults $$$$, ages 6–10 $$$. Call about special pass rates. All tickets require one-time purchase of reusable ski key. $. Summer gondola rides 10:00 A.M.–5:00 P.M. Monday through Thursday, until 8:00 P.M. Friday through Sunday. $$$ adults, $$ ages 6–18, $ ages 5 and under.

You'll find daytime and night skiing on many groomed runs and one of the best ski instruction programs for children anywhere. Skiing begins when the snow covers the slopes, usually in December. There are also several miles of groomed cross-country trails. The Cascade Summit Lodge has a restaurant for skiers who need to warm up with a cup of steaming cocoa and a bite to eat. Both downhill and cross-country ski rentals are available, and child care is offered.

Where to Eat

IN ALBANY

Novak's Hungarian Restaurant. 2306 Heritage Way Southeast; (541) 967–9488. A legend in Albany, Novak's warm and inviting ambience is obvious right when you walk in the door. Delicious homemade breads and noodle dishes will appeal to the kids while Mom and Dad experiment with some of the more exotic cuisine. $–$$

Wine Depot & Deli. Two Rivers Market, 300 Second Avenue; (541) 967–9499. This is a good spot to pick up sandwiches for a picnic lunch or salads and desserts for a quick family dinner. $

IN CORVALLIS

Nearly Normal's. 109 Northwest Fifteenth Street; (541) 753–0791. A casual eatery in an old house near Oregon State campus, it offers a nice variety of vegetarian and international cuisine. Ingredients are as fresh as can be. Kid-friendly. $

New Morning Bakery. 219 Southwest Second (541–754–0181). Open for desserts, breakfast, lunch, and dinner. Incredibly decadent pastries are available. Affordable monster-size cookies and delicious salads and soups give everybody

something to savor. A children's play area is equipped with toys, books, and kid-size tables and chairs. $

IN EUGENE

Glenwood Restaurant. 2588 Willamette (541–687–8201) and 1340 Alder (541–687–0355). Casual food and atmosphere; voted best family dining by *Eugene Weekly* four years in a row. $–$$

Newman's Fish Company. 1545 Willamette Street; (541) 344–2371. It's an easy location to miss, but don't pass up the opportunity to have truly fresh and delicious fish and chips. Outdoor counter service and seating. $

Oregon Electric Station. Fifth and Willamette; (541) 485–4444. This is the splurge restaurant—meals are good but pricey. Kids will adore eating in an old train boxcar or the 1912 train depot. $$$$

Taco Loco. 900 West Seventh Avenue; (541) 683–9171. A lively and visually stimulating eating establishment that serves Mexican and Salvadorean food, it was voted People's Choice Best Mexican for several years in local restaurant surveys. $–$$

IN SALEM

Applebee's. 747 Lancaster Drive Northeast; (503) 581–8040. Varied menu has something for everyone, including children's meals. $–$$

Macleay Country Inn. 8362 Macleay Road Southeast; (503) 362–4225. Along with steaks and seafood, Spud-fish is the restaurant's signature dish—fish and chips with a batter made from potatoes. $–$$

Mill Creek Station. 1313 Mill Street; (503) 370–8855; www.millcreekstation.com. You can eat soup and sandwiches on the deck outdoors, which is right in the middle of Mission Mill Village. $

Where to Stay

IN ALBANY

Econolodge. 1212 Price Road Southeast; (541) 926–0170 or (888) 321–3352. Cable TV. Pets welcome. Seasonal pool. $$

La Quinta Inn & Suites. 251 Airport Road Southeast; (800) 531–5900 or (541) 928–0921; www.laquinta.com. Cable TV. Pets welcome. Pool and spa available. $–$$$

IN CORVALLIS

Corvallis Inn. 1550 Northwest Ninth Street; (541) 753–9151. Just 2 miles from the Oregon State University campus, the motel has an outdoor pool that kids especially appreciate in the summer. Pet-friendly. $$–$$$.

Super 8 Motel. 407 Northwest Second Street; (800) 800–8000 or (541) 758–8088; www.super8.com. Located on the banks of the Willamette River, this budget motel is close to downtown. Indoor pool and spa. Small pets welcome. $–$$

IN EUGENE

Best Western New Oregon Motel. 1655 Franklin Boulevard; (541) 683–3669. Reasonably priced rooms have refrigerators,

and there's a complimentary continental breakfast. Families will also appreciate the indoor pool, whirlpool tub, sauna, and exercise room after a day of traveling. $$–$$$

Campus Inn. 390 East Broadway; (877) 313–4137 or (541) 343–3376; www .campus-inn.com; e-mail: eugene@ campus-inn.com. Centrally located. In-room refrigerators, coffee, Internet access. Free breakfast, parking, newspaper. $$

Phoenix Inn Suites. 850 Franklin Boulevard; (800) 344–0131 or (541) 344–0001; www. phoenixinn.com; e-mail: phoenixinn @uswest. net. At this centrally located hotel, you'll receive a complimentary breakfast and have access to a pool, Jacuzzi, and fitness center. $$–$$$

IN SALEM

Best Western Mill Creek Inn. 3125 Ryan Drive Southeast; (800) 346–9659 or (503) 585–3332. Fitness room, pool; restaurant next door. In-room fridge, microwave. Free shuttle to Salem Airport. $$$–$$$$

Econolodge. 3195 Portland Road Northeast; (503) 585–2900. Free in-room coffee; outdoor heated pool. Refrigerators and microwaves. $$–$$$

IN WOODBURN AND SILVERTON

Champoeg State Heritage Area. (800) 452–5687 for reservations; www.oregon stateparks.org. The campground and park are northwest of Woodburn, due west of Wilsonville; take exit 278 from I–5 and follow signs to the park. $

For More Information

Albany Visitors Association. 250 Broadalbin Street Southwest, Suite 110, Albany, OR 97321; (800) 526–2256 or (541) 928–0911; www.albanyvisitors.com; e-mail: albanyinfo@albanyvisitors.com.

Aurora Chamber of Commerce. 21558 Highway 99E, Aurora, OR 97002; (503) 939–0312; www.auroracolony.com

Corvallis Tourism. 553 Northwest Harrison Boulevard, Corvallis, OR 97330; (800) 334– 8118 or (541) 753–2664; www.visit corvallis.com/about_ccvb.html; e-mail: info@visitcorvallis. com.

Eugene Area Chamber of Commerce. 1401 Willamette Street, Eugene, OR 97401; (541) 484–1314; www.eugene chamber.com; e-mail: info@eugene chamber.com.

Eugene Convention & Visitors Association of Lane County. 754 Olive Street, Eugene, OR 97441; (800) 547–5445 or (541) 484–5307; www.cvalco.org; e-mail: info@cvalco.org.

McKenzie River Chamber of Commerce. P.O. Box 1117, 44643 McKenzie Highway, Leaburg, OR 97489; (541) 896–3330; www.el.com/to/mckenzierivervalley; e-mail: mcrvco@aol.com.

Monmouth-Independence Chamber of Commerce. 355 Pacific Avenue N., Suite A, Independence, OR 97351; (503) 838–4268; www.micc-or.org/; e-mail: micc@open.org.

Newberg Chamber of Commerce. 415 East Sheridan, Newberg, OR 97132; (503) 538–2014; www.chehalemvalley.org.

Salem Convention & Visitors Association. 1313 Mill Street Southeast, Salem, OR 97301; (800) 874–7012 or (503) 581–4325; www.salemvisitorcenter.com.

Woodburn Area Chamber of Commerce. 2241 Country Club Road, Woodburn, OR 97071; (503) 982–8221; www.woodburnchamber.org.

Central Oregon and the Cascades

I n many ways central Oregon is the state's playground. It's here that we can find virtually any kind of outdoor recreation that teases our ambitions—mountain climbing, rock climbing, white-water rafting, canoeing, kayaking, windsurfing, skiing, swimming, hiking, bicycling, fishing, and horseback riding. The area's climate is ideal for the outdoor-bound. In summer less rain falls here than in many other areas of the state. Winter brings snow to the mountains, but a well-equipped highway department keeps roads passable.

Posh family resorts at Sunriver, Black Butte, Seventh Mountain, and Eagle Crest, among others, draw visitors every season of the year. The forests, rivers, and lakes of the region create a lush backdrop for camping and outdoor recreation. And there is a wealth of educational opportunities for outings to lava fields, museums, and historic sites. You'll want to take your time here and then return to see what new experiences each season has to offer.

Bend

Drake Park Mirror Pond (all ages) 🏕 👥
Take Bond Street and turn on Franklin Street heading west to Northwest Riverside Boulevard; (541) 389–7275; www.bendparksandrec.org. Always open. Free.

A wide variety of waterfowl plays a predominant role in this aptly named section of the Deschutes River, which flows through the town of Bend. There is even a pair of swans from Queen Elizabeth's royal swannery here. A broad green parkland hugs the shore, and a children's playground sits just across the bridge at Harmon Park.

CENTRAL OREGON AND THE CASCADES

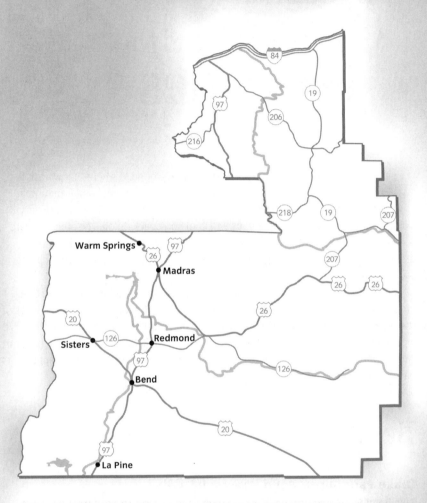

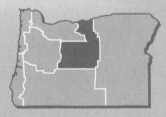

Sawyer Park (all ages) 🏕️

Located just 0.5 mile northwest of the Bend River Mall; (541) 389–7275; www.bend parksandrec.org. Day use. Free.

This sixty-six-acre park has both developed and natural settings, with picnic tables, drinking water, and toilets.

Deschutes River (all ages) 🎣 🚲 🚶

(541) 389–7275. Day use. Free.

Equally enticing for fishing and hiking, the 3-mile-long **Deschutes River Trail** follows the Deschutes from Northwest First Street in Bend to **Sawyer Park** and nearly all the way to **Tumalo State Park.** You'll see lots of joggers, mountain bikers, and walkers on this popular trail. Off Century Drive (Cascade Lakes Scenic Highway), Forest Road 41 leads to several trailheads within the Deschutes National Forest, with 9 miles of trail through lava flows and pine forests. The paths range from easy to moderate. A Northwest Forest Pass is required for parking at the trailheads. For more information, visit the Web site at www.fs.fed.us/r6/centraloregon and search for Deschutes River Trail.

Family Favorites in Central Oregon

1. High Desert Museum, Bend
2. Museum at Warm Springs, Warm Springs
3. Lava Lands Visitor Center, Bend
4. Lava River Cave, Bend
5. Lava Cast Forest, Bend
6. Mt. Bachelor Ski Resort (winter and summer), Cascade Lakes Scenic Highway
7. Pine Mountain Observatory, Bend
8. Osprey Observation Point, Cascade Lakes Scenic Highway
9. Three Creek Lake, south of Sisters
10. Reindeer Ranch at Operation Santa Claus, Redmond

Pilot Butte State Scenic Viewpoint (all ages) 👥

Take Northeast Greenwood, which winds to the top of the butte; (800) 551–6949; www.oregonstateparks.org. Always open. Free.

To get a great view of the Cascades and the surrounding area without going far from town, take a short trek to this volcanic cinder cone within the city's limits. It provides a perfect 360-degree view of the various peaks—Mt. Hood, Jefferson, Washington, Three-Fingered Jack, Broken Top, Bachelor, Newberry Crater, and the Three Sisters—as well as the Deschutes River as it wends its way north. Bring your own thirst quencher as there is no water in the park.

Des Chutes Historical Center (all ages) 🏛

129 Northwest Idaho; (541) 389–1813. Open Tuesday through Saturday 10:00 A.M.– 4:30 P.M. $, children under 12 free with a paid adult admission.

Exhibits of artifacts of the county's colorful history give insight into the lives of Native Americans and pioneers. The timber industry's early days are also explored in displays.

High Desert Museum (all ages) 🏛 🐃

59800 South Highway 97, located just off U.S. Highway 97, 3.5 miles south of Bend; (541) 382–4754; www.highdesertmuseum.org. Open daily 9:00 A.M.–5:00 P.M. except major holidays. Admission for two consecutive days $$, children under 4 free.

Besides the spectacular array of exquisite dioramas, there's a Desert-arium with live animals scurrying about in their natural habitats, a homestead exhibiting the details of harsh pioneer life in the central desert, and a forestry exhibit with a working sawmill. The museum also sponsors special programs and live animal presentations at regular intervals throughout the day (May through September).

Lava Lands Visitor Center (ages 5 and up) 👥 🚌

Located 11 miles south of Bend on US 97; (541) 593–2421; www.fs.fed.us/r6/ centraloregon. Visitor center is open daily mid-April to mid-October 9:00 A.M.–5:00 P.M. $ car entrance fee (Northwest Forest Pass).

You'll feel as though you're in another world entirely, as if you've somehow landed on the moon on this volcanic cinder cone, where the 360-degree view is stunning. Imagine, as you look at the remains of a 9-mile-long, 7,000-year-old lava flow, what it must have looked like as a molten river. Two self-guided interpretive trails take you over the lava fields and through an adjoining pine forest. Another trail rims Lava Butte, which rises 500 feet above the visitor center. Regular programs include guided walks, demonstrations, and talks on the human and volcanic history of the region.

Lava River Cave (ages 10 and up) 🚹🚺

Located about 12 miles south of Bend off US 97 (1 mile south of the Lava Lands Visitor Center); (541) 383–5300 or (541) 593–2421; www.fs.fed.us/r6/centraloregon. Open May through mid-October. $, children 12 and under free.

How would you like to take your kids out for a bit of spelunking? One of the more fascinating discoveries around central Oregon happened when a trapper stumbled across a huge cave while hunting in 1889. In 1923 geologists studying the cavern realized that it continued underground far deeper than any cave previously discovered. This cave is the longest uncollapsed lava tube in Oregon, extending nearly 5,200 feet from end to end, and is part of the Newberry National Volcanic Monument. Bring flashlights and extra batteries or rent propane lanterns at the entrance. Wear sweaters and long pants because the cave is always about forty-two degrees. Get ready for an experience that will have your kids shivering, not from the cold, but because it's a bit spooky to be underground in a long cavern lighted only by your flashlights. Their imaginations will run riot. Stairs take you down into the cave, where ice stalactites and stalagmites form in winter. Children love the echo chamber, where you can hear voices from farther ahead return as strange sounds.

An Adventure to Remember

You'll have a deeper knowledge of the hardships early pioneers faced after visiting central Oregon's High Desert Museum, a veritable treasure chest of natural-history, anthropology, and wildlife displays. A rustic cabin, tiny as today's fabricated toolshed, reflects the pioneer settlers' keen ability to make use of every nook and cranny. The spare multipurpose room holds cast-iron pots and pans, a wooden washboard, a pine-framed bed, and an open pantry, demonstrating among other things how dramatically complex our society has become since the turn of the twentieth century. During the live raptor program, kids can view injured or orphaned birds of prey. Afterwards wildlife educators give kids a chance to feel a hawk's wing and examine a kestrel's skull. Also on the museum grounds are a tiny stream and pond where large rainbow trout swim and rocky beds where otters frolic and porcupines lounge. An old sawmill, a Basque sheepherder's wagon, and exhibits on Native American and pioneer history all reflect the museum's painstaking attention to detail. If you go nowhere else during your stay in central Oregon, be sure to visit this extraordinary museum.

Lava River Cave **Trivia**

- The 22.5-acre Lava River Cave was donated to the State of Oregon for use as a park in 1926 by the Shevlin-Hixon Lumber Company.

- The cave is about 6,200 feet long and as wide as 50 feet in places, and the ceiling is as high as 60 feet in some areas.

- The Lava River Cave area has three ecosystems: warm and dry climate surrounding the entrance; warm and moist microclimate at the entrance; and the cool, moist, and dark environment of the cave itself.

- At the point where the cave crosses beneath US 97, its roof is 50 feet thick.

(Source: USDA Forest Service)

Lava Cast Forest (ages 5 and up)

Located 14.8 miles south of Bend; take US 97 south, then turn east directly across from the Sunriver turnoff for 9 miles to the trailhead; (541) 383–5300 or (541) 593–2421. Open daily May through October dawn to dusk. $ vehicle permit (Northwest Forest Pass).

Somewhat deceptively named, this isn't really a forest of trees embedded in a lava flow 7,000 years ago. Rather, you'll find the hollow impressions left by trees caught in the path of a flow, casting molds in the hardening lava. Explore the area on a paved, self-guided mile-long nature trail.

Mt. Bachelor (ages 5 and up)

Located 22 miles west of Bend on Cascade Lakes Highway; (800) 829–2442 or (541) 382–2442; www.mtbachelor.com; (541) 382–7888 for ski report. Open daily; call for hours. $$$$, children 5 and under free. Surcharge on holidays.

Families can find both summer and winter recreation at Mt. Bachelor, now Oregon's largest ski area, with 3,686 acres of skiing and an average of 370 inches of fresh snow per year. Ski rentals are available, including a complete selection of children's alpine and Nordic skis. Six day lodges let you warm up with a cup of hot chocolate or a piping-hot lunch. The cafe remains open in the summer, too, and the rental shop switches from skis to mountain bikes. The summer excursion chair takes you on a scenic trip to Pine Marten Lodge at the 7,200-foot level, where you can enjoy lunch or dinner with incredible views. Several designated hiking trails at the top allow you to explore the full panorama of central Oregon.

Trail of Dreams Sled Dog Rides (ages 3 and up) 🛷

Located at Mt. Bachelor, operating hours vary during winter season; (800) 829–2422 or (541) 382–2442; www.mtbachelor.com. $–$$$.

A variety of sled-dog rides are offered, including a 1-mile Children's Mini-Thriller Expedition that lasts about ten minutes for kids eleven and under. Kids can also go on standard trips that last about an hour.

Rafting (ages 8 and up) △

A number of outfitters in the area offer white-water rafting trips on the Deschutes, one of Oregon's most challenging white-water rivers. Most trips average about $$$$ per person. In addition to those operating from area resorts, other outfitters include:

- **All Star Rafting.** (800) 909–7238; www.asrk.com.
- **River Drifters.** (800) 972–0430; www.riverdrifters.com.
- **High Desert River Outfitters.** (800) 461–5823; www.highdesertriver.com.
- **Sun Country Tours.** (800) 770–2161 or (541) 382–6277; www.suncountrytours.com.
- **Imperial River Co.** (541) 395–2404 or (800) 395–3903; www.deschutesriver.com.

Pine Mountain Observatory (ages 12 and up) 🔭

Located 30 miles southeast of Bend. Take U.S. Highway 20 to Millican, then turn 9 miles south from the marked road; (541) 382–8331 (after 3:00 P.M.); http://pmo-sun .uoregon.edu. Open to the public late May through September Friday and Saturday evenings or by special appointment, weather permitting. Call first. Suggested donation $.

The University of Oregon's astronomical research facility features 15-, 24-, and 32-inch telescopes. Scientific discoveries made here have been published worldwide. This is the only major observatory in the northwestern United States. There's a primitive campground (no water) across the road. Bring warm clothing when you visit; at 6,500-foot elevation, the evenings are brisk even in summer.

Sunriver Resort (ages 3 and up) 🧗 🚲 🛏️ 🍴 🎿 △

Located about 15 miles southwest of Bend via US 97; (800) 801–8765 or (541) 593–1000; www.sunriver-resort.com; e-mail: info@sunriver-resort.com. Resort always open.

Sunriver, one of the first resorts to combine a lodge with private home development, is a premier family resort. From horseback riding to ice-skating, mountain biking to white-water rafting, the resort offers an array of recreational opportunities with something to please everyone.

- **Bike Shop.** (541) 593–3721; rent a bike here to explore 30 miles of paved paths.
- **Fort Funnigan.** (541) 593–4609; daily programs for kids ages three to ten.
- **Marina.** (541) 593–3492; canoe, kayak, and raft rentals plus shuttle pickup/delivery.

- **Paintball Paradise.** (541) 388–0129; paintball exploits for the twelve and over set.
- **Saddleback Stables.** (541) 593–6995; various rides for ages ten and up.
- **Wanderlust Tours.** (800) 962–2862 or (541) 389–8359; www.wanderlust.tours .com; guided canoe, hiking, and volcano tours.

All these activities cost extra, of course, but the advantage is a well-planned "one-stop-shopping" approach located in the heart of Oregon's lovely high desert region. **Goody's Soda Fountain** (541–593–2155), with the aroma of fragrant home-made waffle cones wafting through the air, is the refreshment stop of choice for families.

Sunriver Nature Center & Observatory (ages 5 and up)

Located 18 miles south of Bend in Sunriver Resort; turn right on Abbott Drive, follow signs to Circle 3, then take River Road; if you reach the marina and stables, you've gone too far; (541) 593–4394; www.sunrivernaturecenter.org. Open daily 9:00 A.M.– 5:00 P.M. in summer, Tuesday through Saturday 10:00 A.M.–4:00 P.M. rest of year. $. The observatory is open 10:00 A.M.–2:00 P.M. and 9:00–11:00 P.M. daily in summer; call for hours rest of year. $ adults, $ children 12 and under.

Families can learn more about astronomy at the observatory and about wildlife and natural and cultural history through living-history programs, nature trails, a botanical garden, and interpretive exhibits. Call for classes and special events.

Working Wonders Children's Museum (all ages)

520 Southwest Powerhouse Drive #624, upstairs in the shops at the Old Mill District; (541) 389–4500; www.workingwonders.com. Open 10:00 A.M.–5:00 P.M. Wednesday through Saturday, 11:00 A.M.–5:00 P.M. Sunday. $.

Working Wonders provides fun, creative activities and hands-on exhibits where kids—and grownups—can play, explore, imagine, and learn. Activities include creating make-believe pizzas, pretending to be a vet, shopping for groceries, building a house, and climbing a rock wall.

Sun Mountain Fun Center (ages 5 and up)

300 Bend River Mall; (541) 382–6161; www.sunmountain fun.com. Open Sunday through Thursday 10:00 A.M.– 4:00 P.M., Friday and Saturday 10:00 A.M.–1:00 P.M. $–$$$.

This 5.5-acre indoor and outdoor facility offers a variety of activities for kids of various ages, including go-karts, minigolf, water wars, batting cages, bowling, billiards, video arcade, snack bar, and rooms for parties.

Top Bend **Events**

July
Cascade Cycling Classic. Racers from around the globe compete in challenging cycling events. Spectators especially favor the evening criterium races. (541) 385–8655; www.cascade-classic.org.

August
Sunriver Music Festival. Classical and pops music plus a children's concert are a sure bet for your resort stay. (541) 593–1084; www.sunriver music.org.

Cascade Festival of Music. Classical and world music are satisfying offerings at this annual event in Drake Park; the children's musical parade is a sure hit. (541) 383–2022 or (888) 545–7435; www.cascade music.org.

Shevlin Park (all ages) 🛶 🚶 🚫

Located 3 miles west of Bend on Shevlin Park Road; (541) 389–7275; www.bendpark sandrec.org. Open all year dawn to dusk. **Free.**

Over 600 acres of forested land offers several trails that wander up Tumalo Creek, where kids enjoy exploring in the water in summer. Several new facilities offer pleasant picnic spots. This is also a popular site for cross-country skiing in winter.

Cascade Lakes Scenic Highway (all ages)

To reach the highway from Bend, take Franklin Avenue west past Drake Park, then follow the signs; (800) 905–2362 or (541) 383–5300; www.byways.org. The road beyond Mt. Bachelor is closed in winter and often doesn't open until June. **Free.**

Also called Century Drive because it's almost 100 miles of beautiful scenery, this road circles a chain of impressive mountain lakes. Take a week or two to explore the area, if you can, stopping at a different lake every night or getting to know one or two very well. The highway runs through the heart of what was once a "ring of fire" chain of volcanic mountains. You'll see a wide range of geologically significant volcanic features, from stratovolcanoes and lava domes to cinder cones, ashflow tuffs, shield volcanoes, and large deposits of pumice and ash. **North and South Twin Lakes** are considered perfect examples of maars: round, deep volcanic crater lakes with no inlet or outlet. **Devil's Garden** is a small spring-fed meadow at the edge of a barren lava flow where astronauts once trained for the Apollo moon missions.

Fun Fact

Part of the film *How the West Was Won* was shot on location at Dutchman Flat, an unusual pumice desert just west of Mt. Bachelor.

Todd Lake (ages 5 and up)

Located about 25 miles west of Bend off the Cascade Lakes Scenic Highway; (541) 383–4000; www.fs.fed.us/r6/centraloregon. Call for hours and winter closures. $ day-use fee (Northwest Forest Pass).

You'll have to carry your camping gear in from the parking area about 200 yards, but the reward is a beautiful wedge of clear mountain water in an alpine meadow, with a view of **Broken Top** in the background. A path circles the lake and provides a perfect opportunity for exploring. In August the lakeshore comes alive with frogs, which guarantee the kids extra fun. Tables on the west shore provide shady spots for having lunch, but you can also take your picnic basket and blanket and dine in a sunny meadow on the north shore.

Boating (ages 8 and up)

You can rent canoes, kayaks, and other watercraft at **Alder Creek Kayak & Canoes**, 345 Southwest Century Drive, (541) 317–9407; www.aldercreek.com. Guided trips, lessons, and classes also available.

Elk Lake (ages 5 and up)

Located 33 miles southwest of Bend on Cascade Lakes Highway; (541) 383–5300; www.fs.fed.us/r6/centraloregon; resort: (541) 480–7228; www.elklakeresort.com. $ day pass, $$ camping.

Three Forest Service campgrounds and two picnic areas provide a base of operation if you're camping, or the resort is the place to stay if you want a bit more comfort. This 390-acre lake is popular for small sailboats and sailboards as well. In summer the lodge offers canoe, pedalboat, rowboat, and kayak rentals. In winter the lodge will bring you in from the Mt. Bachelor Sno-Park by Sno-Cat for cross-country ski holidays. The **Pacific Crest Trail** runs adjacent to the resort, and there are numerous mountain-bike trails to explore.

Osprey Observation Point (all ages)

Located on the west shore of Crane Prairie Reservoir, 45 miles southwest of Bend; (541) 383–5300; www.fs.fed.us/r6/centraloregon. $ day-use fee (Northwest Forest Pass).

Watch ospreys circling over the lake and listen to their piercing cries calling to one another as they seek their dinner from the lake below. The osprey was once an endangered species, but with the ban on DDT and with protected habitats such as this one, they are now a more common sight on Oregon lakes and rivers. This area remains one of a handful of designated osprey nesting sites in the United States. Take the 0.25-mile nature trail from the parking lot and help your kids spot the huge nests atop tall poles. It's quite a sight to observe an osprey make a successful dive, then return to the nest with a wriggling trout clutched in its talons.

La Pine

The **Cascade Lakes Scenic Highway** turns east again on State Highway 42, toward La Pine. On the way, take State Highway 43 to **Pringle Falls** along the Deschutes River.

Newberry National Volcanic Monument (all ages) 🏃

Located 24 miles south of Bend on US 97; (541) 383–5300; www.fs.fed.us/r6/central oregon. Call for hours and winter closures. $ car entrance fee (Northwest Forest Pass).

Newberry was designated a national monument in 1990 for its unique geologic, scenic, recreational, and scientific value. The giant caldera within Newberry Crater holds two crystal-clear alpine lakes, Paulina and East, as well as the Big Obsidian Flow. Native Americans used the sharp black obsidian to make tools and spear- and arrowheads. If you come across a historical or cultural artifact along the trail, such as an Indian arrowhead, feel free to pick it up and hold a piece of history in your hands for a moment, but then replace it so those who follow you might also appreciate its significance. To remove any such artifact is against federal law.

Walk with your kids along the 1-mile interpretive trail through the center of the flow, but caution them about the cutting edges of this dense volcanic glass. In August this area is alive with frogs migrating up the flow from Lost Lake—your kids will go wild!

Throughout the summer, park naturalists at Newberry National Volcanic Monument offer **free** educational and interpretive programs, usually at a small outdoor amphitheater near the Big Obsidian Flow.

Fun Fact

The Big Obsidian Flow at the Newberry Volcano was created 1,300 years ago and now covers 700 acres.

Sisters

When first driving into this small western town, you could be forgiven for thinking the calendar has dropped about a hundred years. If it weren't for the cars, the town's clapboard false-front buildings and wooden boardwalks would make you believe you were back in the Old West. Many of the shops are geared for tourists, but your kids will appreciate the ice-cream parlor on Main Street.

Metolius River Recreation Area (all ages) 🚶🚻
Just 8 miles west of Sisters; (541) 595–6711 (Camp Sherman Store); www.metolius river.com. **Free.**

The headwaters of the Metolius River rush full force out of the ground, a sight that will amaze your kids and rekindle your own appreciation of the wonders of nature. This is one of the premier fly-fishing rivers in the state, completely set aside for catch-and-release angling. Good places to get a look at some lunkers are on the small viewing platform near the bridge where the river flows in front of the **Camp Sherman Store,** about 5 miles north of US 20, and at the state hatchery about 5 miles beyond. The store also has one of the best selections of hand-tied flies I've come across.

Hoodoo Ski Area (ages 5 and up) ⛷🚶
Located 22 miles northwest of Sisters; (541) 822–3799 or (541) 434–8114; (541) 822–3337 (snow report); www.hoodoo.com. Call for hours. $$$$, children under 5 **free.**

Hoodoo, which offers excellent downhill skiing with a variety of slopes, is the second–oldest ski area in Oregon. The groomed cross-country trails at the resort can be enjoyed for a fee, but equally fun trails take off from the Sno-Park below the mountain. Sometimes you'll see mushers racing their sled-dog teams on broad stretches of Forest Service roads in the summer. A new lodge has delighted skiers with dining options for a variety of tastes. Sledding and tubing hills are always family favorites.

Black Butte Ranch (all ages) 🚴⛺🚶🎣🏊⛷🚶
Off US 20, 13 miles east of Sisters; (800) 452–7455 or (541) 595–6211; www.blackbutte ranch.com. Open daily year-round: $–$$ recreation, $$$–$$$$ lodging.

The ranch offers a variety of recreational activities: four swimming pools, twenty-three tennis courts, 16 miles of bicycle paths, an equestrian center, an arcade, a climbing wall, basketball courts, boating, and fly-fishing (catch-and-release only), as well as playgrounds and recreation programs. In winter, cross-country skis and snowshoes can be rented at the Sports Shop for use at nearby Sno-Parks or on the ranch, as long as there's at least 6 inches of snow.

Many hiking trails are available on and off the ranch, including some with spectacular views leading to the top of Black Butte. Area trails range in difficulty from easy walks to distinctly challenging. The recreation center has a guidebook that outlines the options. A chain of spring-fed lakes provides a waterway for boating, and you can rent canoes, kayaks, or paddleboats at the lodge pool for use on Phalarope Lake. If you want to take canoes or kayaks to nearby Suttle or Clear Lakes, you can rent them from the recreation center. Life jackets are provided with the rental.

Guided trail rides take off daily in summer from the Black Butte Stables (541–595–2061). Wear long pants and sturdy shoes or boots with heels. Riders must be at least seven years old and meet size, strength, and balance requirements. Riding lessons are available by appointment only. Call about special options such as wilderness rides, wagon rides, chuckwagon dinners, and cattle drives.

Three Creek Lake (ages 5 and up)

Located about 17 miles south of Sisters on Forest Road 16; (541) 549–7700 or (541) 345–7665 (resort store); www.fs.fed.us/r6/deschutes. Call for hours and snow closures. $ day-use fee (Northwest Forest Pass).

You'll find this lake is a beautiful spot to spend a weekend, a week, or just an afternoon. The shore of the lake has a shallow, gradual shelf that is perfect for wading, and the small marina rents rowboats by the day or the hour. The water in this lake is so clear that you can see to the bottom at its deepest point, some 30 feet below the surface. A small stream runs into the lake from **Little Three Creek Lake** above. Walk along the stream in search of brook trout, crawdads, or other critters. The lush green meadow surrounding Little Three Creek comes alive during August when tiny frogs make their way from the lake to the forest. In winter several Sno-Parks offer cross-country skiers access to the backcountry.

Top Events in Sisters

June

Sisters Rodeo. A parade, pancake breakfast, and four rodeo performances draw people from all over the state. (541) 549–0121 or (800) 827–7522; www.sistersrodeo.com.

Wizard Falls Kids Day. Usually held the second Saturday in June, this event lets kids ten and under fish in the big pond for lunker trout. (541) 579–7700 or (541) 595–6611.

July

Sisters Quilt Show. All the buildings in town are festooned with quilts. (541) 549–0251; www.stitchinpost.com.

Fun Fact

Sisters is Oregon's llama capital and is literally surrounded by llama ranches.

Wizard Falls (ages 5 and up)

Located about 5 miles north of Camp Sherman on US 20; just east of Black Butte, turn north at sign for Metolius River and drive to Forest Road 1419; (541) 549–7700. Open as weather permits. **Free.**

The Metolius River passes through a narrow channel of deep rock and forms these grand falls. The spot is as hazardous as it is beautiful, so keep your kids on the bridge when you stop to admire it. Take a walk up the **Canyon Creek Trail** along the Metolius for some gorgeous scenery.

Wizard Falls Fish Hatchery (all ages)

Located just across the bridge at Wizard Falls, 5 miles downstream from Camp Sherman; (541) 549–7700 or (541) 595–6611. Open 8:00 A.M.–7:00 P.M. year-round as weather permits. **Free.**

The kids can feed the enormous brook trout, including some unusual specimens like albino trout, with food available from a coin-operated dispenser. Interpretive displays describe the life of a trout and how the hatchery helps enhance the native populations of brown and rainbow trout and kokanee salmon in the river.

Redmond

Crooked River Railroad Company Train (ages 6 and up)

Three miles north of Redmond off US 97 and O'Neil Road; (541) 548–8630; www .crookedriverrailroad.com. Train runs for Friday and Saturday dinner and Sunday brunch and supper. $$$$, children 2 and under $$–$$$.

This 1800s-era dinner train rides 19 miles through the Crooked River Valley, past rim-rock canyons and high desert. Entertainment features Wild West characters who take you back in time to the era of train robberies and adventure. Special holiday and mur-der-mystery trains are also offered.

Smith Rock State Park (all ages)

Off Crooked River Drive, 9 miles northeast of Redmond; from US 97 north of Red-mond, follow signs to the park; (800) 551–6949 or (541) 548–7501; www.oregon stateparks.org. Open year-round dawn to dusk. $ day-use fee.

This is a mecca for rock climbers and photographers. Your kids are probably too young to climb, but you can watch climbers scale the rock faces in the park, then rappel down on brightly colored ropes. The 641-acre park is filled with dramatic rock spires rising above the Crooked River Canyon. Walk along 2 miles of developed trails to the river or ridge (keep to the trail to reduce erosion) and watch for wildlife such as mule deer and nesting geese, hawks, falcons, golden eagles, and ospreys (keep an eye open for rattlesnakes). On your way, stop at the **Juniper Junction** store, 9297 Northeast Crooked River Drive, (541) 548–4786, for a huckleberry ice-cream cone, a store specialty for thirty-five years.

Petersen Rock Garden and Museum (all ages)

Located off US 97 at 7930 Southwest Seventy-seventh; (541) 382–5574. Open 9:00 A.M. daily, closing time varies by season. $, children under 6 free.

The late Mr. Petersen spent seventeen years creating this four-acre park of miniature bridges, lily ponds, towers, and gardens, using varicolored rocks to create the designs.

Operation Santa Claus (all ages)

4355 West State Highway 126; located 2 miles west of Redmond; (541) 548–8910. Open daily dawn to dusk. Free.

Christmas in July? Make that Christmas all year at Operation Santa Claus reindeer ranch. More than a hundred reindeer live at this ranch, where the owners believe in keeping the spirit of the holiday going all year. Take a self-guided tour or wander through the gift shop. Come see the newborns in May and June.

Halligan Ranch (ages 5 and up)

Located at 9020 South Highway 97; (541) 389–6855; www.halliganranch.com. Call for information on operating hours, reservations, and rates.

The Halligan Ranch offers day hikes and overnight trips for families with llamas. The ranch has more than fifty llamas, and visitors of all ages can experience hands-on grooming, petting, feeding, and leading. The walks take place on a portion of the 230-acre ranch, with guides providing information on local history, rock fences, ranch structures, and, of course, llamas.

Cascade Swim Center (ages 5 and up)

465 Southwest Rimrock Drive; (541) 548–7275; www.coprd.org; e-mail: coprd@coprd.org. Children $, adults $$.

The swim center features a 25-meter pool, basketball and sand volleyball courts, a preschool park, horseshoe pits, and picnic areas.

Top Redmond **Events**

July

Fourth of July Parade. If you're here during Fourth of July weekend, help this friendly community celebrate Independence Day by cheering participants in an old-fashioned parade. (541) 923–5191.

July and August

Chamber Music on the Green. Concerts offered outdoors July through August. (541) 923-5191; www.redmondcofc.com.

Borden Beck Wildlife Preserve (ages 4 and up)

Located 5 miles west of Terrebonne on Lower Bridge Road; (541) 548–7275; www.co prd.org; e-mail: coprd@coprd.org. Free.

The newest addition to Redmond's recreational facilities is the Borden Beck Wildlife Preserve. Through the annual donations of the Beck family, the preserve is maintained in its natural state for local residents and visitors to enjoy. It features nature and hiking trails, picnic areas, fishing and swimming in the Deschutes River, and wildlife viewing.

Madras

Lake Billy Chinook (all ages)

Two miles southwest of Madras; take US 26 to Culver Highway, then follow signs to the lake; (800) 551–6959; www.oregonstateparks.org. Call for hours and winter closures. $ vehicle permit.

Three rivers feed into the waters of Lake Billy Chinook, named for an Indian guide who helped Captain John Frémont in his mapping expeditions to Oregon. The lake is now a haven for summer water fun in the midst of Oregon's high desert country.

Cove Palisades State Park (all ages)

On Lake Billy Chinook at 7300 Southwest Jordan Road; (800) 551–6949 or (541) 546–3412; (800) 452–5687 for reservations; www.oregonstateparks.org. Open daily. $ day-use fee.

The park straddles the Deschutes and Crooked Rivers arms of the lake and is the center of much recreational activity. Boat ramps, swimming beaches, campgrounds, and picnic tables are provided. The two campgrounds, one on the Deschutes River and another overlooking the Crooked River from above on the cliffs, are closed in winter.

There are three public day-use areas and a private restaurant that's open May through September. Rustic lakeshore cabins are available for rent, and there are 10 miles of hiking trails to explore.

Cove Palisades Marina (541–546–3412), on the Crooked River arm of the lake, rents fishing and waterskiing boats, patio boats, and jet skis. In summer, park rangers offer interpretive programs. Just up from the **Deschutes Campground** to the northeast, you'll find a large boulder of basalt with Indian petroglyphs. You can walk to the beach along a trail across from the entrance station at the campground, but keep the eyes and ears open for rattlesnakes.

Round Butte Overlook Park (all ages) 🛱

Located 15 miles southwest of Madras off Belmont Lane; (503) 464–8515. Open daily May 25 through September 30 8:00 A.M.–dusk. Free.

The park includes a picnic area and interpretive center overlooking Round Butte Dam and Lake Billy Chinook.

Richardson's Recreation Ranch (all ages) 🪨

Located 11 miles north of Madras (off US 97) near milepost 81; (541) 475–2680; www .richardsonrockranch.com. Open daily 7:00 A.M.–5:00 P.M. weather permitting; arrive by 3:00 P.M. if you want to dig. $.

Kids of all ages can enjoy an afternoon of rockhounding here, digging for thunder eggs—those drab, round rocks that, when split in two, reveal formations like miniature worlds in crystal, opal, agate, or cinnabar.

The thunder egg is the Oregon state rock, and its name comes from an Indian legend about a battle between the thunder spirits residing in Mt. Jefferson and Mt. Hood. When they became angry at each other, the spirits hurled the agate-filled balls at one another, sounding their thunder with each toss. The result of their ire is resting in rock beds, about 4,000 acres of which are within the Richardson family ranch. Digging is available daily, weather permitting, and rock picks are provided. Thunder-egg splitting services are also available at the shop, and finished rock products are sold. Rocks are just 50 cents, but you can also pay by the pound for what you take out.

Top Madras **Event**

May

Collage of Culture. Country music, hot-air baloons, Latin salsa, traditional Native American dances, and ethnic food—what more could you want in this event that celebrates cultural diversity? (541) 475–2350 or (800) 967–3564; www.collageofculture.com.

Warm Springs Indian Reservation

Kah-Nee-Ta Resort (all ages) 🌊 👫 🐟 ⛰ 🚐 🚲

To get to Warm Springs and the resort, take US 26 for 25 miles northwest from Madras or 119 miles southeast from Portland; (800) 554–4786 or (541) 553–1112; www.kah-nee-ta resort.com. $–$$ (recreation), $$$–$$$$ (lodging).

Everyone will enjoy the traditional aspects of a stay at this tribal-owned and-operated resort that retains the rugged natural beauty of its surroundings. Kids love swimming in the pools, one fed by hot springs and the other with a fountain depicting bears holding salmon spouting water. Activities include salmon bakes and fry bread, dancing and drumming, and storytelling and singing. You can rent cabins, lodge rooms, tepees, or campsites for RVs. Recreation also includes fishing and kayaking on the Deschutes, hiking along trails, horseback riding, working out at the fitness center, and playing tennis and golf.

Museum at Warm Springs (ages 3 and up) 📷 👫

2189 US 26; (541) 553–3331; www.warmsprings.biz/museum. Open daily year-round, 9:00 A.M.–5:00 P.M. $$ adults; $ ages 5–12, 4 and under free.

The homeland for more than 3,400 members of the Warm Springs, Wasco, and Northern Paiute tribes, Warm Springs Reservation has developed a thriving tourist industry as well as a center that seeks to enlighten visitors about the rich traditions of Northwest Native American culture. The stunningly beautiful museum is one place you won't want to miss. Completed in 1993, the 25,000-square-foot facility was created to provide a legacy to the generations that follow and houses the largest collection of Native American artifacts under one roof in the United States. The history of the Confederated Tribes unfolds in a state-of-the-art permanent exhibit of audiovisual presentations and displays, which include prized heirlooms from tribal families, historic photographs, and murals. Traditional dwellings—a tule mat lodge, wickiup, and plankhouse—show how people lived in ancient villages. Beadwork, basketry, cloth-

Fun Fact

Kah-Nee-Ta Village was named for an Indian woman, Xnitla, which means "root digger." She was a scout and a spiritual leader who used the natural hot springs and indigenous plants and roots for medicinal purposes and religious ceremonies.

ing, and other artifacts are also displayed. A multimedia exhibit draws you into the traditional singing, drumming, and dancing of the tribes, which is a marvelous experience to appreciate with your family. Walking trails along Shitike Creek lead to picnic areas and an amphitheater where performances and demonstrations are staged in the summer.

Olallie Lake National Scenic Area (ages 5 and up) 🌊 ⛺ 👥

Located 32 miles south of US 26 off Forest Road 42; (541) 822–3381; www.fs.fed.us/r6/ mthood or www.olallielake.com. Call for hours and seasonal closures. $ vehicle fee (Northwest Forest Pass).

This area covers nearly 11,000 acres in both the **Mt. Hood National Forest** and the **Warm Springs Reservation.** The many lakes that dot the region of pine and fir forests reflect the grandeur of Mt. Hood to the north and Mt. Jefferson to the west. A resort on Olallie Lake offers small cabins for rent, as well as a store with fishing and camping supplies and boat rentals. No motors or swimming are allowed on the lake because it provides drinking water for local residents. You can swim in **Head Lake** and **First Lake,** both just off the road to the north of Olallie Lake. **Breitenbush Lake** is on reservation land and is difficult to access by road without a high-clearance vehicle; tribal fishing permits are required (541–553–2000).

Olallie Trail circles Olallie Lake, and spur trails lead to several other lakes. You can pick up a map of area trails from the ranger station near the entrance to the scenic area or at the resort store on Olallie Lake. Access to Olallie Lake is not suitable for trailers and requires a car in good condition.

Top Warm Springs **Events**

February

Lincoln's Pow-Wow. Celebrated in Simnasho on the weekend of Lincoln's birthday, the event features authentic Native American arts and crafts, food, stick games, traditional dancing, and singing.

June

Pi-Ume-Sha Pow-Wow. This annual celebration of the treaty that established the Warm Springs Reservation is held on the weekend closest to June 25 and includes Native American dancing, singing, an endurance horse race, food, crafts, a parade, a rodeo, and a golf tournament.

For both events, contact the Confederated Tribes of Warm Springs at (541) 553–3243; www.warmsprings.com; e-mail: info@warmsprings.com.

Where to Eat

IN BEND

Legends Publick House. 125 Northwest Oregon Avenue; (541) 382–5654. Upscale dining in a casual setting makes this a popular place for locals and visitors. $$

Tumalo Feed Company. 64619 West US 20; (541) 382–2202; www.tumalofeedcompany.com. Listed as one of *Sunset Magazine*'s "11 Great Steakhouses of the West." Kids receive crayons and paper, and they can choose a prize out of the saddlebags if they clean their plates (or do their best). Children under five eat free, and up to age twelve eat for $4.95.

Westside Bakery and Cafe. 1005 Northwest Galveston; (514) 382–3426. On the way out of town, heading toward the Cascade Lakes Scenic Highway, you'll come across this dining establishment with unusual and eclectic decor that includes a red-nosed moose head, old movie posters, and Native American paraphernalia. The menu offers a wide variety of options for both parents and children. You can even grab goodies to go from the bakery. $

IN SISTERS

Bronco Billy's Ranch & Grill. 190 East Cascade Street; (541) 549–7427; www.broncobillysranchgrill.com. At this favorite watering hole, you can also find lunch and dinner with a western flair. Barbecued ribs, links, and chicken are renowned rib-sticking entrees. $–$$$

Kokanee Cafe. 13173 Southwest Forest Road 1419; located 15 miles west of Sisters in Camp Sherman; (541) 595–6420. Many would agree that this hidden gem offers the best of Northwest cuisine. Fresh local ingredients are always featured in the small but carefully chosen list of featured dinner entrees. Closed in winter; call first. $$$–$$$$

Papandrea's Pizza. 442 East Hood; (541) 549–6081. This cozy pizza parlor has a very local, friendly feel. $$–$$$

Where to Stay

IN BEND

Bend Riverside Motel. 1565 Northwest Hill Street; (800) 284–2363 or (541) 389–2363; www.bendriversidemotel.com. The large property sits on the Deschutes River next to Pioneer Park. Less-expensive rooms are cramped, but for slightly more you get room to stretch out and views of the river. An indoor pool, sauna, and a tennis court are available. $$–$$$

Black Butte Ranch. P.O. Box 8000, Black Butte Ranch, OR 97759; (800) 452–7455 or (541) 595–6211; www.blackbutteranch.com; email: info@blackbutteranch.com. The year-round resort offers lodge rooms and condominiums, as well as private homes rented by the day or week. Cycling on miles of paved trails, plus tennis, swimming, and golf, round out many a family vacation. $$$–$$$$

Entrada Lodge. 19221 Century Drive; (800) 528–1234 or (541) 382– 4080; www.entradalodge.com. Situated a few miles west of Bend among tall pine trees, this peaceful place is close to Mt. Bachelor. It doesn't offer all the fanfare that other establishments do, but it includes a continental breakfast, an outdoor pool, and a whirlpool. $$–$$$

Sunriver Lodge and Resort. 1 Center Drive; (800) 801–8765 or (541) 593–1221; www.sunriver-resort.com; e-mail: info@sunriver-resort.com. Private homes and condos are for rent on a nightly and weekly basis. Horseback riding, ice-skating, mountain biking, and white-water rafting make this a perfect "one-stop" resort site. $$$–$$$$

IN LA PINE

Best Western Newberry Station. 16515 Reed Road and US 97; (800) 210–8616 or (541) 536–5130. Continental breakfast, an indoor swimming pool, and a spa give families a pleasant respite. $–$$

Paulina Lake Resort. East Paulina Lake Road; (541) 536–2240; www.paulinalake resort.evisionsite.com. The resort is open May through September and mid-December through mid-March. Camping is available along the lakes and Paulina Creek. Paulina Lake Resort and **East Lake Resort** (541–536–2230; www.eastlakeresort.com) both offer cabins. They also provide boat rentals and restaurants serving breakfast, lunch, and dinner (Paulina only). Paulina is also open for winter recreation. $$–$$$$

West View Motel. 51371 US 97 South; (541) 536–2115. Pets are allowed. Some kitchenettes are available. $

IN MADRAS

Best Western Rama Inn. 12 Southwest Fourth Street; (541) 475–6141; www.bw madrasinn.com. Continental breakfast, a sauna, and an exercise room are offered here. $$–$$$

Sonny's Motel. 1539 Southwest US 97; (800) 624–6137 or (541) 475–7217. Kitchenettes and laundry facilities are available. Pets allowed. $$–$$$

IN REDMOND

Eagle Crest Resort. 1522 Cline Falls Road; (800) 682–4786 or (541) 923–9644; www .eagle-crest.com. Exercise rooms, indoor and outdoor pools, kitchenettes, and a restaurant give families plenty of options. $$$–$$$$

Historic New Redmond Hotel. 521 Southwest Sixth Street; (541) 923–7378; www.newredmondhotel.com; e-mail: nrdh@bhghotels.com. Although the hotel was built in 1927, the rooms are modern and comfortable. Exercise room, spa, free continental breakfast, and free parking. $–$$$

IN SISTERS

Best Western Ponderosa Lodge. 500 US 20 West; (541) 549–1234 or (800) 549–1234; www.bestwesternsisters.com. Continental breakfast, a swimming pool, and spa pool are offered to guests, who will also appreciate the proximity to downhill skiing, golf, and fishing. $$–$$$

Comfort Inn at Sisters. 540 US 20 West; (541) 549–7829 or (800) 228–5150. Continental breakfast is available here, and pets are allowed with prior approval. You'll also find an indoor swimming pool and laundry facilities. RV spaces are available at the adjacent Mountain Shadow RV Village. $$–$$$$

Sisters Historic Motor Lodge. 511 West Cascade; (541) 549–2551; e-mail: sisml@ uci.net. Full breakfast is provided, and you'll be close to golf, skiing, tennis, and fishing. Kitchenettes are also available. Pet-friendly. Nonsmoking. $$–$$$$

IN WARM SPRINGS

Kah-Nee-Ta Resort. P.O. Box K, Warm Springs, OR 97761; (800) 554–4786 or (541) 553–1112; www.kah-nee-taresort.com. Choose from lodge rooms, cabins, tepees, and RV sites. Kayaking and white-water rafting opportunities are available on the Deschutes, along with hiking, horseback riding, working out at the fitness center, and playing tennis or golf. Two restaurants serve American and Northwest cuisine. The resort museum is outstanding. $$–$$$$

For More Information

Bend Chamber of Commerce. 777 Northwest Wall Street, Bend, OR 97701; (541) 382–3221; www.bendchamber.org.

Bend Visitor & Convention Bureau. 917 Northwest Harriman, Bend, OR 97701; (877) 245–8484; www.bisitbend.com.

Central Oregon Visitors Association. 572 Southwest Bluff Drive, Suite C, Bend, OR 97702; (800) 800–8334 or (541) 389–8799; www.visitcentraloregon.com or www.covisitors.com.

Confederated Tribes of Warm Springs. 1233 Veterans Street, Warm Springs, OR 97761; (541) 553–3333; www.warmsprings .com; e-mail: info@warmsprings.com.

La Pine Chamber of Commerce. On US 97 at the south end of town; P.O. Box 616, La Pine, OR 97739; (541) 536–9771; www .lapine. org; e-mail: info@lapine.org.

Madras Chamber of Commerce. P.O. Box 770, 274 Southwest Fourth Street, Madras, OR 97741; (541) 475–2350 or (800) 967– 3564; www.madraschamber.com.

Prineville-Crook County Chamber of Commerce. 390 Northeast Fairview, Prineville, OR 97754; (541) 447–6304; www.prineville-crookcounty.org; e-mail: pchamber@prineville.org.

Redmond Chamber of Commerce. 446 Southwest Seventh Street, Redmond, OR 97756; (541) 923–5191; www.redmond cofc.com; e-mail: rcc@empnet.com.

Sisters Area Chamber of Commerce. P.O. Box 430, 352 West Hood Avenue, Sisters, OR 97759; (866) 549–0252 or (541) 549–0251; www.sisters chamber.com; e-mail: info@sisterschamber.com.

Sunriver Area Chamber of Commerce. P.O. Box 3246, Sunriver, OR 97707; (541) 593–8149; www.sunriverchamber.com; e-mail: sunrivercc@coinet.com.

Southern Oregon

The southern region of Oregon encompasses the diversity of the whole state: coast, mountains, valleys, high desert. Your choices for family fun are equally diverse—from bird-watching on Oregon's largest lake to exploring its only national park, from riding a wild river to watching Shakespeare performed in one of the world's preeminent Shakespearean theaters. In winter southern Oregon is transformed into a frosty playground. In summer the warm, dry weather provides an open invitation to outdoor recreation.

Ashland

Ashland's population of 19,000 swells to more than 50,000 when the renowned Shakespearean festival season is at its peak. While we wouldn't recommend introducing your children to Shakespeare with a play like *King Lear,* the theater inevitably offers three of the Bard's twelve comedies on its playbill each year. Experiencing a play in the open-air Elizabethan Theatre is wonderful, but spend a little extra to rent a cushion and lap robe—it will make all the difference if the night becomes chilly. Another enjoyable pastime in Ashland is dining, and for a town this size, there are a number of remarkably good restaurants.

Oregon Shakespeare Festival (ages 8 and up) 🎵
15 South Pioneer Street, P.O. Box 158, Ashland, OR 97520; (541) 482–2111 (for brochure and information); (503) 482–4331 (tickets); www.osfashland.org. Plays run February through October. Call for prices and schedules.

Three theaters, the **Elizabethan Theatre,** the **Angus Bowmer Theatre,** and the **New Theatre,** which replaced the Black Swan Theater, all offer top-notch productions. The Bowmer offers both Shakespeare and contemporary plays, while the Elizabethan is primarily dedicated to the Bard.

SOUTHERN OREGON

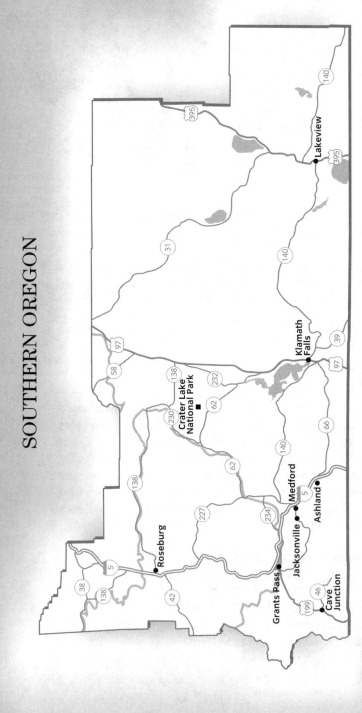

Crater Lake
National Park

Klamath
Falls

Lakeview

Medford

Ashland

Jacksonville

Grants Pass

Cave
Junction

Roseburg

Oregon Shakespeare Festival Backstage Tours (ages 5 and up) 🎵

15 South Pioneer Street; (541) 482–4331. Reservations required. Open Tuesday through Sunday late February to late October, 10:00 A.M. Prices range from $ to $$, depending on the season.

With an actor as a guide, you get a behind-the-scenes look at how a theatrical production is put together. Your kids will especially enjoy the costumes and props, which they're allowed to touch.

Oregon Cabaret Theatre (ages 8 and up) 🎵

First and Hargadine Streets, P.O. Box 1149, Ashland, OR 97520; (541) 488–2962; www.oregoncabaret.com. Plays run February through December. Call for prices and schedule.

This theater presents entertaining musicals, revues, and comedies in a nightclub setting in a historic church. Preshow gourmet dinners are available by reservation, and beverages and desserts are offered at intermission.

Emigrant Lake (all ages) 🚶 🚴 ⛺ 🏊 ⚓

Located 6 miles southeast of Ashland, on State Highway 66; (541) 774–8183. Open dawn to dusk. $ vehicle pass.

Emigrant Lake has long been a popular spot for waterskiing, fishing, and swimming. This reservoir has a 270-foot twin-flume waterslide that will keep your kids squealing and happy for hours. Camping is also available here.

Top Ashland Events

June

Feast of Will. This celebration dinner in Lithia Park, complete with period music and dancing, marks the opening of the Elizabethan Theatre each season. (541) 482–4331.

December

Holiday Festival of Lights. Be sure to attend the community's yuletide festival if you're in the area during the holidays. It lasts the whole month. (541) 482–3486.

Year-round

Southern Oregon University Theatre Arts. The university presents a variety of classics, musicals, and contemporary plays each academic year. (541) 552–6348; www.sou.edu/THTR/season.html.

Hyatt Lake (all ages)

Located farther along State Highway 66; (541) 482–2031. Open dawn to dusk. $ day-use fee; camping $$.

You'll find more water recreation as well as winter fun at Hyatt Lake, a high Cascade lake that will reward you with a view of Mt. McLoughlin. There are two private resorts on the lake as well:

- **Hyatt Lake Resort.** 7979 Hyatt Prairie Road; (877) 411–3331 or (541) 482–3331; www.hyattlake.com; e-mail: hyattlake@hyattlake.com. Restaurant and convenience store plus cabins, RV sites, tent sites, and boat, canoe, and paddleboat rentals.
- **Camper's Cove Resort.** 7900 Hyatt Prairie Road; (541) 482–1201; www.members .aol. com/badentinc/cmprcve.htm; e-mail: badentinc@aol.com. Restaurant and RV spaces.

Mt. Ashland (ages 5 and up)

1745 State Highway 66, located 18 miles from the city center heading south; (541) 482–2897; www.mtashland.com. Usually opens Thanksgiving weekend; call for hours. Lift tickets $$$–$$$$.

With four chairlifts and more than twenty ski runs on a 1,150-foot vertical slope, Mt. Ashland should be on the to-do list for any family that enjoys downhill skiing. A ski school and rental shop cater to those interested in giving the slopes a try for the first time, and the day lodge offers meals and great views. Summer hiking is terrific here, too. The **Pacific Crest Trail** crosses Mt. Ashland Inn's parking area, and several spur trails lead to scenic viewpoints and picturesque streams.

Wild and Scenic Rogue River Rafting (ages 8 and up)

Many local outdoor operators run trips out of Ashland, including:

- **Noah's River Adventures.** 53 North Main Street; (800) 858–2811 or (541) 488–2811; www.noahsrafting.com; e-mail: noahs@mind.net. Call for schedule. Half-day Rogue River trip $$$$; one-day Rogue River or Upper Klamath trip $$$$. Family discount plans available. Noah's offers half-, full-, and multiday floats and family scenic "sunsoaker" trips without the white water.
- **Adventure Center.** 40 North Main Street; (800) 444–2819 or (541) 488–2819; www.raftingtours.com. Call for schedule; runs early spring to early fall. Half-day or all-day trip $$$$. Discounts available for families. This company runs eight different rivers, including the Rogue and wild Upper Klamath, and supplies transportation, gear, and food. It also offers a simple float trip for families with preschool-age children.
- **Raft the Rogue.** 21171 State Highway 62, Shady Cove; (800) 797–7238 or (541) 878–3623; www.rafttherogue.com; e-mail: rafttherogue@earthlink.net. Call for schedule; runs early spring to early fall. Raft trip $$$$. This company rents the rafts and delivers you to the river—you do the rest!

Lithia Park (all ages)

Located just off Siskiyou Boulevard; (541) 488–5340; www.ashland.or.us. Open dawn to dusk. Free.

A green and lovely place with Ashland Creek creating a musical backdrop, Lithia Park is at the heart of this romantically small town. Designed by John McLaren, the architect who gave San Francisco Golden Gate Park, Lithia Park is now a recognized National Historic Site. Near the entrance to the park is a small fountain, bubbling forth mineral water from Lithia Springs, which has been said to have curative powers.

ScienceWorks Hands-On Museum (all ages)

1500 East Main Street; (541) 482–6767; www.scienceworksmuseum.org. Open Wednesday through Saturday 10:00 A.M.–4:00 P.M., Sunday noon–4:00 P.M. $.

This is a state of the art museum for explorers of all ages. It offers interactive exhibits, science shows, and an outdoor garden.

Medford

Medford's prosperity turned from gold in the 1800s to agricultural activity—it's still a major world center for pears—and it is a major business and medical center in southern Oregon.

Butte Creek Mill (ages 5 and up)

402 Royal Avenue North, Eagle Point; (541) 826–3531; www.buttecreekmill.com; e-mail: info@buttecreekmill.com. Open Monday through Saturday 9:00 A.M.–5:00 P.M., Sunday 11:00 A.M.–5:00 P.M. Free.

Oregon's only original water-powered gristmill has been operating continuously since 1872, when two 1,400-pound French buhr millstones were brought around Cape Horn by ship, then transported over the mountains by wagon. The building itself, open for self-guided tours, is a living museum. Your kids will be intrigued by the way the waterwheel turns the stones to grind the grains into flour. To continue the old-fashioned family entertainment, bring a picnic to enjoy in the park across the stream, and walk across the Antelope Creek Covered Bridge, also nearby. You can buy Butte Creek Mill products online and at the Country Store located on the property.

Top Medford **Events**

April

Pear Blossom Festival. Among the activities are the 10-mile Pear Blossom Run, bicycle races, arts and crafts, and a parade. (541) 734–7327.

Summer

Bear Creek Park Concerts. Concerts are held in the park on Sunday evenings. (541) 774–2400.

October

Medford Jazz Jubilee. More than a hundred performances give families plenty of options for a weekend of great music entertainment. (800) 599–0039 or (541) 770–6972; www.medfordjazz.org.

Harry and David (ages 8 and up) 🔒

1314 Center Drive #A; (877) 322–1200; (541) 864–2278 or (541) 776–2277; www.harry anddavid.com. Tours are offered four times a day on weekdays, 9:15 A.M.–1:45 P.M. by reservation. $, children 12 and under free.

If your kids love fruit, take them on a tour of one of the largest mail-order companies in the world. The tour takes you through the plant that packages gift baskets of delectable fruits, from Oregon-grown ruby silk pears to ruby cream bananas; to the candy kitchen where an assortment of chocolate truffles are created before your eyes; and on to the bakery where baklava, loaf cakes, and fruit pastry confections will get your mouths watering—just in time to return to the retail store. You can also visit the store on your own, without the benefit of a guided tour.

Fun Fact

When Medford sprang up in the wake of the Oregon and California Railroad, nearby Jacksonville, unhappy with the competition, referred to it as Chaparral City, perhaps as a means of depressing the pretensions of the upstart rival community.

Medford Railroad Park (ages 3 and up) 🏞

Located near the Rogue Valley Mall on Berrydale Avenue off Table Rock Road; (541) 774–2400; http://sorcnrhs.railfan.net/medfordrrpark.htm; e-mail: sorcnrhs@railfan.net. Open second and fourth Sundays April through October 11:00 A.M.–3:00 P.M. Free, but donations appreciated.

Train buffs have put together miniature steam, diesel, and electric trains that run along a mile of track. Parents and kids are welcome to take rides. Bring lunch to eat in the picnic pavilion.

Joseph P. Stewart State Recreation Area (all ages) 🚶 🚴 🏊 ⛺

Located 35 miles northeast of Medford on State Highway 62; (800) 551–6949 or (541) 560–3334. Always open. Free.

The park has a marina with a cafe and store and a swimming beach for cooling off during the summer. It also features 5.5 miles of hiking trails and a 6-mile bike trail. Campsites are available, too ($).

Southern Oregon History Center (ages 5 and up) 🏛

106 North Central Avenue; (541) 773–6536; www.sohs.org; e-mail: info@SOHS.org. Open Tuesday through Friday 9:00 A.M.–5:00 P.M. Free.

Exhibits include traditional collections of pioneer artifacts and informative displays on early farming and mining in the region.

Crater Rock Museum (ages 5 and up) 🏛

2002 Scenic Avenue, Central Point; located 6 miles north of Medford off State Highway 99; (541) 664–6081; www.craterrock.com. Open Tuesday, Thursday, and Saturday 10:00 A.M.–4:00 P.M.

The museum offers amazing displays of rocks, minerals, and gems, and it has a gift shop.

Fish Lake Resort (all ages) 🍽 🚶 🎣 🎿 ⛺ ⛺ 🏊

Located 30 miles west of Medford and 39 miles east of Klamath Falls off State Highway 140; (541) 949–8500; www.fishlakeresort.net. Open year-round. $$–$$$

You'll find this resort by a Cascade lake near the foot of Mt. McLoughlin. It includes cabins, RV and tent sites, a cafe, store, game room, and boat rentals. The lake offers fishing and swimming, but no speedboats or waterskiing. The site is located near hiking, mountain-biking, and cross-country ski trails.

Jacksonville

Located just west of Medford, Jacksonville was at the heart of southern Oregon's gold rush that began in 1852, and the entire town has since been put on the National Register of Historic Places. If you'd like to explore Jacksonville and learn more about its history, take a narrated carriage or trolley ride through town.

Jacksonville Museum of Southern Oregon History (ages 5 and up)

206 North Fifth Street; (541) 773–6536; www.sohs.org. Open Wednesday through Sunday 10:00 A.M.–5:00 P.M. $ (covers Children's Museum also).

Exhibits feature Native American artifacts and pioneer pottery.

Children's Museum (all ages)

206 North Fifth Street; (541) 773–6536. Same hours as Jacksonville Museum of Southern Oregon History, above. $

This child-oriented attraction is located in the adjoining County Jail. Kids appreciate the pioneer exhibit area, where the usual museum refrain "Look but don't touch" doesn't apply. The collection of antique toys is also a favorite.

Top Jacksonville **Events**

June through Labor Day
Britt Festivals. Renowned musicians converge here to wow audiences in a peaceful outdoor setting. (800) 882–7488 or (541) 773–6077; www.britt fest.org.

July
Children's Festival. Held on the Britt grounds, this event is especially fun for children ages two to twelve. The whole family can enjoy arts and crafts, food, and live entertainment. (541) 776–7286.

December
Victorian Christmas. Strolling carolers and horse-drawn carriage rides add a festive holiday atmosphere in this famous gold-rush town. (541) 899–8118.

Jacksonville History Store (ages 5 and up) 🔵

California and Third Streets; (541) 773–6536. Open Wednesday through Sunday 11:00 A.M.– 4:00 P.M.

Offerings include wonderful replicas of children's toys from long ago and a good selection of folk art.

Gin Lin Mining Trail (ages 5 and up) 🔵 🔵

Located 15 miles south of Jacksonville in the Rogue River National Forest; (541) 776–7001 or (541) 899–1812; www.fs.fed.us/r6/rogue. Always open. Free.

The trail tells the story of a Chinese miner whose claim on this stretch of the Siskiyous yielded more than a million dollars in gold dust. An interpretive brochure, available at the trailhead, describes numbered stops along the way. A guide is also available online. The easy 0.75-mile walk takes off from the Flumet Flat Campground in the Rogue River National Forest.

Applegate Lake (all ages) 🔵 🔵 🔵 🔵

Located in the Rogue River National Forest, 23 miles southwest of Medford; (541) 899–1812. Always open; water levels may restrict recreational activity. Some free sites; others require a $ fee.

This is a great place to spend the day swimming, boating, fishing, or hiking on one of several trails around the lake. Hartish Park, on the west shore, is a charming spot for picnicking.

Grants Pass

The **Rogue River** is one of the most popular destinations in Oregon, and it runs through Grants Pass. Immortalized by writer Zane Grey, this mighty 215-mile river is famous worldwide for its stunning beauty, from the headwaters in Crater Lake National Park to the Pacific Ocean. The wild and scenic section of the river brings thousands to challenge its white-water canyons in rafts and kayaks.

Hellgate Jetboat Excursions (ages 8 and up) 🔵

966 Southeast Sixth Street; (800) 648–4874 or (541) 476–2628; www.hellgate.com; e-mail: info@hellgate.com. Operates May through September; call for schedules. Hellgate Quick and Scenic Trip (two hours, 36 miles): $$$$ adults, $$$ children, 3 and under free.

The original jet boat tour company on this part of the river, Hellgate trips leave from the Riverside Motel, off Seventh Street, to either Hellgate Canyon (made famous by

John Wayne's *Rooster Cogburn*) or Grave Creek. The brunch and dinner trips include a meal at the OK Corral.

Wildlife Images Rehabilitation Center (ages 8 and up) 🐾

11845 Lower River Road, 13 miles west of Grants Pass; (541) 476–0222. Tours offered daily at 11:00 A.M. and 1:00 P.M.; call *at least a day* ahead for reservations. Donations gratefully accepted.

Visitors to this wildlife rescue program get a close-up look at how the center aids and nurtures injured and orphaned animals, including bears, cougars, raccoons, and birds of prey.

Grants Pass–**Area Parks**

Take both your picnic and a Frisbee to any of four parks in and near town where your family can play Disc Golf. You toss your whirling disc at the "holes," which are actually wire baskets mounted atop poles.

- **Riverside Park** (all ages). Located downtown on the Rogue River; (541) 471–6435. Open dawn to dusk. Riverside Park has a nine-hole course that is perfect for beginners.

- **Tom Pearce Park** (all ages). Located off Foothill Boulevard about 5 miles from Grants Pass's town center; (541) 474–5285. Open dawn to dusk. This park has a "pro" eighteen-hole course that's used in competitions.

- **Indian Mary Park** (all ages). Located on Merlin-Galice Road about 10 miles from exit 61 off I–5; (541) 474–5285. Open dawn to dusk. There's a nine-hole course as well as camping and picnicking facilities.

- **Wolf Creek Park** (all ages). Located in the small town of Wolf Creek about 18 miles north of Grants Pass off exit 76; (541) 474–5285. Open dawn to dusk. Here you'll also find a nine-hole course as well as camping and picnicking facilities.

- **Lake Selmac** (all ages). Located 25 miles southwest of Grants Pass off Lake Shore Drive; (541) 474–5285; www.co.josephine.or.us/parks. Open daily year-round. Free for day use; camping $. This 160-acre lake has the only lakeside park in the county system. It's a beautiful spot for fishing, sailing, swimming, hiking, and camping, and there are picnic shelters, ball fields, a playground, and boat ramps. Special fishing derbies are held here in June and July, along with the Iron Horse Rodeo.

Top Grants Pass **Events**

May

Boatnik Festival. Adventurous white-water buffs compete over a 50-mile course on the Rogue River. A parade, art shows, and carnival are also a part of this lively weekend event. (800) 547–5927 or (541) 476–7717; www.boatnik.com.

July and August

Concerts in the Park. Make your way to Riverside Park downtown on Tuesday evenings, 6:30–8:30 P.M., for a variety of entertainers. (541) 476–7717.

August

Josephine County Fair. This old-fashioned event with carnival rides and pig races is certain to entertain your brood. A favorite event is the four-wheel-drive log pull. (541) 476–3215; www.jocofair.com.

August through September

Jedediah Smith Mountain Man Rendezvous. The rendezvous takes you back to another era, one filled with brawny mountain adventurers and pioneer women who forged a new life in this vast, wild land. It includes demonstrations of the firearms, lifestyle, clothing, and crafts of that period. (541) 476–2040 or (541) 476–5020.

Howling Acres Wolf Sanctuary (ages 8 and up)

Located on Davidson Road south of Williams, about 25 miles southwest of Grants Pass off State Highway 238; (541) 846–8962; www.howlingacres.org; e-mail: wolves@howlingacres.org. Tours given daily every hour on the hour 10:00 A.M.–4:00 P.M. $–$$, children 5 and under free.

This thirteen acres of timbered hillside is dedicated to the preservation of wolves and the education of humans. You'll hear about the wolf in Native American lore, the history of wolves in this region, and current efforts to preserve habitat for and raise awareness about these fascinating canines.

Grants Pass Historical Walking Tour (ages 5 and up)

(800) 547–5927, (541) 476–5510, or (541) 479–7827; www.grantspasschamber.org. Always open. Free.

Take a self-guided walking tour of the town's historical neighborhoods, where you will see some of the most impressive early-twentieth-century architectural styles in southern Oregon. Downtown Grants Pass is now a National Historic District, and many of these buildings also house irresistible antiques shops and restaurants. On Saturday from mid-May through Thanksgiving weekend, stop by the Grower's Market, 9:00 A.M.–1:00 P.M., for fresh produce and local crafts. During summer the market operates on Tuesday as well.

Valley of the Rogue State Park (all ages)

Located about 10 miles east of Grants Pass, just off I–5 near the town of Rogue River; (800) 452–5687 for reservations; (800) 551–6949 or (541) 582–1118 for information; www.oregonstate parks.org. Open year-round for camping, dawn to dusk for day use. **Free** day use; $$$ for camping, depending on season and type of accommodation.

Perhaps one of the most popular campgrounds in the state as a result of its proximity to I–5, Valley of the Rogue also offers a picnic area along the river, which lets you watch boaters launch rafts and kayaks into this placid body of water. Across the river is the site of a fort, and the land around the park itself was once used briefly as a reservation for Takilma Indians.

House of Mystery at the Oregon Vortex (all ages)

4303 Sardine Creek Road, Gold Hill; past Valley of the Rogue State Park about 3 miles on I–5; (541) 855–1543; www.oregonvortex.com. Open daily March through May and September through October 9:00 A.M.–5:00 P.M. (last tour at 4:15 P.M.), June through August 9:00 A.M.–6:00 P.M. (last tour at 5:15 P.M.). $$ adults, $ ages 5–11, under 5 **free**.

This is the spot of the Oregon Vortex, which proprietors claim is the area of unusual phenomena that Native Americans called the Forbidden Ground. Kids love the strange sensations produced by trying to stand up straight when the walls and floors around all seem slanted. The visual phenomena are fun to experience, and, who knows, maybe it's not just an optical illusion.

Cave Junction

Cave Junction, Oregon's third-oldest town, sits in what is called the Illinois Valley, where the east and west forks of the Illinois River join on the journey down the Siskiyou mountainsides toward the Rogue River and the sea. More than a dozen creeks find their way into the Illinois in Cave Junction, making rushing waters a common sound just about anywhere in town. **Illinois River Forks State Park** lies less than a mile south of Cave Junction along the West Fork Illinois River. On hot days your kids will appreciate the cooling water and will enjoy splashing among the rocks. There are picnic tables for a leisurely riverside lunch.

Oregon Caves National Monument (ages 6 and up) (symbols)

19000 Caves Highway, located 19 miles from Cave Junction on State Highway 46; (541) 592–2100; www.nps.gov/orca. Cave tours closed winter; trails open year-round. Call for tour times, which vary seasonally. $$ adults, $ ages 6–11, under 6 free.

Your children will be awestruck in this underground wonderland. The cavernous spaces, the strange formations, and the sound of water echoing off the cave walls all combine to produce an eerie, yet wondrous, experience. Have your kids look for the "ghosts," spectral shapes that hang from the cave ceilings. Cave temperature is a constant forty-one degrees, so wear a sweater and slacks and also sturdy shoes. Camera tripods and walking aids such as canes are not allowed in the cave, nor are strollers. Children under six are permitted only if they are at least 42 inches tall and can handle the sometimes steep stairways on their own. There's a special free twenty-minute tour for those under 42 inches in height.

While you wait for the tour to start, explore aboveground, where a nature trail leads you on a cliff-top loop about 0.1 mile long. Trailside signs identify the plant life, and you're likely to encounter a little wildlife along the way as well. **No Name Trail,** about 1.1 miles round-trip, takes you past gurgling mountain streams and mossy cliff sides, through dense forest with wildflowers in the undergrowth. Another trail follows **Cave Creek** 1.8 miles to Cave Creek Campground. Allow several hours for your visit.

Oregon Caves Chateau (all ages) (symbols)

20000 Caves Highway; (541) 592–3400, (877) 245–9022; http://ivcdo.projecta.com/ sectionindex.asp?sectionid=2; e-mail: robert@jvcdo.org. Call for hours. Closed late October through mid-April. Free for day visitors.

This 1934 chateau is a treasure trove of the past and a designated National Historic Landmark. The six-story lodge is nestled among waterfalls in the rugged Siskiyou Mountains. Most of the furnishings have been making people comfortable for more than sixty years. Park rangers hold slide talks here, and you can treat your kids to an ice-cream cone at the beautiful old wooden soda fountain. Lodging is available from early May through late October, and you can make reservations online.

Fun Fact

The Illinois River got its name from three 1847 pioneers from Peoria, Illinois, who discovered gold on the river. Samuel, John, and Phillip Althouse were among the early placer miners to find gold in southern Oregon.

Out 'N' About Treesort (ages 5 and up) ⊖ ⊜ ⊛

300 Page Creek Road; (541) 592–2208; www.treehouses.com; e-mail: treesort@tree houses.com. Tours, rentals, horseback riding per hour, tree climbing/rappelling. Call for rates.

One of the most unusual places to stay is a bed-and-breakfast that rents a standard ground-level cabin (very cozy, sleeps five), and, thanks to revised permits, the proprietor can allow people to spend the night in the lofty perch of a white oak tree. The family tree house has two cabins linked by a swinging bridge. Kids think this is the next thing to heaven—or Disneyland. The freshwater swimming pool is fed by river water. Horseback riding is available, with guided trail rides (for ages eight and older). Tours are offered daily in summer and off-season weekends from noon–5:00 P.M. You can tour unoccupied tree houses and experience the Mountain View Treeway—a high-rise walkway that includes 90-foot and 45-foot suspension bridges.

Roseburg

Douglas County Museum of History and Natural History (ages 6 and up) ⊛

123 Museum Drive, located next to the County Fairgrounds; follow signs from I–5 at exit 123; (541) 957–7007; www.co.douglas.or/museum. Open weekdays 9:00 A.M.–5:00 P.M., Saturday 10:00 A.M.–5:00 P.M., Sunday and holidays noon–5:00 P.M. $.

This is a surprisingly large museum with a nationally acclaimed collection in four separate wings. Exhibits range from the prized million-year-old saber-toothed tiger to an 1890 steam donkey used in local logging camps. Native American artifacts that predate Crater Lake, a "mud wagon" that traveled the roads of nineteenth-century southern Oregon, and a large collection of historic photographs (the largest in the state) will have your kids enthralled. They'll love the hands-on Discovery Room, too.

Wildlife Safari (all ages) ⊛ ⊛

1790 Safari Road, Winston; take exit 119 from I–5 at Winston and follow signs on State Highway 42 for about 5 miles; (541) 679–6761; www.wildlifesafari.org. Open daily except Christmas 9:00 A.M.–5:00 P.M., until 4:00 P.M. in winter. $$$, children 3 and under free.

You'll find an open zoo where emus peck at your car windows and baby pygmy goats in the petting area beg for food in ice-cream-cone cups. African elephants provide entertainment twice daily, and your child can ride one of these giant creatures, pretending to be on a lion hunt in the wilds of Africa. Trains run, weather permitting, within the central Safari Village, and you can grab a bite to eat in the White Rhino restaurant. Check out the botanical gardens, too.

An Adventure to Remember

Snuggled tightly in the rolling hills of western Douglas County, Wildlife Safari has come a long way since its beginnings in the 1970s as a for-profit open-zoo enterprise. Today the 600-acre savanna successfully provides a natural habitat that closely resembles the native homes of elephants, bears, gazelles, rhinos, zebras, and ostriches, among others. And it's now a member of the Safari Game Search Foundation, a non-profit organization dedicated to animal conservation, education, research, and rehabilitation. The grounds provide a marvelous opportunity for you and your family to observe animal interaction in an unrestrained, bucolic setting. If you're near Roseburg, include this destination in your travels.

Diamond Lake (all ages)

Located 76 miles east of Roseburg off North Umpqua Highway. Umpqua National Forest Diamond Lake Ranger District: (541) 498–2531 (weekdays) or (541) 793–3310 (weekends); www.fs.fed.us/r6/umpqua. Three campgrounds with more than 400 campsites; some campsites can be reserved by calling (877) 444–6777 or online at www.reserve USA.com; campsites usually open late May through September. Diamond Lake RV Park: 3 miles from Diamond Lake Lodge on the south end of the lake; (541) 793–3318. Diamond Lake Resort: 350 Resort Drive; (800) 733–7593 or (541) 793–3333; www .diamondlake.net; e-mail: info@diamondlake.net.

Diamond Lake has long been a favorite destination for Oregon families, often discovered while in the area to see the more famous Crater Lake. It's a fabulous year-round destination—swimming, boating, fishing, and hiking in summer; cross-country skiing, snowshoeing, and snowmobiling in winter. The USDA Forest Service maintains several hundred campsites and numerous hiking trails, plus there's an RV park on the south side of the lake. But the true family fun center is **Diamond Lake Resort,** which has it all. It offers lodge rooms, guest cabins, and studios with kitchens, along with a coin-op laundry, grocery store, cafe, dining room, pizza parlor, and service station. The resort's marina, corrals, and bicycling are described below. Call for specific prices.

- **Diamond Lake Marina.** In addition to a full-service bait-and-tackle shop, the marina rents motorboats, patio boats, sea cycles and paddleboats, bumper boats, single or double kayaks.
- **Diamond Lake Bicycling.** Also at the marina, Diamond Back mountain bikes are available to rent for riding the 12-mile Forest Service paved bike path around the lake. You'll also find backcountry dirt roads and trails; ask marina staff for directions to the best sites for your family's interests and skill levels. Helmets are provided with each bike.

- **Diamond Lake Corrals.** Guided horseback rides are available from mid-June until the snow arrives in the fall. One-hour rides leave on the hour from 9:00 A.M.–4:00 P.M. (except at noon). Two-hour rides leave at 9:00 A.M., 10:00 A.M., 2:00 P.M., and 3:00 P.M. The three-hour rides depart at 9:00 A.M. and 2:00 P.M. An all-day ride takes you to the top of Tipsoo Peak. Suppers from the Chuck Wagon and group wagon and buggy rides are also available. The corrals are closed Sunday, except for holiday weekends.
- **Winter Recreation.** In winter the resort offers guided snowmobile tours. There are 8 miles of groomed cross-country ski trails, plus more than 50 miles of marked backcountry trails for all ski abilities. The 12-mile path circling the lake also makes a great ski trail. The North Store offers skis, boots, and poles for rent. Call for prices.

Rafting and Bicycling (ages 10 and up) ⚠ 🚲

A number of outfitters offer guided fishing and white-water trips on the North Umpqua River. Two local outdoor specialists are:

- **North Umpqua Outfitters.** 222 Oakview Drive; (541) 673–4599 or (888) 454–9696; www.nuorafting.com/; e-mail: info@umpquarivers.com. Call or e-mail for schedules and prices.

Top Roseburg **Events**

June

The Land of Umpqua Discovery Days and Rodeo Parade. This street fair includes pie-eating contests, a bed race, music, entertainment, and a pet parade. A rodeo parade showcases horses and participants in the weeklong rodeo at the Douglas County Fairgrounds.

Umpqua Valley Roundup and Parade. This event features the only summertime Professional Rodeo Cowboy's Association rodeo, plus arts and crafts and dancing. (541) 672–2648.

June through August

Music on the Half Shell. Located in lovely Stewart Park, this free summer series features a variety of music programs ranging from zydeco and Cajun to African. Pack a picnic dinner and relax! (800) 444–9584, ext. 10, or (541) 672–2648; www.halfshell.org.

July

Graffiti Week. 1950s car owners from the West Coast gather for car shows, a fun run, concerts, and '50s-style fun. (800) 444–9584.

- **Oregon Ridge and River Excursions.** P.O. Box 495, Glide, OR 97443; (541) 496–3333 or (888) 454–9696; www.umpquarivers.com. Call for schedules and prices. The Oregon Ridge part of the name refers to mountain–bike excursions, which they also offer.

Stewart Park (all ages) 🛝 🚗 🏛 🍁

Located on Stewart Parkway on the west side of town, off Garden Valley Road; (541) 672-7701. Open dawn to dusk. Free.

Kids love climbing on the old steam locomotive in the large playground. The 230-acre park also has horseshoe pits and tennis courts, wide green fields, and a nature trail leading from the wildlife pond through an old orchard and along the North Umpqua River. On summer Tuesday evenings take your kids to an outdoor concert at the band shell.

Stewart Park also has an excellent skate park at Northwest Goetz Street. For more information, you can check in with the Umpqua Skaters Association (541–673–1414) or visit the Web site at www.skateoregon.com/Roseburg/Roseburg.html.

Susan Creek Falls Trail (ages 5 and up) 🚶 ⛺

Starts in the day-use area of the Susan Creek Campground, off State Highway 138 about 28 miles east of Roseburg; (541) 440–4930; www.or.blm.gov. Always open. $; day use free.

This trail leads to a group of fascinating Indian mounds. You'll walk through a young forest of mixed conifers and madrones with a thick undergrowth of salal, fern, and huckleberry. At 0.75 mile the falls cascade nearly 70 feet down a cliff side into a boulder-bordered pool. Beyond the falls, follow the footbridge up a fairly steep hill for another 0.5 mile to the mounds—ceremonial rock piles prepared by young men in spiritual quest. These are cultural treasures that should not be disturbed. The campground also houses thirty-one campsites that are open May through October.

Crater Lake National Park

Crater Lake National Park (all ages) 🏨 👫 ⚠ 🚐 🛶 🎿 🍴

P.O. Box 7, Crater Lake, OR 97604; (541) 594–3100; (541) 830–8700 (lodge) for lodging and boat-tour information; www.craterlakelodges.com or www.nps.gov/crla. Park is open year-round; camping available when snow clears in early summer; lodging available mid-May through mid-October. $$ for a seven-day vehicle pass. North entrance is located off State Highway 138, from Roseburg; two visitor centers, Steel Information Center, at the junction of the south entrance road and Rim Drive, and the Rim Village Visitor Center, near the east end of the parking area, provide a wealth of informational materials. The park entrance at the south gate is off State Highway 62, which runs between Medford and Klamath Falls. In winter, access to the park is by way of State Highway 62 only. Rim Drive is closed in winter, but intrepid Nordic skiers can take the 33-mile unplowed road circling the rim of the lake on skis. Watch for ice, and check with park rangers for avalanche warnings before you begin.

It's difficult not to describe Crater Lake in superlatives: The bluest water, the most dramatic contrasts, and the clearest air all leave visitors invigorated for days. Away from the lake itself, the forests are rich with surprises—deep river canyons, sparkling waterfalls, bright and delicate wildflowers. You'll want to take your time exploring here. The geology and history of the area are equally fascinating. In the last 750,000 years, explosive eruptions created a series of volcanic peaks along what we now call the Cascade Range. Mt. Mazama, which holds Crater Lake in its peak, was one of these, and for 500,000 years it erupted regularly. About 7,700 years ago the most violent eruption of all took place in a series of massive explosions forty-two times more powerful than Mt. St. Helens's 1980 blast. The winds scattered as much as 6 inches of ash over 5,000 square miles, covering eight states and three Canadian provinces. In the **Pumice Desert,** north of the rim, the ash is 50 feet deep. The eruptions emptied the mountain of magma, removing the support for the mountain peak. The peak collapsed, forming the bowl-shaped caldera that, at first, was too hot to

Free Things to Do at Crater Lake

- **Mazama Campground Amphitheater.** Your family will enjoy the public programs offered in the amphitheater in summer, including guided nature walks and evening talks.

- **Steel Information Center.** The center shows the movie *Crater Lake* every half hour in summer. (541) 594–3100.

- **Sinnott Memorial Overlook Museum.** This museum has exhibits and displays on the origin and history of the lake. There are also scheduled ranger talks.

Fun Fact

Crater Lake is the deepest lake in North America, the second-deepest in the Western Hemisphere, and the seventh-deepest in the world.

hold water. As volcanic activity slowed, the caldera filled with water. The volcano has been silent for 4,000 years.

Many children prefer the Klamath Indian version of events that created the mountain lake. A battle began between the god of the world above, Skell, who lived on Mt. Shasta to the south, and the evil god of the world below, Llao. Skell won the battle, beheading the mountain of Llao and forever ridding the world of his evil influence, leaving in his place a beautiful mirrored lake that reflects the sky. Look for **Llao Rock,** which dominates the northwest portion of the lake and faces **Skell Head,** across the lake on the east side. From the parking lot at the rim, walk the paved path down to the **Sinnott Memorial Overlook,** where a rock shelter hewn from the side of the caldera provides a breathtaking view. A topographical relief map of Mt. Mazama shows the lake, **Wizard Island,** and the surrounding area. Along the park's south entrance road on State Highway 62, stop at one of several pullouts or picnic areas to view a breathtaking canyon through which Annie Creek runs more than 250 feet below.

To explore the environs of Crater Lake more deeply, take the **Annie Creek Trail,** which leaves between Loops D and E in the Mazama Campground and follows a 1.7-mile loop descending 200 feet to the valley floor and along the stream before ascending the rim to complete the circuit. Other trails to explore are the **Castle Crest Wildflower Trail,** a 0.4-mile loop that begins across from the Steel Information Center just beyond the junction of East and West Rim Drives, and the **Godfrey Glen Nature Trail,** about 1 mile beyond Mazama Village on the road to the rim. Rangers sometimes lead walks, or you can purchase inexpensive leaflets at the trailhead. The only safe—and legal—access to the lake is the 1-mile **Cleetwood Cove Trail,** on West Rim Drive about 13 miles from Rim Village. You must be in good physical condition to attempt this steep hike down the walls of the caldera. Once there, you can dip your feet in the water or try your hand at catching some of the kokanee salmon or rainbow trout that remain in the lake, which was stocked with these species between 1888 and the 1940s, when park rangers decided to allow the lake to return to its natural state. During the summer, boat tours of the lake offer up-close views with trips leaving from the Cleetwood Cove dock. The Volcanic Cruise Boat Tour is the only company allowed to have boats on the lake. The trips provide views from inside the caldera. You can also stop and spend some time on Wizard Island, returning on a later tour. The two-hour narrated tour takes you past the **Phantom Ship,** remnants of an older volcano and dike that were exposed after the great eruption. The boat tours operate daily late June through mid-September, weather permitting. The Annie Creek Restaurant & Gift Shop near the south entrance is open from early June through October. Construction has been ongoing at Rim Village, so contact the park for updated information on concession facilities available.

Klamath Falls

Klamath Falls sits on the southern tip of Upper Klamath Lake, the largest lake in the state at 58,992 acres, with Mt. McLoughlin casting its reflection in the waters. In the summer you can hop aboard a restored 1906 trolley for a ride through the downtown area to get a sense of the area and its history.

Baldwin Hotel Museum (ages 5 and up)

31 Main Street; located in the old Baldwin Hotel; (541) 883–4207. Open June through September Tuesday through Saturday 10:00 A.M.–6:00 P.M. $. Family rates available.

Guided tours take you back to the early 1900s, with the original furnishings and many photographs by the builder's talented daughter.

Favell Museum of Western Art and Indian Artifacts
(ages 5 and up)

125 West Main Street; (541) 882–9996; www.favellmuseum.org. Open Monday through Saturday 9:30 A.M.–5:30 P.M. $, children 6 and under free.

Arrowheads, ceremonial knives, stone- and beadwork, basketry, and pottery captivate the kids. See the silver treasure from an abandoned wagon train and tour the walk-in vault display of miniature working firearms, including a Gatling gun.

Volcanic Legacy Scenic Byway

As the name implies, this roadway has been designated a scenic byway for the beauty created by millennia of volcanic activity. In 1999 the federal government awarded All American Road status to this spectacular byway, which includes Crater Lake National Park, the most dramatic feature of the drive. Along the way you'll see a pumice desert, ancient natural chimneys (called fumaroles) along Annie Creek, canyons, and the lush wildlife refuge of Upper Klamath Lake. (800) 445–6728; www.travelklamath .com or www.sova.org/volcanic.

Klamath County Museum (ages 5 and up) 🌡️

1451 Main Street; (541) 883–4208. Open Tuesday through Saturday 9:00 A.M.–5:00 P.M.
$, children 4 and under free.

Natural history, Indian and pioneer history, and agricultural development are all on
display in the museum. Your kids will see up close some of the birds and animals they
might encounter in the natural areas around Klamath Falls, and they'll learn about the
geothermal energy resources that have been used in the area for centuries.

Lake of the Woods (all ages) 🌊🏕️🎣🚴🚶🛏️⛺⛷️

Located 42 miles east of Medford and 32 miles west of Klamath Falls off State Highway 140; (866) 201–4194; www.lakeofthewoodsresort.com or www.fs.fed.us/r6/
frewin/. Hours vary by season; call ahead. Lodging: $$$; restaurants: $$–$$$.

This is a high-mountain lake in the Cascades with Forest Service campgrounds, sum-
mer camps, private cabins, picnic area, resort with cabins, restaurant, store, and
boat rentals. Swimming, waterskiing, fishing, and canoeing are available.

Upper Klamath Canoe Trail (all ages) 🏕️

Begins at Malone Springs launch 4 miles from the junction of State Highway 140 and
West Side Road (take Rocky Point turnoff), northwest of Klamath Falls; (530) 667–2331;
www.klamathbasinrefuges.fws.gov/ukcanoe.html. Open dawn to dusk. Free.

The canoe trails meander through marshland on the edge of Upper Klamath Lake.
You can rent canoes at **Rocky Point Resort** on Rocky Point Road (541–356–2287;
www.rockypointoregon.com).

Over the Hill Live Steam Club (all ages) 🏞️🚂

Located 27 miles north of Klamath Falls at 36851 South Chiloquin Road in Chiloquin;
(541) 783–7763; www.sscom.org/oth.html. Open Sunday 10:00 A.M.–3:00 P.M. Memorial
Day through Labor Day. Call for prices.

The club operates a one-eighth-scale train park that is open to the public during sum-
mer months. Bring a picnic to enjoy at tables set up for guests. The trains, a mixture
of diesel and live steam engines, pull cars with comfortable seats, roomy enough for
adults, along thousands of feet of track.

Sun Pass Ranch (all ages) 🌊🛏️🚴⛷️🎣🏕️

52125 State Highway 62, P.O. Box 499, Fort Klamath, OR 97626; (888) 777–9005 or
(541) 381–2259; www.virtualcities.com/ons/or/c/orc4701.htm; e-mail: sunpass@aol
.com. Open year-round. Bed-and-breakfast $$; guided horseback tours $$$$ per person for the first hour.

Located in a pristine rural setting, the ranch offers horseback riding and river float
trips, pony rides, mountain-bike rentals, cross-country skiing, fly-fishing, and a ranch-
style bed-and-breakfast.

Fun Facts

- The area boasts the largest wintering population of American bald eagles in the forty-eight contiguous states.
- Upper Klamath Lake, at 58,992 acres, is the largest lake in Oregon.

Collier Memorial State Park and Logging Museum (all ages)

Located 30 miles north of Klamath Falls; (800) 551–6949 or (541) 783–2471; www .oregonstateparks.org. Open dawn to dusk; call for museum hours. Free.

The museum side of the park is open year-round and houses rotating exhibits; camping is closed in winter. Straddling the highway, the park has a beautiful picnic area in a shaded ponderosa pine forest alongside the Williamson River and an open-air logging museum across the highway that some claim has the largest collection of logging equipment in the nation. Children appreciate the sense of scale and the absence of "do not touch" signs. There's also an authentic pioneer village with buildings relocated from their original sites.

Fort Klamath Museum (all ages)

Located on State Highway 62, 2 miles south of Crater Lake; (800) 445–6728, (541) 381–2230, or (541) 883–4208. Open Thursday through Monday 10:00 A.M.–6:00 P.M. June through August. Free, but donations appreciated.

The museum is housed in a military post that was established in 1863. The displays depict the Modoc Indian War of 1872–73. In the park are the graves of the fearless Modoc chief Captain Jack and three braves who fought against the U.S. Army in the most extensive Indian war in the West.

Top Klamath Events

August
Klamath County Fair & Jefferson Stampede Rodeo. You'll receive a two-for-one series of events that fill your entire weekend. (541) 883–3796; www. kcfairgrounds.org; e-mail: KCFAIR@kcfairgrounds.org.

December
Snowflake Festival. A holiday bazaar, parade, toy show, holiday play, and tree lighting help usher in the season. (541) 883–5368.

Lakeview

First settled in the 1870s by sheep and cattle ranchers, Lakeview calls itself the "tallest town in Oregon" because it has the highest elevation above sea level of any incorporated town in the state.

Schminck Memorial Museum (ages 5 and up)

128 South E Street; (541) 947–3134. Open Tuesday through Saturday 1:00–4:00 P.M.; closed December through January. $, children under 13 free.

Kids love the doll and toy collection in the basement, and the old vacuum cleaners behind the kitchen area will bring on a few giggles. Baseball fans will covet the silk baseball cards of such early players as Ty Cobb and Rebel Oakes.

Warner Canyon Ski Area (ages 8 and up)

Located 11 miles northeast of Lakeview off State Highway 140 in the Fremont National Forest; (541) 947–6040; www.lakecountychamber.org/skihill.html. Call for hours and lift prices.

With fourteen downhill runs and several miles of Nordic trails, as well as great sledding opportunities, this county-run ski area is a great place for families with a hankering for some outdoor winter fun.

Fort Rock State Natural Area (all ages)

Located north of Silver Lake, 7 miles off State Highway 31; (800) 551–6949; www.oregonstateparks.org. Always open. Free.

This area rises nearly 400 feet from the desert shelf. Archaeologists discovered 9,200-year-old woven sandals here, and one is now housed in the Lake County Museum.

Fort Rock Cave (all ages)

Located 1 mile north of the rock, within the Fort Rock State Natural Area; (541) 938–6055 or (800) 551–6949; www.oregonstateparks.org. Open daily, year-round. Free.

A 0.5-mile trail takes you inside an ancient volcanic maar that rose within a 40-mile-wide lake, which Native Americans lived by more than 10,000 years ago.

Lake County Museum (ages 5 and up)

118 South G Street; (541) 947–2220. Open May through October Monday through Saturday 9:00 A.M.–4:30 P.M., February through April Wednesday through Friday 10:00 A.M.–4:00 P.M. Closed November through January. $, children free.

Historical displays with artifacts portray the Native American culture indigenous to the area. One room features the region's Irish traditions.

Top Lakeview **Events**

June
Junior Rodeo. For a chance to see young people compete on horseback, come to this event held early in the summer. (541) 947–6040.

September
Lake County Round-Up. The event is held during the Lake County Fair. A wild-cow milking contest is guaranteed to have your kids roaring with laughter. (541) 947–6040.

Fremont National Forest
Located 8 miles west of Lakeview on State Highway 140; (541) 947–2151; www.fs.fed .us/r6/frewin/. Always open. Free.

Fremont National Forest has an abundance of lakes and streams for you to explore with your kids. **Drews Reservoir** is a popular spot for waterskiing as well as fishing and swimming. **Cottonwood Meadow Lake,** north of State Highway 140, is surrounded by aspen and pine forests, with a trail that circles the lake and connects two camping areas. South of the highway, **Lofton Reservoir, Heart Lake,** and **Holbrook Reservoir** are accessible from various Forest Service roads, and all are well maintained even though some are gravel.

Family Favorites in Southern Oregon

1. Oregon Shakespeare Festival, Ashland
2. Rogue River, Grants Pass
3. Oregon Caves National Monument, near Cave Junction
4. Crater Lake National Park
5. The House of Mystery, near Grants Pass
6. Favell Museum of Western Art and Indian Artifacts, Klamath Falls
7. Fremont National Forest, near Lakeview
8. Susan Creek Falls Trail, near Roseburg
9. Wildlife Safari, Winston
10. Douglas County Museum of History and Natural History, Roseburg

Hart Mountain National Antelope Refuge (all ages)

Located 65 miles northeast of Lakeview and 25 miles west of Plush; the road surface becomes gravel just before climbing the escarpment; (541) 947–3315; www.fws.gov. Open daily, year-round. Free.

Hart Mountain is accessible on mostly paved roads from the southern Oregon town of Lakeview. The refuge was established in 1936 to protect then dwindling herds of pronghorn antelope. It now also protects mule deer, sage grouse, California bighorn sheep, golden eagles, prairie falcons, and more than 250 other species of game and birds. Features include undeveloped camping, fishing, hiking, historic cabins, and hot-springs bathing.

Warner Wetlands (all ages)

Located 39 miles northeast of Lakeview and 5 miles from Plush; (541) 947–2177; www.or.blm.gov/lakeview. Open daily, year-round. Free.

The wetlands are a series of pothole lakes along the western base of Hart Mountain and were established to protect the Warner Valley's unique features and restore critical wildlife habitat. The lakes and ponds go through a natural cycle of drying and filling that increases productivity by recycling nutrients and invigorating plant communities. At Hart Lake walking footpaths provide a nice trip along dikes to bird-viewing blinds. Bring binoculars and a bird identification book. Commonly seen birds include Canada geese, great blue herons, cinnamon teals, cormorants, white egrets, white pelicans, sandhill cranes, and yellow-headed blackbirds. Boating in the area depends on fluctuating water levels.

Christmas Valley **Back Country Byway**

This drive takes you through vastly different scenery than most "scenic" drives, and it covers some of the most geologically interesting country in the state. The area is riddled with caves, a 325-foot rock towering over the desert, a "lost" forest of pines in the middle of the desert, the largest inland sand dune in the state, a giant crater, and a fissure in the earth approximately 2 miles long and up to 70 feet deep. The signed route departs from State Highway 31 at the Fort Rock turnoff and follows a variety of roads (paved, gravel, and ghastly) before returning to Highway 31 just south of Silver Lake. A number of alternate routes are marked to help you avoid the ghastly roads if your vehicle doesn't have high clearance.

About 5 miles north of the Fort Rock cutoff and 1 mile off the highway, you'll come across a scene reminiscent of a science-fiction film—**Hole-in-the-Ground.** This massive crater, some 500 feet deep and covering a quarter acre, was formed by an explosion caused when molten lava hit water. In 1966 a group of astronauts used this spot to experience something close to what they expected the moon's surface to be like.

Some 5 miles farther down Highway 31, follow signs to **Fort Rock State Natural Area,** formed more than five million years ago when a volcanic explosion of molten rock erupted through a lake. It was in **Fort Rock Cave** near here that the oldest shoes in the world were found in 1938— seventy-five sagebrush sandals made by people who inhabited the valley more than 9,000 years ago. The cave is a National Heritage Site and is open only by a state-park guided tour; call (541) 536–2428 at least three days in advance to arrange a tour. In the town of Fort Rock, stop by the Homestead Village Museum, open weekends and holidays from Memorial Day weekend through September (541–576–2327).

Derrick Cave, located off Derrick Caves Road northeast of Fort Rock, is a 30-foot-high lava tube nearly 0.25-mile long with "rooms" nearly 40 feet wide and 60 feet high. It served as a fallout shelter during the Cuban missile crisis, with provisions for 1,000 people in case of a nuclear war.

About 2 miles east of Christmas Valley is an area that was a huge lake 10,000 years ago. Now referred to as **Fossil Lake,** it covered the entire basin. This is one of the most significant sites in North America for ice age (Pleistocene) fossils. Note, however, that it is illegal to remove fossils from the area, but you can wander the dusty grounds and imagine the mammoths, camels, and miniature horses that once drank from the lakeshore here.

An alternate route from the byway takes you about 6 miles north of Christmas Valley along a graded gravel road to a fascinating place: **Crack-in-the-Ground**. Nearly 2 miles long and 12 feet wide, the 1,000-year-old fissure reaches a depth of 70 feet in some places. From the parking area, a 0.25-mile trail takes you to the opening of the crack, from there descending about 400 yards into the earth. You can walk along an unofficial path at the top if you prefer.

Some 20 miles northeast of Christmas Valley, the **Lost Forest** seems misplaced more than lost—a 9,000-acre pine and juniper forest in the middle of a giant desert. Still, the forest is several thousand years old despite the minimal annual rainfall. The forest borders the largest sand dune in the state that's not next to the ocean. Composed of ash and pumice blown into the valley after Mt. Mazama erupted seven millennia ago, the dunes cover 16,000 acres and sometimes reach as high as 60 feet.

For more information about the Christmas Valley Back Country Byway, call the Bureau of Land Management at (541) 947–2177 or Oregon State Parks at (800) 551–6949; additional information is online at www.or.blm .gov/lakeview.

Where to Eat

IN ASHLAND

Alex's Plaza Restaurant. 35 North Main Street; (541) 482–8818. Sitting alongside Ashland Creek, Alex's has a diverse menu sure to please everyone. $–$$$

Ashland Bakery and Cafe. 38 East Main Street; (541) 482–2117. Enjoy pastries and cappuccino at breakfast or a lunch of delicious home-style soup and bread; dinner also served. $$

Ashland Creek Bar and Grill. 92½ East Main Street; (541) 482–4131. Also nestled along the creek, this place serves burgers, sandwiches, and salads. $$

Pangea Grill & Wraps. 272 East Main Street; (541) 552-1630. A friendly place for lunch or dinner with healthy wraps, fresh soups, and other homemade delights. $–$$.

Señor Sam's. 1634 Ashland Street; (541) 488–1262. The specialty is healthy Mexican food. The restaurant received the "Best Burritos" in Ashland vote. $

Zoey's Café. 199 East Main Street; (541) 482–4794. From delicious ice creams—try the Rogue Valley Pear and Oregon Trail—to calzones, wraps, and sandwiches, this is a family-friendly place for freshly prepared foods. $–$$

IN CRATER LAKE NATIONAL PARK

Annie Creek Restaurant. In Mazama Village near the park's south entrance; (541) 594–2255; www.craterlakelodges.com; open June through mid-September. This new restaurant opened in 2006 and features pizza, pasta, salads, soups, and self-serve ice cream. $$–$$$

IN GRANTS PASS

The Laughing Clam. 121 Southwest G Street; (541) 479–1110. The menu at this casual family restaurant is varied enough to make everyone happy. $

Wild River Brewing & Pizza Co. 595 Northeast E Street; (541) 471–7487. Here's a pizza place that serves its specialty with a flair. Parents appreciate the local micro-brews. $–$$

Yankee Pot Roast. 720 Northside Sixth Street; (541) 476–0551. Fine family dining in comfortable surroundings. $$–$$$

IN JACKSONVILLE

Bella Union Restaurant. 170 West California; (541) 899–1770; www.bellau.com. It may be housed in the building where the Bella Union Saloon was one of seven local bars in 1868, but you won't find typical saloon fare in this upscale spot. Instead your choices will include pasta, pizza, steak, and seafood. $$

IN KLAMATH FALLS

The Creamery Brew Pub and Grill. 1320 Main Street; (541) 273–5222. Locally owned brewpub offering specialty salads, pastas, pub meals, items from the grill, and Klamath Basin Brewing Co. beers and ales. $$

The Klamath Grill. 715 Main Street; (541) 882–1427. The place where locals meet for hearty breakfasts, including "home-grown pancakes," and lunches. $–$$

Mia and Pia's Pizzeria and Brewhouse. 3545 Summers Lane; (541) 884–4880. Recently remodeled, the family pizza parlor features an outdoor patio, kids' games, and glimpses of local history in the décor. It was Klamath County's first microbrewery. $$

IN LAKEVIEW

Happy Horse Deli & Antiques & Collectibles. 728 North Fourth Street; (541) 947–4996. Along with freshly made soups, salads, and sandwiches, this lunchtime gathering place features rooms filled with precious and not-so-precious antiques, including many regional items. $–$$

Pizza Villa. 44 South G Street; (541) 947–2531. This family-operated pizza parlor also offers hot sandwiches and features a kids' game area. $–$$

IN MEDFORD

Hometown Buffet. 1299 Center Drive; (541) 770–6779; www.buffet.com. Nothing fancy, just plenty of choices and the largest salad bar in town. It's a very affordable place to feed the whole family. $$

IN ROSEBURG

Brutke's Wagon Wheel. 227 Northwest Garden Valley Boulevard; (541) 672–7555. This pasta and prime-rib eatery is a local family favorite. $$$–$$$$

Cafe Espresso. 368 Southeast Jackson; (541) 672–1859. This is a good place to stop for a snack of cookies or pastries and good java. $

La Hacienda. 940 Northwest Garden Valley Boulevard; (541) 672–5330. Good Mexican food. $–$$

Where to Stay

IN ASHLAND

Bed-and-breakfast referrals are available through two different agencies in Ashland: **Ashland B&B Clearinghouse,** (800) 588–0338 or (541) 488–0338; www.bbclearing house.com; **Ashland's B&B Network,** (800) 944–0329; www.abbnet.com.

Hyatt Lake Resort. 7979 Hyatt Prairie Road; (541) 482–3331. RV and tent sites are available plus all kinds of activities to enjoy with your kids, including horseback riding, boating, mountain biking, and fishing in summer and cross-country skiing and general snow play in winter. $

Mt. Ashland Inn. 550 Mt. Ashland Ski Road; (800) 830–8707 or (541) 482–8707; www.mtashlandinn.com. Located in a large log chalet; all five rooms have private baths. The inn's owners will shuttle guests to the ski lodge, only 3 miles up the road. $$–$$$

Stratford Inn. 555 Siskiyou; (800) 547–4741 or (541) 488–2151; www.stratford innashland.com. Just 5 blocks from the Shakespeare festival, this inn provides continental breakfast and has laundry facilities, a pool, and a spa. $$$

Windmill Inn of Ashland. 2525 Ashland Street; (800) 547–4747 or (541) 482–8310. The inn offers kitchenettes and refrigerators plus continental breakfasts. Pets are welcome. $$$–$$$$

IN CAVE JUNCTION

Oregon Caves Lodge. 20000 Caves Highway; (541) 592–3400; call for open season. This rustic six-story lodge was built in 1934. Nestled deep in the Siskiyou National Forest, there are plenty of opportunities for outdoor activities, including nearby hiking and cave exploration. $$$–$$$$

IN CRATER LAKE NATIONAL PARK

Crater Lake Lodge. Reservations from Xanterra Parks & Resort, 1211 Avenue C, White City; (541) 830–8700; www.crater lakelodges.com. The historic lodge is located in Rim Village and overlooks the lake. It is open May through October. The restaurant offers breakfast, lunch, and dinner. $$$$

Mazama Campground and Lost Creek Campground (tents only). First-come, first-served. Campground spaces cannot be reserved and usually fill up by early afternoon in summer. Open mid-June through September. Note that weather may affect campground opening and closing dates. Call (541) 594–3100 for more information. $

Mazama Village Motor Inn. (541) 830–8700; www.craterlakelodges.com. The inn is located in the Mazama Village complex. Open June through September. $$$–$$$$

IN GRANTS PASS

Riverside Inn Resort & Conference Center. 971 Southeast Sixth Street; (800) 334–4567 or (541) 476–6873; www.river sideinn.com. This full-service inn stands next to the Rogue River, where the Hellgate jet boats take off. It has an outdoor pool, a spa pool, and a restaurant. $$$$

Travelodge. 1950 Northwest Vine Street; (888) 515–6375 or (541) 479–6611; www .travelodge.com. A restaurant, continental breakfast, and laundry facilities make this a convenient place for families. $$$

IN JACKSONVILLE

The Stage Lodge. 830 North Fifth Street; (800) 253–8254 or (541) 899–3953; www .stagelodge.com. Resembling a nineteenth-century stage stop, this two-story lodge has attractive decor that matches the rest of the town's ambience. They serve a continental breakfast, too. $$–$$$$

Wolf Creek Inn. 100 Front; (541) 866–2474; www.thewolfcreekinn.com. Eight rooms. One of the state's oldest hostelries, the inn originally opened for business in 1880 as a stop along the Oregon-to-California stagecoach line. The rooms have been restored to reflect the authentic pre-1900 style. Includes continental breakfast. $$

IN KLAMATH FALLS

Best Western Klamath Inn. 4061 South Sixth Street; (877) 882–1200 or (541) 882–1200. Continental breakfast and indoor pool. $$–$$$

Maverick Motel. 1220 Main Street; (800) 404–6690 or (541) 882–6688. You can cool off in the summer in the outdoor pool. They serve a continental breakfast and welcome pets, too. $

Quality Inn & Suites. 100 Main Street; (800) 732–2025 or (541) 882–4666. The facility offers a wide range of accommodations, some of which have kitchenettes. Continental breakfast is served, and there's a restaurant on the premises. $$–$$$

Rocky Point Resort. 28121 Rocky Point Road; located on upper Klamath Lake off State Highway 140 and Forest Road 34, 25 miles from Klamath Falls; (541) 356–2287; www.rockypointoregon.com. Boat rentals, tent sites, and RV hookups as well as dining rooms, showers, and laundry facilities are offered. $

IN LAKEVIEW

Aspen Ridge Resort. Located off Forest Road 3790 about 16 miles south of State Highway 140; P.O. Box 2, Bly, OR 97622; (800) 393–3323 or (541) 884–8685; www.aspenrr.com; e-mail: aspenr@starband.net. Lodge rooms and self-catering cabins overlook a meadow where the ranch's cattle and buffalo roam. Horseback trips take you into the surrounding forest. In winter you can strap on cross-country skis or hop on a snowmobile. $$$–$$$$

Lakeview Lodge Motel. 301 North G Street; (541) 947–2181. The motel has a spa pool and an exercise room. Pets are welcome. $$–$$$

IN MEDFORD

Best Western Pony Soldier Inn. 2340 Crater Lake Highway; (800) 634–7669 or (541) 779–2011; www.bestwestern.com. There's a restaurant on the complex, and continental breakfast is available. It also has an outdoor pool and a spa pool. $$–$$$

Cedar Lodge Motor Inn. 518 North Riverside; (800) 282–3419 or (541) 773–7361. A restaurant and continental breakfast are conveniences available to inn guests. Pets are welcome. $–$$$

Windmill Inn of Medford. 1950 Biddle Road; (800) 547–4747 or (541) 779–0050. A playground nearby makes parents and kids happy. Laundry facilities and kitchenettes are available, too. $$–$$$

IN ROSEBURG

Big K Guest Ranch. 20029 State Highway 138 West near Elkton, about 40 miles northwest of Roseburg; (800) 390–2445 or (541) 584–2295; www.big-k.com. The Kesterson family welcomes guests in twenty modern, log-sided cabins on their ranch, which rests along 10 miles of the Umpqua River. They offer horseback riding, fishing, horseshoes, and lots of exploring possibilities. $$$–$$$$

Diamond Lake Campground. West off State Highway 138 about 80 miles east of Roseburg on Forest Road 4795; (877) 444–6777 or (541) 793–3310; www.reserveusa.com. Fireplaces, running water, flush toilets, and showers provide a little extra luxury to this camping experience. $

Diamond Lake Resort. 76 miles east of Roseburg along the North Umpqua Highway; (800) 733–7593 or (541) 793–3333; www.diamondlake.net; e-mail: info@ diamondlake.net. The resort offers the sparkling solitude of a Cascade mountain lake but with amenities to enhance your family's fun. Hiking, biking, and horseback riding are all available in the vicinity. Motel rooms $$–$$$; cabins $$$$.

East Lemolo Campground. North off State Highway 138, located 75 miles east of Roseburg on Forest Road 2610; (541) 498–2531; www.fs.fed.us/r6/umpqua. Fifteen pretty sites are located on Lemolo Lake. The campground has vault toilets, picnic tables, and fire rings, and the lake offers fishing and waterskiing opportunities. $

Howard Johnson Express Inn. 978 Northeast Stephens Street; (541) 673–5082 or (800) 446–4656. The full-service inn offers continental breakfasts, kitchenettes, an indoor swimming pool, and laundry facilities. $$–$$$

Windmill Inn of Roseburg. 1450 Northwest Mulholland; (800) 547–4747; www .windmill inns.com. It has a swimming pool, whirlpool and sauna, guest bicycles, and a complimentary continental breakfast. Family packages available. $$

For More Information

Ashland Visitor Information Center. 110 East Main Street, Ashland, OR 97520; (541) 482–3486; www.ashlandchamber.com.

Grants Pass–Josephine County Chamber of Commerce/Grants Pass Visitors and Convention Bureau. 1995 Northwest Vine Street, Grants Pass, OR 97526; (800) 547– 5927 or (541) 476–7717; www.visit grants pass.org or www.grantspass

chamber.org; e-mail: gpcoc@grants pass.com or vcb@visitgrantspass.org.

Travel Klamath. 205 Riverside Drive, Klamath Falls, OR 97601; (800) 445–6728 or (541) 882–1501; www.travelklamath.com; e-mail: dawn@greatbasinvisitor.info.

Illinois Valley Chamber of Commerce. P.O. Box 312, 201 Caves Highway, Cave Junction, OR 97526; (541) 592–2631 or (541) 592–3326.

Jacksonville Chamber of Commerce. P.O. Box 33, 185 North Oregon Street, Jacksonville, OR 97530; (541) 899–8118; www.jacksonvilleoregon.org; e-mail: jville chamber@wave.net.

Klamath County Chamber of Commerce. 706 Main Street, Klamath Falls, OR 97601; (877) 552–6284 or (541) 884–5193; www.klamath.org; e-mail: inquiry@klamath .org.

Lake County Chamber of Commerce. 126 North East Street, Lakeview, OR 97630; (541) 947–6040; www.lakecountychamber .org.

Medford Visitors & Convention Bureau. 101 East Eighth Street, Medford, OR 97501; (800) 469–6307, (541) 772–6293, or (541) 779–4847; www.visitmedford.org; e-mail: medjacc@magick.net.

Roseburg Visitors and Convention Bureau. 410 Southeast Spruce Street, Roseburg, OR 97470; (800) 444–9584 or (541) 672–9731; www.visitroseburg.com.

Southern Oregon Visitors Association. 548 Business Park Drive, Medford, OR 97501; (800) 448–4856 or (541) 779–4691; www.sova.org; e-mail: sova@jeffnet.org.

Eastern Oregon

The rolling wheatlands of the Columbia River Valley give way to the high Blue Mountains and Wallowa Mountains before dropping sharply into Hells Canyon of the Snake River. Grande Ronde River's colorful carved canyons, the sage-scented high desert, and the painted hills around the John Day Fossil Beds testify to vast changes wrought over fifty million years of geological evolution. The landscape recalls the days of cowboys and bronco-busting, pioneers and wagon trains, sometimes so vividly that one feels transported back in time. One of the least-populated areas of the state, much of northeastern Oregon remains untouched, the terrain preserved as early pioneers would have encountered it. Walking in the actual path of the wagon trains and reading the words of the pioneer women and men who trod these paths impart a sense of the past your kids won't find in any history books.

Baker City

This Old West gold-mining town has recaptured its history by resurrecting its original name: Baker City. For years the name had been shortened to Baker, but with the approach of the Oregon Trail sesquicentennial celebrations, the town mined its roots for a wealth of historic interest. For a while in the 1960s, Baker was known as the site of "No Name City," the fictional location created for filming *Paint Your Wagon*, with Clint Eastwood and Lee Marvin. A complete frontier town was constructed for the filming, and a replica is displayed at the Oregon Trail Regional Museum.

National Historic Oregon Trail Interpretive Center (all ages)
(museum icon) (icon)

Located at Flagstaff Hill, about 5 miles from Baker City on State Highway 86; (541) 523–1843; www.endoftheoregontrail.org; e-mail: Nhotic_Mail@or.blm.gov. Open daily April through October 9:00 A.M.–6:00 P.M., November through March 9:00 A.M.–4:00 P.M. $, children under 6 free.

EASTERN OREGON

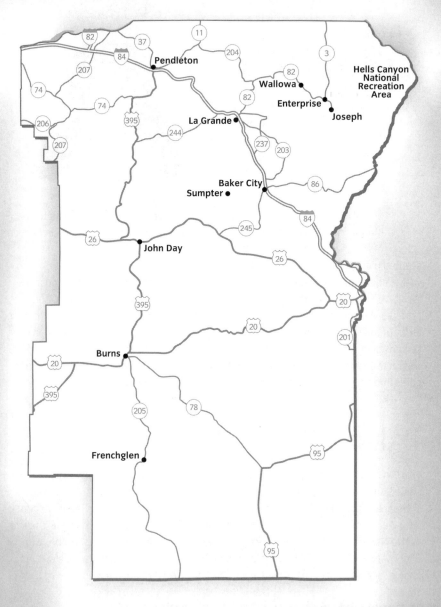

Plan to spend all day here. At the heart of the center are exhibits of life-size figures speaking out as if you're overhearing their conversations along the trail. The historical accuracy and details are absorbing for both parents and children. In three mini-theaters, well-made films integrated into a scenic backdrop provide insight into the experience of Oregon's early pioneers. Your kids can try to pack a miniature wagon with all the supplies needed to make the journey, having to make some tough choices about what to leave behind—a puzzle that can keep determined youngsters occupied for hours! Walking trails take you down the hill to several spots where wagon ruts are visible among the sagebrush. Some of the 4.2 miles of trails are quite steep, so you'll want to be in good shape. Ticks, rattlesnakes, and scorpions are local pests to be aware of on your walk. Take water, too, especially if you're walking in the heat of the day. A pioneer encampment and an old mine site are additional attractions.

Oregon Trail Regional Museum (ages 5 and up)

2480 Grove Street; (541) 523–9308. Open daily 9:00 A.M.–5:00 P.M. March through October and by appointment. $, $$ family.

Often confused with the National Historic Oregon Trail Interpretive Center, this museum, too, is worth a visit. A schoolroom replica includes some old schoolbooks your children will have fun looking through. An impressive rock and mineral collection, a fire wagon, and old carriages are other favorites. The replica of the complete frontier town built for the filming of *Paint Your Wagon* is on display here.

Adler House Museum (ages 5 and up)

2305 Main Street; (541) 523–9308. Open May 15 through September 15 Friday through Monday 10:00 A.M.–2:00 P.M. $, $$$ family, children under 16 free.

You can take a guided tour of this fully refurbished turn-of-the-twentieth-century Victorian home, which once belonged to Leo Adler, Baker City's greatest benefactor.

Top Baker City Event

Memorial Day, Fourth of July, Labor Day weekends

Sumpter Valley Country Fair. This outdoor flea market spreads from the fairgrounds to the town area. The tiny town of Sumpter comes to life when literally thousands of visitors come through to look at the wares or enjoy an old-time fiddler's show. When the kids have had enough browsing, they can buy fresh American Indian fry bread or barbecued beef sandwiches at one of the food stands set up for the occasion. (541) 894–2314.

Fun Fact

In the 1860s gold was discovered just outside Baker City, spawning a gold rush that lasted more than fifty years. In the early 1900s Baker City was known as the "queen city" of the Pacific Northwest because it was the cultural center between Salt Lake City and Portland, with several exquisite hotels and restaurants, ballrooms for dancing, and an opera house.

Leo Adler Memorial Parkway (all ages) 🚶 🎣 🚲
Contact Baker County Visitors Bureau, (800) 523–1235, (541) 523–3356; www.visitbaker.com. Open daily, year-round. Free.

This trail along the Powder River was built in memory of Leo Adler, a bachelor who died in 1993 and left his $20 million estate to the community. Fishing, running, and bird-watching are among the trail's attractions.

Elkhorn Drive National Forest Scenic Byway (all ages) 🏛
Travels in a 106-mile loop from Baker City through the Blue Mountains to the not-so-ghostly ghost towns of Sumpter and Granite and the more ghostly Auburn; (800) 523–1235 or (541) 523–3356. An illustrated brochure is available from Wallowa Whitman National Forest; (541) 523–1405; www.fs.fed.us/r6/w-w/rog/byway/byway.elkhorn.htm. Always open. Free.

Once a wild frontier town where laws were posted on trees, Auburn grew to become the second-largest town in Oregon. Now it's marked only by the grave sites of those left behind. Be sure your gas tank is full. Gas is available only in Baker City, Haines, Sumpter, and Granite.

Sumpter

Sumpter, one of the most interesting of area "ghost towns," can be reached by State Highway 7, south of Phillips Lake. You'll pass the **Sumpter Valley Dredge** (541–894–2486), a state park where a massive machine was used to dredge up the valley floor to be processed for gold. Point out to your children the long rows of rock piles left by the dredge all along the road. More than $10 million in gold came from dredging the Sumpter Valley alone.

What to Do If You Encounter
a Cattle Drive

Do

• Slow down.

• Watch the herders for signals on when to proceed.

• If you follow a herder or another vehicle, stay close to prevent cows from moving in between.

• Watch for cow-herding dogs.

Don't

• Honk your horn or make other loud noises.

• Stop more than 50 feet from the herd. If you stop, the cows might stop, too.

• Get out of your vehicle. It's OK to roll down a window and take photographs.

Gold Post Groceries & Museum (all ages)
150 Northeast Mill Street; (541) 894–2362. Open daily 7:30 A.M.–7:30 P.M.

This mercantile doubles as grocery store, gift shop, sporting-goods store, and museum. You'll see old photos and artifacts of the region's gold-mining days.

Sumpter Valley Railroad (all ages)
Leaves from the McEwen Station, 5.5 miles down the valley toward Phillips Lake to the south end of Sumpter and back; (541) 894–2268 or (866) 894–2268; www.svry.com; e-mail: webmaster@svry. com. Operates the 5 miles between McEwen Station and Sumpter on weekends and holidays May through September; call or check Web site for schedule and special events. $$, $$$$ family, children 5 and under free. Tickets can be purchased at either end.

No trip to Sumpter is complete without taking a train ride on the narrow-gauge steam locomotive as it whistles down 5 scenic miles of track. Vital to the settlement and development of eastern Oregon, the Sumpter Valley Railroad was one of the most colorful and longest-lived narrow-gauge railroads in the nation. Take a trip back in time to an era when steam locomotives were the main mode of transportation, and logging and mining were the mainstays of the local economy.

John Day

John Day Fossil Beds National Monument is one of the best reasons for traveling to this part of the state. Aside from their vivid beauty, the canyons of the John Day River provide a window on prehistory that will give your children a better understanding of the expanse of time captured in the region's geography. For more information, visit the Web site at www.nps.gov/joda.

Kam Wah Chung State Heritage Site (ages 5 and up) 👁

Located adjacent to Gleason Park; (541) 575–0028 or (800) 551–6949; www.oregon stateparks.org. Open May through October Sunday through Saturday 9:00 A.M.–5:00 P.M. Free.

On personal tours the museum director explains the purpose of some of the more unusual items housed in the museum, which is maintained to preserve the legacy of the Chinese workforce in Oregon. Shrines in each room seek to appease various deities, such as the kitchen god. Do you have any aspiring doctors in the family? They'll be especially fascinated with the collection of more than 500 Chinese medicinal herbs that were once dispensed in the building.

John Day River (ages 10 and up) 🏊 ⚠️

John Day Middle Fork intersects State Highway 19 about 45 miles west of Baker City; www.nps.gov/rivers/johnday.html. Always open. Free.

Recreation, from fishing to float trips, is a highlight of this region. Most of the river is smooth-flowing enough for canoes and beginning rafters. Some of the canyon walls bear evidence of previous residents: petroglyphs from the Tenino Indians.

John Day Fossil Beds National Monument, Sheep Rock Unit (all ages) 👁 👫

Located 7 miles northwest of Dayville on State Highway 19, just beyond the junction with U.S. Highway 26; (541) 987–2333; www.nps.gov/joda/tours/srutour.htm. Visitor center open daily 9:00 A.M.–5:00 P.M.; closed weekends Thanksgiving through February. Monument open daily dawn to dusk. Free.

This historic visitor center and museum is a good place to begin accumulating information about the area. The museum has fossil displays of prehistoric creatures that once roamed this region—from saber-toothed cats to elephants and rhinos—between six and fifty million years ago. A fifteen-minute film presents a synopsis of the area's geological history in terms your children will understand. The grounds of the center make a perfect picnic spot. At a small laboratory in an old log shed, park rangers demonstrate some of the tools and techniques used to remove fossil specimens from the stone encasing them. Your children will be fascinated by the tiny jackhammers and will enjoy the idea of dental tools being used to scrape fossil teeth rather than their teeth. Park rangers guide walks on some of the trails throughout the summer. Pick up trail maps and program schedules at the center, then head up the road to explore. The monument covers 14,000 acres in three separate units, the largest of which is the **Sheep Rock Unit.** Trails in this section include two in the **Blue Basin,** with its stunning blue-green canyons, just 2.5 miles north of the visitor center. About 3 miles farther north on State Highway 19, you'll see the striations of **Cathedral Rock,** one of the hallmark images of this area.

An Adventure to Remember

The Kam Wah Chung & Co. building was constructed in the 1860s and served as a trading post on the main east–west highway during that period. The dim lighting that casts an eerie glow in the museum's rooms also beckons the curious to come explore its exotic ambience. You will see that Kam Wah Chung & Co. served as an efficient multipurpose pharmacy, doctor's office, general store, religious shrine, and opium den. The museum has been left in almost the same state that proprietor "Doc" Ing Hay left it when he locked the doors in 1948. Hay and fellow proprietor Lung On purchased the building in the 1880s, and the two men soon became important members of the local community. Lung On was a respected entrepreneur, and Hay was considered the most famous herbal medicine doctor between Seattle and San Francisco. You can spend well over an hour under this tiny roof as your imagination runs wild contemplating the clandestine opium exchanges and examining sundries that now lay dormant on dusty shelves. More than 500 Chinese medicinal herbs, along with gold-mining and logging tools, are wedged next to canned goods, tobaccos, and notions. Several Buddhist shrines still coated with incense are housed here, too, giving testimony to Hay's position as the region's chief priest for the Chinese. Don't miss this museum, the contents of which are said to provide the best historical account of the integration of Oriental and Occidental cultures in the United States, in addition to the prosperous gold-mining era in northeastern Oregon.

Fun Facts

- The John Day River has more miles of wild and scenic designation than any other river in the United States. It's the second-longest undammed river in the country.

- After gold was discovered in 1862, $26 million of the shiny stuff was mined from the John Day–Canyon City region.

Painted Hills (all ages) (※)
Located northwest of Mitchell; (541) 987–2333; www.nps.gov/joda/tours/putour.htm. Open daily dawn to dusk. Free.

The monument's Painted Hills offer a close-up look at the eroded hills of multimillion-year-old colorful volcanic ash. The best views are at dawn and dusk after a rain, when the moisture brings out the spectacular hues in the mineral-rich clays. A 0.75-mile hike leads to an outstanding rim view, and a short self-guided walk to **Painted Cove** offers a close view of the colorful clay stones.

Strawberry Mountain Wilderness (ages 8 and up) (※)(A)
Located 11 miles southeast of John Day; (541) 820–3311; www.fs.fed/r6/malheur. Closed due to snow during the winter and spring. Free.

Located in the **Malheur National Forest,** the Strawberry Mountain Wilderness has more than 100 miles of hiking trails as well as several campgrounds. **Strawberry Lake** is one of the more accessible lakes in the wilderness, although the trail climbs steadily for about 1.3 miles and can be tiring for little ones. From Prairie City head south on Forest Road 60 to the **Strawberry Lake Campground,** about 12 miles south of US 26. You can set up camp here and take a day trip to the lake or backpack into one of several wilderness sites near the lake, where you must leave behind no trace of your visit.

Top John Day **Events**

August
Grant County Fair and NPRA Rodeo. This county fair has all the fixings for a family weekend of fun. (541) 575–1900.
Grant County Kruzer Car Show. Classic cars are celebrated with activities at the fairgrounds and in the streets of Prairie City. (541) 575–2533.

Burns

When you get into the southeastern corner of Oregon, you're entering one of the least-populated areas of the country. Harney and Malheur Counties together account for 20,154 square miles of land—more than Massachusetts and New Jersey combined—and only 34,900 people, fewer than the student population of some universities. That's part of the reason you feel as if you've entered deep Australian outback when you're driving through this country of broad sagebrush deserts and lonely mountain crags. As the major population center in the southeast, Burns is a natural place from which to begin exploring the vast range of outdoor opportunities that awaits visitors. The city received its name because of the fondness early postmaster George McGowen, one of the town's founders, had for Scottish poet Robert Burns.

Rockhounding

An activity for all ages, rockhounding is one of the major tourist attractions in this area. Government-managed properties do not charge a fee for removing rocks, but call the Harney County Chamber of Commerce first (541–573– 2636) about the requirements for each area.

- **Steens Mountain**. Located 60 miles south of Burns; (541) 573–2636. Agate, jasper, obsidian, and thunder eggs can be dug near Buchanan Road at the base of the mountain.

- **Burns.** Located off State Highway 205; (541) 573–2636. Agates are abundant at the quarry just south near the Narrows, the strip of land between Harney and Malheur Lakes.

- **Glass Butte.** Located 55 miles west of Burns on US 20; (541) 573–2636. The butte is so named because it is composed almost entirely of volcanic glass, or obsidian. This area was used extensively by Native Americans for gathering obsidian used to make arrowheads. Collecting arrowheads is against federal law, so if you find any, leave them for the next person to appreciate. All kinds of obsidian can be found near here—lace, rainbow, mahogany, gold sheen, black, and banded.

Fun Fact

Close to Delintment Lake in Ochoco National Forest is the largest Douglas fir in the continental United States—standing more than 158 feet tall with a 23.5-foot base.

Harney County Historical Museum (ages 5 and up)

18 West D Street; (541) 573–5618; www.burnsmuseum.com. Open Tuesday through Saturday 9:00 A.M.–5:00 P.M. April through September. $, family of four $$, children under 6 **free.**

Look for the armored wagon at the edge of the parking lot. Once a brewery, it's now a hands-on museum where your kids can turn the apple peeler and lift the hand irons to get a feel for the work that had to be done to keep a family together a century ago.

Ochoco National Forest, Delintment Lake (all ages)

3160 Northeast Third Street; lies 42 miles northwest of Burns via Forest Road 41; (541) 416–6500; www.fs.fed.us/r6/centraloregon. Always open. **Free** forest access; Delintment Lake $ day-use fee, $ camping fee.

This lake was created by damming Delintment Creek. Campsites in the ponderosa pine forest are suitable for tents and RVs. A picnic area and boat ramp are also available.

Top Burns **Events**

April

John Scharff Migratory Bird Festival and Art Show. Watch thousands of birds as they rest and feed during their spring migration. You'll see everything—waterfowl, shorebirds, cranes, raptors, waders, songbirds. (541) 573–2636.

June

Old-Time Music Jamboree. There's an endless stream of music during this event. Don't miss it. (541) 573–2863.

September

Harney County Fair, Rodeo & Race Meet. Rides, exhibits, food concessions, and broncos will fill your entire weekend. (541) 573–1616.

Crystal Crane Hot Springs (ages 5 and up) 🌊 🛏️ 🏕️
Located 25 miles southeast of Burns on State Highway 78; (541) 493–2312; www.crane hotsprings.com. Open Monday through Saturday 9:00 A.M.–9:00 P.M., Sunday 2:00–9:00 P.M. $$

There's a naturally hot mineral-water swimming pool and bathhouse/spa for families and kids. Rustic cabins as well as tent and RV sites are available.

Sagehen Hill Nature Trail (ages 5 and up) 🥾 🏕️
Located 16 miles west of Burns at the Sagehen Rest Area on U.S. Highway 20. Contact Bureau of Land Management, 12533 U.S. Highway 20W, Hines, OR 97738; (541) 573–5241. Always open. **Free.**

The half-mile-long nature trail has eleven stations along the route that provide information on the trees, cultural history, plants, and, of course, sage hens, also called sage grouse. The trail goes through sagebrush, bitterbrush, and western juniper. Watch for sage grouse in May.

Frenchglen

Both the Steens Mountain Loop Road and the Malheur National Wildlife Refuge loop tours take you through this tiny town, perhaps best known for its century-old hotel.

Frenchglen Hotel State Heritage Site (all ages) 🛏️ 🍴 🏕️ 🏛️
State Highway 205, Frenchglen; (800) 551–6949 or (541) 493–2825; www.oregonstate parks.org. Operates March 15 through November 15. Call for rates.

Part of a State Historic Wayside Park, the eight-room hotel is an oasis for travelers to this region where many miles separate even the closest towns. The hotel provides lodging and meals for visitors coming to enjoy bird-watching and wildlife. Whether or not you stay at the hotel, you can stop by for sodas or coffee, or just enjoy a picnic in the shaded yard. Breakfast, lunch, and dinner are served daily to residents and drop-in guests. Reservations are a must for dinner meals.

McCoy Creek Inn (all ages) 🛏️ 🐾
Located 10 miles south of State Highway 205 from Diamond Junction; (541) 493–2131. Reservations required. Call for rates.

The inn is a working ranch that's been in the same family for five generations. Children can explore McCoy Creek Canyon, wade in the stream, or feed the ducks, peacocks, turkeys, chickens, and calves. Watch for the raccoons, beavers, porcupines, and deer that inhabit the canyon and come to the meadows around the ranch to feed.

Fun Fact

The town of Frenchglen was named for Peter French and Dr. Hugh Glenn, who established a 150,000-acre livestock ranch at the base of Steens Mountain in 1872. After French married Glenn's daughter, Glenn was killed by a man named Miller in 1883 on his Jacinto Ranch in California, where French once worked for him. French also met a violent end—he was shot and killed over a land dispute near his P Ranch. A large section of the ranch is now in the Malheur National Wildlife Refuge.

Fish Lake (all ages) 🔺 🔺 👥

Located about 18 miles east of Frenchglen; (541) 573–4400; www.or.blm.gov/burns. Open dawn to dusk during season; closed November through April. $ camping fee, free day use.

There's a boat ramp for nonmotorized boats, as well as twenty campsites in both shaded and open areas. A trail joins two sections of the campground on opposite sides of the lake. The wildflowers here—and all along the loop road—are stunning, especially in July. **Page Springs,** another campground, is just 4 miles east of Frenchglen. Open year-round, it has thirty campsites, toilets, water (seasonally), fireplaces, and limited firewood. There's a $ camping fee when water is available. Watch for rattlesnakes, ticks, and stinging nettles in summer.

Peter French Round Barn (all ages) 🏛

Located southeast of Burns and Malheur Lake near New Princeton; road signs direct you to the site from State Highway 205; (541) 573–2636. Hours change seasonally; call first. Free.

The barn is worth a stop for both historic and architectural reasons. Built before 1884 of native rock and juniper trees, the structure is fascinating. It's shaped like a Chinese umbrella, with timbered "spokes" leading to a central truss. Peter French used the barn as a winter livestock shelter and for breaking saddle horses.

Diamond Craters (ages 8 and up)

Located 55 miles south of Burns on State Highway 205; (541) 573–4400; www.or.blm .gov/burns. Always open. Free.

The craters were created in the last 25,000 years. They have been described as having the nation's most diverse basaltic volcanic features. There are craters, domes, lava floors and pits to explore.

Oard's Museum and Café (ages 3 and up) 🍴 🧃 🔒

Located 23 miles east of Burns off U.S. Highway 20; (541) 493–2535 or (800) 637–0252. Open seven days a week; call for hours. Free.

This old-fashioned museum features authentic American Indian art and historic pioneer collectibles while the shop has contemporary arts and crafts. It's a fun break during a long day on the road.

Wild Horse Corrals (all ages) 🐘

Just west of Hines, on U.S. Highway 20 near milepost 122; (541) 573–4456 or (541) 573–4400; www.or.blm.gov/Burns. Open weekdays year-round 7:30 A.M.–3:00 P.M. Free.

More than 2,600 wild horses are free-roaming, unbranded descendants of horses turned loose by, or escaped from, the U.S. Cavalry, ranchers, prospectors, or Indian tribes from the late 1800s to the 1930s. At certain times of the year, you can see wild horses in the corrals operated by the Bureau of Land Management or at various viewpoints around the Steens Mountain area. The BLM operates an "adopt a wild horse program" to help control their population.

Malheur National Wildlife Refuge (all ages) 🐘 🧃

From Burns take State Highway 78 south, turn right on State Highway 205 for 28 miles, then left at refuge sign; (541) 493–2612; www.r1.fws.gov/malheur. Visitor center open Monday through Friday 8:00 A.M.–4:00 P.M.; museum and refuge open daily dawn to dusk. Free.

Located in the Blue Mountains south of Burns, Malheur is one of the best places to view birds and waterfowl in the state. Before leaving Burns, be sure to fill the gas tank. The refuge encompasses both Malheur and Harney Lakes, as well as a narrow stretch of land bordering State Highway 205 south of Burns. Established by President Theodore Roosevelt in 1908, the refuge covers 183,000 acres and is home to more than 320 species of birds and 58 mammal species. Obtain a list of species at the

Fun Fact

The greater sandhill cranes that return each year to nest at the Malheur National Wildlife Refuge belong to one of the oldest living bird species. Today's flocks descended from birds that lived more than nine million years ago. One particular crane was banded in 1969 and is still alive as of this writing, making it the oldest living wild crane known to science.

headquarters, located on the south shore of Malheur Lake, 5 miles from State Highway 205 along a paved road. The headquarters consists of both a visitor center and a museum, which contains nearly 200 mounted bird specimens. It's a great opportunity for your children to see up close the birds they might spot through binoculars on the refuge. The Web site has a "Bird Arrivals" page that lists approximate dates of arrival for migrating species. The big show of the year happens in August, when more than 200 pairs of greater sandhill cranes nest at the refuge.

Steens Mountain (ages 10 and up) (%)
Located 60 miles south of Burns on State Highway 205 toward Frenchglen; (541) 573–4400; www.or.blm.gov/steens. Road open July through September. Check road conditions before you visit. Free.

Steens Mountain Loop Road is the best way to explore the mountain; take a full day—or more—and drive the gravel-topped road, which is open only in summer. The road is rough in places, so you'll want to make sure your car is in good condition and has a full tank before you set out. One of the most dramatic geological features of the region, Steens Mountain is a 30-mile-long fault block that rises to an elevation of more than 9,700 feet. A breathtaking view from the rim looks down through the deep gorges of Kiger, Wildhorse, Big Indian, and Little Blitzen Canyons, carved by glaciers a million years ago, into the dry Alvord Desert more than a mile below. The highest road in the state, it stops just short of the mountain's 9,733-foot summit. A short climb on foot takes you to the top of the jagged peak. Be prepared for dramatic shifts in the weather, and keep a close eye on the children—the walls of the mountain are rocky and steep, and high winds can disrupt balance with surprising swiftness.

La Grande

One of the towns settled by pioneers traveling the Oregon Trail, La Grande takes its name from the lush Grande Ronde Valley and the river that flows through its center.

Meacham Divide (ages 8 and up)
Located 19 miles northwest of La Grande near Meacham; (541) 963–7122. Open late April through mid-December. Call for snow levels and opening status. Free.

Winter weather blankets the area with snow, making cross-country skiing a popular activity. You and your children can set out on 9 miles of groomed trails here, with diagonal and skate lanes. Hike or bike on trails in summer.

Top La Grande Events

June

Eastern Oregon Livestock Show and PRCA Rodeo. Take the opportunity to enjoy the oldest rodeo in the Northwest—since 1908! The event also includes horse racing, a carnival, and dancing. (800) 848–9969 or (541) 963–8588.

July

Elgin Stampede. Located in Elgin, 20 miles northeast of La Grande. Pro rodeo and a draft-horse pulling contest are featured, plus a carnival, dances, a parade, and races. (541) 437–4007.

August

Oregon Trail Days, Rendezvous, and Old-Time Fiddler's Contest. Besides good old-fashioned fiddlin', Trail Days features a pioneer encampment, a buffalo barbecue, and a Dutch-oven cookoff. (800) 848–9969.

Anthony Lakes Mountain Resort (ages 5 and up)

Located 50 miles southwest of La Grande on I–84, 19 miles west of the North Powder exit; (541) 856–3277; www.anthonylakes.com. Open 9:00 A.M.–4:00 P.M. Thursday through Sunday in winter, daily during Christmas and spring break. Lift tickets $$$–$$$$.

The resort has rope tows or Pomalifts for beginners, chairlifts for experienced skiers, ski and snowboard rentals, and meals on-site. Anthony Lakes also offers 40 kilometers of groomed Nordic trails looping the lake. Downhill, cat, and cross-country skiing are offered.

Lehman Hot Springs (ages 5 and up)

Located in Ukiah, 38 miles west of La Grande on State Highway 244; (541) 427–3015; www.lehmanhotsprings.com. Open year-round; call for hours; closed Monday for cleaning. $$ admission for swimming, children 3 and under free.

The large hot swimming pool, an unheated pool, and two smaller pools give you many choices for an afternoon soak. This used to be a gathering place for the Nez Percé.

Eastern Oregon Fire Museum (ages 5 and up)

Located on the corner of Elm and Washington Streets; (541) 963–8588; call for hours and admission costs.

The museum is housed in La Grande's historic fire station, which was used from 1899 to 2002. Along with the usual displays, the museum offers chances to climb on vintage and historic fire trucks.

Hot Lake RV Resort (ages 5 and up)

65182 Hot Lake Lane; take I–84 to exit 265 and State Highway 203, driving southeast about 4 miles; (541) 963–5253. Open year-round; call for hours and rates.

A hot spot for summer and winter visitors, the site was once a thriving health spa. The resort now offers RV camping as well as a few tent sites. The natural hot spring produces two million gallons a day at 186 degrees, which provides heat for the mineral baths, hot tub, steam sauna, and heated pool. Several shallow ponds contain fish that you can try catching. You can also take walks along several trails.

Lions' Birnie Park (all ages)

Located at the corner of Old Oregon Trail (B Avenue) and Gekeler Street; (800) 848–9969 or (541) 963–8588. Open dawn to dusk. Free.

Once a pioneer encampment, where wagon trains circled to rest and reenergize for the steep climb up the Blue Mountains to the west, the park now houses symbolic ceramic columns that mark the route taken by wagons as they climbed out of the valley and a life-size wrought-iron pioneer play wagon. Interpretive displays contain excerpts from pioneer diaries, extolling the beauty of the valley and describing the hardships of the journey.

Union County Museum (ages 5 and up)

333 South Main Street, Union, 15 miles southeast of La Grande; (541) 562–6003. Open daily Mother's Day through mid-October 10:00 A.M.–4:00 P.M., Sunday 1:00–4:00 P.M. $. Special tours by request.

Natural history and a Cowboys Then and Now exhibit will give you a glimpse into the region's early days and its cultural and geographic evolution.

Grande Ronde River (ages 8 and up)

Runs through La Grande parallel to State Highway 244; (800) 848–9969 or (541) 963–8588; www.nps.gov/rivers/wsr-grande-ronde.html. Always open. Free.

Summer temperatures in this high-country town call for cooling swims in one of several swimming holes along the banks of the river or in nearby lakes and reservoirs. The Grande Ronde River is a natural selection, especially at any of the parks or campgrounds along its shores. Mule deer, elk, black bears, cougars, and bighorn sheep inhabit the river corridor.

Fun Fact

The Grande Ronde River, at 180 miles long, is Oregon's second-longest free-flowing river and has been designated "Wild and Scenic."

Pendleton

History truly comes alive once a year in this cowboy town when the **Pendleton Round-Up** rears its raucous head. But if you're not in town for the rodeo or didn't plan well enough in advance to get tickets, your children can still get a taste of the Old West with a visit to the **Pendleton Round-Up Hall of Fame.**

Umatilla County Historical Society Museum (ages 5 and up) 🐾

108 Southwest Frazer; (541) 276–0012; www.umatillahistory.org; e-mail: uchs@oregon trail.net. Open Tuesday through Saturday 10:00 A.M.–4:00 P.M. $.

Exhibits trace the region's history, beginning with the Native American tribes that settled along the Umatilla River and leading through the arrival of missionaries, sheepherders, ranchers, farmers, soldiers, and loggers. The museum, housed in the restored 1909 railway depot, contains a large collection of photographs and artifacts to accompany the tales from the Old West. Your children might enjoy what's next door most of all. Kids can compare contemporary classrooms with the restored one-room schoolhouse—an elementary, middle, and high school all in one.

Tamástslikt Cultural Institute (ages 3 and up) 🐾

72789 Highway 331 (take exit 216 off I-84 and follow signs to Wildhorse Resort); (541) 966–9748; www.tamastslikt.com. Open daily 9:00 A.M.–5:00 P.M. $$ adults, seniors, and students, children under 5 free.

The word *tamástslikt* means "interpret," and this center interprets the story of three distinct native peoples—the Cayuse, Umatilla, and Walla Walla tribes—whose histories came together over the past 150 years toward an alliance called the Confederated Tribes of the Umatilla Indian Reservation. The museum looks at the region from the perspective of these tribes—often a very different outlook than that traditionally taught in textbooks. Permanent and changing exhibits and regularly scheduled talks and demonstrations provide a rich experience in history. Permanent artifact collections and photography archives look to the past, while contemporary art exhibits display works by local and regional tribal artists. The store offers local tribal crafts, and there's a cafe for light meals.

Fun Fact

This area is known as Nicht-yow-way, homeland of the Cayuse, Umatilla, and Walla Walla—three distinct tribes now combined to form the Confederated Tribes of the Umatilla Indian Reservation. These tribes once numbered 8,000 people; now they have 2,300 enrolled tribal members.

Pendleton Underground Tours (ages 5 and up) 🏛

37 Southwest Emigrant; (800) 226–6398 or (541) 276–0730; www.pendletonunder groundtours.org. Call for ninety-minute tour dates and times, March through October between 9:30 A.M. and 3:30 P.M. (reservations recommended). $$ adults, $ children.

Descend below street level and get a glimpse of remnants of a time when Pendleton was part of the rootin' tootin' Wild West, once boasting thirty-two saloons and eighteen bordellos. The tours are tastefully presented, but parents of young children might not want to have to explain some of the references. Twice yearly, the underground comes to life. Actors dressed as dance-hall girls, cowboys, Chinese laborers, and gamblers provide entertainment along the tour.

Pedaler's Place Cycle & Ski Shop (ages 8 and up) 🚲

318 South Main Street; (800) 567–0060 or (541) 276–3337; e-mail: ppcs@uci.net. Open year-round 9:30 A.M.–6:00 P.M. Monday through Friday, 10:00 A.M.–5:00 P.M. Saturday. Adult-size bicycle rental $$$ per day.

When the weather's fine—as it usually is throughout the summer—rent bicycles and explore the **Pendleton River Parkway.** The illuminated paved pathway borders the Umatilla River as it flows through town. You can also rent skateboards for the **Pendleton SK8 Park** in May Park, Southeast First and Isaac.

Fun Fact

Pendleton's underground tunnels, dug by Chinese immigrants between 1870 and 1930, cover more than 70 miles underneath Pendleton's historic district.

Clockworks

If you walk to the corner of Southeast Fourth and Court, you can view the century-old clockworks through glass panels in the clock tower. The Seth Thomas clock is located in front of the Umatilla County Courthouse.

Bar M Dude Ranch (all ages)

58840 Bar M Lane, Adams; located 31 miles east of Pendleton in the Blue Mountains; (888) 824–3381 or (541) 566–3381; www.guestranches.com/barm; e-mail: barmranch@eoni.com. Ranch open to guests mid-May through mid-September. Cost is $$$$ per week per person.

Home-style accommodations are offered on this working ranch. The main ranch house has eight guest rooms. Other accommodations include three two-room suites and two cabins. Horseback riding, a recreation barn, natural hot springs, and meals to make any ranch hand's mouth water are all part of the experience.

Blue Mountain Crossing Interpretive Site (ages 5 and up)

Located just south of Emigrant Springs; (541) 963–7186. Call for seasonal hours. $ trailhead fee (Northwest Forest Pass).

During summer weekends you can meet some pioneers camped with their wagon at the 4,193-foot summit, awaiting the rest of their wagon train. Dressed as characters drawn from the past, the living-history pioneers tell tales sketched from diaries left by the emigrants. Three short trails take you past signs of their passage. Give your child the interpretive brochure to guide you to the numbered stops along the way.

Hat Rock State Park (all ages)

Located on the shore of a lake formed by McNary Dam, 29 miles northwest of Pendleton via State Highway 37 and U.S. Highway 73; (800) 551–6949 for information; (800) 452–5687 for reservations; www.oregonstateparks.org. Closed in winter except for boat ramp. Free day use. Call for camping and picnic area reservations and fees.

This is the first Oregon landmark recorded by Lewis and Clark on their journey. The park has camping and picnicking facilities as well as boat access to the Columbia River. A private campground across from the park has a swimming pool. The large pond is a great place to picnic and spot waterfowl that inhabit the area—great blue herons, kingfishers, and friendly ducks and geese are among those you will be able to spot.

Top Pendleton **Event**

September

Pendleton Round-Up. One of the largest rodeos in the country, the Round-Up includes unusual events such as wild-cow milking and Indian and baton races. You'll want to don your ten-gallon hat and your cowboy boots (or your baseball cap and sneakers—there's no dress code) and join in the festivities. The nightly **Happy Canyon Show,** in which members of the local Umatilla, Cayuse, Walla Walla, and Nez Percé tribes present pageantry and tradition, is a spectacle to capture even the most jaded teenage interests. (800) 45–RODEO or (541) 276–2553; www.pendleton roundup.com or www.happycanyon.com.

Pendleton Round-Up Hall of Fame (ages 5 and up)

1205 Southwest Court Street; (800) 45–RODEO, (541) 276–2553, or (541) 278–0815; www.pendletonroundup.com. Open Monday through Saturday 10:00 A.M.–5:00 P.M. Free, but donations appreciated. Tours available.

Displays of photographs of famous bronco riders and rodeo stars line the walls that commemorate the Wild West. There's even an old rodeo bucking horse, Warpaint, in full-body mount—a real kid–pleaser.

Pendleton Woolen Mills (ages 5 and up)

1307 Southeast Court Place; (800) 568–3156 or (541) 276–6911; www.pendleton-usa .com. Open Monday through Saturday 8:00 A.M.–5:00 P.M., Sunday 11:00 A.M.–3:00 P.M. Free twenty-minute tours available Monday through Friday at 9:00 A.M., 11:00 A.M., 1:30 P.M., and 3:00 P.M.

When some people hear the word *Pendleton,* they have visions of soft woolen shirts and blankets instead of rodeos. Although your kids may not be thrilled to look inside a woolen mill, they might at least appreciate the benefit of the warm winter clothing that can be purchased at the outlet here.

Hells Canyon National Recreation Area

What is the deepest river gorge in North America? Nope, not Arizona's Grand Canyon. It's right here in eastern Oregon: **Hells Canyon** on the Snake River. Forming the border between Oregon and Idaho, the Snake River carved a gorge more than a mile deep over the last twenty million years. The canyon's oldest rocks were formed as long as 280 million years ago at the bottom of a vast inland sea.

Designated in 1975 as a National Recreation Area, Hells Canyon offers many opportunities for family fun. The highest point on the Oregon rim of the canyon is **Hat Point,** rising 6,982 feet above sea level. A new road into the scenic overlook has made this vista available to motorists from mid-June through October. From Imnaha drive east on Hat Point Road. Gas up before leaving Enterprise or Joseph and carry drinking water; you'll drive 23 miles from Imnaha one-way to the Hat Point Overlook.

Hells Canyon National Recreation Area (ages 5 and up)

(541) 523–6391 or (541) 426–5546; www.fs.fed.us/hellscanyon/. Check first for road access during winter months. Free.

To explore the Hells Canyon National Recreation Area more deeply, look into guided trips by boat, on the back of a horse, or with a pack mule or llama. You can take your own float or powerboat trip along the "Wild and Scenic" Snake River if you are an experienced white-water boater.

Hells Canyon Adventures (note age restrictions below)

Located 80 miles east of Baker City; P.O. Box 159, Oxbow, OR 97840; (541) 785–3352 or (800) 422–3568; www.hellscanyonadventures.com; e-mail: jetboat@hellscanyon adventures.com. Open mid-May through mid-September. Call for schedules and prices.

They are one of the few outfitters offering day trips rather than extended overnight floats. With one exception, the trips—either by raft or jet boat—navigate all of the major white water on the river, including some Class IV rapids (not for the faint of heart). Children must be at least twelve to take a daylong raft trip. For those with hearts and stomachs made of weaker substances than steel, they offer "soft adventures"—two- and three-hour jet boat trips that take you up to but not through the worst of the white water. Younger children are welcome on jet boat trips. All trips involve stops to explore an old homestead, ancient Indian pictographs, an abandoned Indian village, a deserted cave, or the Kirkwood Living Historical Ranch, a museum that was once the home of former Idaho governor and U.S. senator Len Jordan.

Steen's Wilderness Adventures

(ages 6 and up)

64591 Steen Road, Joseph; (541) 432–6545; www
.steens-packtrips.com; e-mail: steens@oregontrail.net.
Trips run late May through early September. $$$$.

Three- to seven-day rafting and horse and mule pack trips
take you into the canyon or into the **Eagle Cap Wilderness.** With five generations of history in the region,
Steen's Wilderness Adventures knows the canyon and its
wilderness well.

Hurricane Creek Llama Treks (ages 6 and up)

1145 Twenty-fifth Avenue, Albany; (800) 528–9609 or (541) 928–7365; www.hcltrek
.com. Call for schedules. Five-day trips $$$$.

Another option for exploring Hells Canyon is one your children (six and older) will
love. Guides and their gentle, brown-eyed, fluffy llamas make hiking a real adventure
on tours into Hells Canyon, on wildflower treks along Bear Creek, or on trips up to the
enchanting Lakes Basin in the high Wallowas.

Back Country Outfitters (all ages)

P.O. Box 137, Joseph, OR 97846; (800) 966–8080 or (541) 426–5908; www.backcountry
outfitters.com; e-mail: bcountry@eoni.com. Wallowas July through early October;
Snake River May through June. $$$$.

One of the most time-honored means of descending into the canyon is on the back of
a mule, those stout and stable but much-maligned creatures with a reputation for
stubborn streaks as deep as the canyon. This company takes you down into the
canyon on three- to twenty-one-day trips. You'll ride horses, and the mules will pack
all the camping gear and supplies, though there are a few riding mules for those
who'd like the experience. Custom trips can include children as young as toddlers.

Nee-Me-Poo National Recreation Trail (ages 8 and up)

Access to the trail by car (high-clearance vehicles strongly recommended) is from
Imnaha, about 20 miles over rough, single-lane gravel-topped Forest Road 4260; (541)
426–4978, ext. 5546; www.fs.fed/hellscanyon. Open year-round. Free.

The 5-mile (one–way) trail gives kids a strong sense of history as it leads into the
Snake River Canyon, downriver from Hells Canyon. Nee-Me-Poo means "the real people." The evocative story of Chief Joseph and his flight from the Wallowa Valley seems
to resonate through the valley as you walk in his footsteps. The trail ends at Dug Bar
on the Snake, where an interpretive sign tells the story of the Nez Percé. When walking here, carry drinking water and be prepared for weather changes. This is a steep
trail, with a 1,000-foot elevation change at each end of the hike. Be watchful for rattlesnakes.

Saddle Creek Viewpoint and Campground (ages 5 and up) Ⓐ 🚻
Located 18.8 miles out of Imnaha; (541) 426–5546 or (541) 425–4978. Open July
through October (caution: never before mid-June), but always check first for snow levels. **Free.**

This area has both camping facilities and terrific viewing spots into Hells Canyon,
where you also get a good view of the Seven Devils Mountains in Idaho. An interpretive sign helps you identify for your children the various geologic features they're seeing, and they'll enjoy scrambling over the rocky surfaces that surround the area. From
here the road climbs in twists and turns another 4.7 miles to Hat Point. If you're not
one for heights, you can enjoy the view from here while your kids climb the 92-foot
lookout tower for an all-around view that spans northeastern Oregon and extends to
northwestern Idaho. If you're camping, bring your own water, as there's no supply at
the campground.

The Wallowas

The lush flatlands of the Wallowa Valley form a contrast to the abrupt rise of the
mountains. The variety of choices for family adventure in this beautiful corner of the
state is surprising for an area with such a sparse population. Magnificent natural
beauty, much of it preserved in the **Wallowa-Whitman National Forest** and **Eagle
Cap Wilderness,** captivates visitors and residents alike throughout the year. Winter
snows cover the Wallowa Mountains—often called the Swiss Alps of Oregon—which
offer downhill and Nordic skiing. Spring brings a time for alpine wildflower walks and
fishing in the area's many lakes and streams. Summer invites hikers, mountain bikers,
horseback riders, water-skiers, and swimmers. Autumn colors are spectacular, and so
is the fishing during fall spawning.

   Wallowa Lake, formed about a million years ago by glacial drift, is bounded on
the east and west by lateral moraines (accumulations of earth and stones collected
and deposited by a glacier) and at the north by a terminal moraine. The teardrop-
shape lake is 283 feet deep and 6 miles long. Its name comes from the Nez Percé

Fun Facts

- When the Wallowa Lake Tramway was constructed, it boasted the
  steepest vertical lift for a four-passenger gondola in all of North
  America.

- Eagle Cap Wilderness is Oregon's largest designated wilderness area.

term for a tripod-mounted fish trap that was used in the lake. The south end of Wallowa Lake was first commercially developed in 1906. A dance pavilion and bowling lanes have given way to numerous resorts and lodges. Floating platforms dot the lake near the shore for swimmers and water-skiers to rest or picnic. Fishing is excellent both in the lake and in nearby streams for rainbow trout, kokanee (landlocked blue-back salmon), Dolly Varden (char), sturgeon, and mackinaw (lake trout). Hiking trails take off into the Eagle Cap Wilderness Area, or you can take horseback trips with a guide. Mule deer roam the area freely and are quite accustomed to people. Please don't feed the deer, as human food is bad for them. Also, these are wild animals, and their antlers and hooves are sharp and powerful.

Wallowa Lake Marina (ages 5 and up) ⏛

P.O. Box 47, Joseph, OR 97846; (541) 432–9115. Open 8:00 A.M.–8:00 P.M. Memorial Day through Labor Day. Call for prices.

Reservations can be made for a one-and-a-half-hour lake tour aboard a pontoon boat, which is also available for rent. The marina rents canoes, rowboats, paddle-boats, and motorboats by the day, half day, or hour. The kids will be delighted to find kiddie rides here.

Wallowa Lake Tramway (ages 5 and up) 🍴 👫 🌿

59919 Wallowa Lake Highway; (877) 994–TRAM or (541) 432–5331; www.wallowalake tramway.com. Open daily June through September 10:00 A.M.–4:00 P.M., to 5:00 P.M. July through Labor Day. Enclosed gondola for backcountry skiing December through March; call for details. $$$, children 3 and under free.

The tram takes you on an alpine ride on an amazingly steep incline. The elevation at the base is 4,450 feet, climbing to a breathtaking 8,200 feet at the crest of Mount Howard. Along the surprisingly brief (about ten-minute) ride, the gondola travels between 3 and 120 feet off the ground—be prepared for children's squeals of mixed delight and terror. From the top the spectacular vista encompasses **Wallowa Lake,** the **Eagle Cap Wilderness,** the **Seven Devils Mountains** in Idaho, the **Hells Canyon** area, and on really clear days the **Bitterroot Mountains** of Montana. Let kids work off pent-up energy walking the 2-mile trail that circles the summit, then stop for a bite to eat at the **Summit Deli and Alpine Patio.** June is the peak month for alpine wildflowers on the mountain.

Joe's Place Pizza & Bumper Boats (all ages) 🎡

72662 Marina Lane, Wallowa Lake; (541) 432–4940. Open daily Memorial Day through Labor Day, usually 11:00 A.M.–10:00 P.M. Call for prices and hours, which change seasonally.

The whole family can load into bumper boats or play mini-croquet or putt-putt golf at Joe's, and the kids will quickly gravitate to the arcade area. Order one of Joe's "gour-met pizzas" in between sessions or tuck into a great hand-dipped ice-cream cone.

Top Wallowa **Events**

July

Tamkaliks Celebration. Held annually, the Tamkaliks Celebration symbolizes the return of Wallowa Band Nez Percé descendants to their homeland. *Tamkaliks* means "from where you can see the mountains." Your children will be wowed by the traditional dancing in ceremonial dress, the rhythm of the drumming and singing, and the experience of a distinctive cultural tradition. The Nez Percé prepare venison, salmon, and traditional fry bread, and other area residents bring potluck dishes to share for the Friendship Feast on Sunday. Visitors are asked to contribute, too, either with a dish or a donation. Tepee, tent, and RV camping available. (800) 585–4121, (541) 426–4622, or (541) 886–3101; www.wallowanez perce.com; e-mail: tamkaliks@eoni.com.

September

Alpenfest. For more than twenty-five years, the Wallowa Lake community has been transformed for one September weekend into a Swiss village. Traditional food, dancing, costumes, and music—yodeling, Swiss cowbells, and 12-foot-long alpenhorns—bring Bavaria alive in eastern Oregon. (800) 585–4121 or (541) 432–4071; www.wallowalake.net.

Eagle Cap Wilderness Pack Station (ages 7 and up)

59761 Wallowa Lake Highway; (800) 681–6222 or (541) 432–4145; www.eaglecap wildernesspackstation.com. Open June through mid-November. Call for pricing on various trips and activities.

This is the oldest horse-packing operation in northeastern Oregon. Your family can take a one-hour, two-hour, half-day, or all-day ride as well as a week-long excursion. All rides are accompanied by experienced guides. Deluxe summer pack trips come complete with camp setup, horses, guide, and wranglers (who take care of the horses and cooking). The outfitter has recently added parasailing to its offerings.

Enterprise

This Old West town, named by a committee of early settlers who hoped the moniker would bring good fortune to the area, forms a gateway for vacationers heading into the Eagle Cap Wilderness.

Eagle Cap Wilderness (all ages)

Begins at the Hurricane Creek Campground, 6 miles south of Enterprise on Forest Road 8205, a rough road suitable for slow travel with a passenger car but not recommended for RVs or trailers; (541) 426–4978; (541) 426–5546 for road conditions; www.fs.fed.us/r6/w-w/ecwild.htm. Call for hours, which vary seasonally (there's often snow in the area until July). $ vehicle fee (Northwest Forest Pass).

Besides an easy hike, you'll have great views of Sacajawea Peak and the Matterhorn, Oregon's sixth- and seventh-tallest mountains, as you pass through meadows and forested areas along Hurricane Creek.

Stangel Buffalo Ranch (all ages)

Located about 1 mile north of Enterprise on State Highway 3 at 65044 Alder Slope Road; (541) 426–4919. Always open. **Free.**

A wide spot on the road's shoulder invites you to stop and view the herd of 150 or more buffalo that are usually found grazing here. It's a far cry from the days of herds of thousands, but it's an opportunity for your kids to see creatures once native and wild in Oregon. Mules are another frequent sight around here.

Top Enterprise **Event**

September

Hells Canyon Mule Days. These long-eared animals are celebrated at this annual event. Mule owners from all over the state come together, and your family can join in a halter and trail class or just watch the parade down Main Street. Races, rodeo competitions, and mule rides are also part of the fun. (541) 426–3271 or (800) 585-4121; www.hellscanyonmule days.com; e-mail: loziers@eoni.com.

Joseph

Named for the famous Nez Percé chief who led his people on a harrowing winter journey to avoid war, the town of Joseph remembers its history. Any resident could tell you the story of young Chief Joseph—the statesman and orator whose Nez Percé name was Hinmut-too-yah-lat-kekeht, which is said to mean "Thunder Rolling in the Mountains"—and his father, Old Joseph, who is buried at the north end of Wallowa Lake, where a roadside historical marker provides a brief history. Young Chief Joseph's peaceful band was ordered in 1877 to leave the Wallowa country, which had been granted to his people by treaty in 1855. After a few angry men seeking revenge for the deaths of two young braves killed some white settlers, Joseph led his people first to seek refuge with the Crow in Montana and then toward Canada and Chief Sitting Bull. They were pursued and captured after a two-day battle within 50 miles of the Canadian border. In surrender, Chief Joseph spoke words that have rung through time: "Hear me, my chiefs! I am tired. My heart is sick and sad. From where the sun now stands, I will fight no more forever."

Manuel Museum Nez Percé Crossing (ages 5 and up)

400 North Main Street; (541) 432–7235; www.davidmanuel.com; e-mail: manuel@ eoni.com. Open Monday through Saturday 8:00 A.M.–5:00 P.M. in summer; call for off-season schedule. $$ adults, $ seniors and children 10 and under.

David Manuel's museum offers a large collection of Native American and historical artifacts—including the first wagon to cross into this area on the great Oregon Trail migration. It also includes Manuel's own bronze sculpture, as well as a children's museum, a miniature tepee encampment, and a wagon train.

Top Joseph **Events**

Summer

Great Joseph Bank Robbery. At 1:00 P.M. nearly every Saturday from Memorial Day through Labor Day, enthusiastic performers reenact the 1896 Robbery (always referred to in capital letters around here). Masked bandits gallop up to the bank, then come out a few minutes later with guns blazing (blanks, of course). (541) 432–1015.

July

Chief Joseph Days Rodeo and Encampment. The events include a five-day rodeo, a ranch-style breakfast, a Nez Percé encampment, a carnival, ceremonial dancing, and parades. (541) 432–1015 or (800) 585–4121; www.chiefjosephdays.com.

Visual Arts

One of the more surprising elements of this small western town is its sizable arts community. While the idea of a trip through an art museum might not excite your children, they'll be enthralled by the bronze sculpture showrooms in Joseph. A number of art foundries specialize in extremely detailed, realistic renderings of western themes, such as wolves, horses, mountain lions, eagles, cowboys, and Native Americans, including:

- **Valley Bronze of Oregon.** 307 West Adler Street (foundry); (541) 432–7551; www.valleybronze.com; e-mail: info@valleybronze.com. Open daily for tours. $ per person. Stop by the foundry or the Joseph Gallery at 18 West Main Street (541–432–7445).

- **Joseph Bronze Foundry.** 83365 Joseph Highway; (541) 432–2278; www.josephbronze.net; e-mail: info@josephbronze.com. Call for hours. Also see the description for **Manuel Museum Nez Percé Crossing,** which offers foundry tours and workshops.

Ferguson Ridge Ski Area (ages 8 and up)
Located 8 miles southeast of Joseph; (541) 426–3494; e-mail: outdoors@eoni.com. Open weekends only 10:00 A.M.–4:00 P.M. in winter. Call for times and prices.

Young downhill skiers can spend all day on the rope tow for a couple of dollars; adults ski from the T-bar for less than $10 a day. Equipment rentals and food are available at the lodge. The hill is owned by the Ferguson Ridge Ski Club and operated by members, so opening times are a bit sporadic.

Wallowa Lake State Park (all ages)
On Wallowa Lake at the edge of the Wallowa River 6 miles south of Joseph; (541) 432–4185 or (800) 551–6949; (800) 452–5687 for campground reservations; www.oregonstate parks.org. Open year-round. $ day-use fee. Camping fees additional for tent, full hookup, yurt, or cabin.

From Memorial Day through Labor Day, this place is packed, so you'll definitely need to reserve your campsite. But if you're staying elsewhere, come out for the day to enjoy swimming, boating, fishing, or hiking the nature trail. There's also a playground, and the area is frequently on the visiting path of the local deer. Never let your children feed or pet the deer. They may seem tame, but they have very sharp hooves and antlers.

Family Favorites in Eastern Oregon

1   National Historic Oregon Trail Interpretive Center, near Baker City

2. Malheur National Wildlife Refuge, near Burns

3. Steens Mountain, near Burns

4. Nee-Me-Poo National Recreation Trail, Hells Canyon

5. Peter French Round Barn, near Burns

6. John Day Fossil Beds National Monument

7. Kam Wah Chung State Heritage Site, John Day

8. Pendleton Underground Tours

9. Umatilla County Historical Society Museum, Pendleton

10. Wallowa Lake Tramway

Wallowa County Museum (ages 5 and up)

110 South Main Street; (541) 432–6095; www.co.wallowa.us/museum. Open daily
10:00 A.M.–5:00 P.M. Memorial Day weekend through the third weekend in September.
Free, but donations appreciated.

The Nez Percé history room contains a large tepee that your children will enjoy sitting
in even if museums in general offer little appeal. Look for "buckskin bucks," money
produced for trading locally during the Great Depression, when real money was
scarce.

Where to Eat

IN BAKER CITY

Baker City Cafe. 1840 Main Street; (541)
523–6099. Signature menu items are "flam-
ing pasta salads"—we won't spoil the sur-
prise—as well as more traditional fare.
$–$$

Inland Cafe. 2715 Tenth Street; (541) 523–
9041. Down-home cooking specialties are
chicken-fried steak and pork chops. $–$$

Oregon Trail Restaurant. 221 Bridge
Street; (541) 523–5844. Family dining with
old-fashioned American fare. $$–$$$

Sumpter Junction. 2 Sunridge Lane; (541)
523–9437. A miniature replica of the
Sumpter Valley Railroad runs on tiny tracks
around the restaurant, alongside booths
and over dining tables. Family dining with
Mexican specialties. $–$$

IN ENTERPRISE

House Cafe. 307 West North; (541) 426–
9055. Family-style meals served in a casual
setting. $–$$

Toma's. 309 South River Street; (541) 426–
4873. Family cooking. $–$$

IN JOHN DAY

Grubsteak Mining Company. 149 East Main; (541) 575–1970. Pizza, steak, fish, and chicken specialties; open for lunch and dinner. $–$$

IN JOSEPH

Cheyenne Cafe. 209 North Main; (541) 432–6300. Country cooking seven days a week. $–$$

Manuel Magnonis. 500 North Main; (541) 432–3663; www.davidmanuel.com/magnonis. Italian specialties served family-style for all you can eat. $$

Old Town Cafe. 8 South Main Street; (541) 432–9898. This tiny lunch and breakfast place offers hearty food at reasonable prices. It's the place to stop and fill up before heading out for a round of outdoor activities in northeastern Oregon. $

IN LA GRANDE

Boulder Creek Café at the Rock. 2301 Cove Avenue; (541) 975–5595. The cafe offers salads, sandwiches, and appetizers along with fish, steak, and seafood dinners.

Foley Station. 1011 Adams Avenue; (541) 963–7473; www.foleystation.com. Open for brunch, lunch, and dinner, this eatery offers gourmet dishes at reasonable prices. $–$$

Ten Depot Street. 10 Depot Street; (541) 963–8766. This casual restaurant is a good place to relax with a tasty meal and get a feeling for this friendly town. The owner also operates **Mamacita's** on the next block (110 Depot Street), which serves Mexican fare ($). $$

IN PENDLETON

The Great Pacific Wine and Coffee Company. 403 South Main Street; (541) 276–1350. Get a good deal for your picnic lunch here and buy tasty sandwiches made on bagels or croissants. Then stuff your picnic basket with baked goodies. $

IN THE WALLOWAS

Bob's Cafe. 216 East First Street; (541) 886–6874. Full breakfast, lunch, and dinner menus, with daily specials. Closed Sunday. $$

Russell's at the Lake. 59984 Wallowa Lake Highway; (541) 432–0591. Open May through October. Grab a hamburger and terrific fries (from potato to plate in ten minutes) at this old-fashioned burger bar that has both outdoor and indoor seating. Russell's is popular for its almost-too-thick-for-a-straw milkshakes as well as its ranch-style breakfasts. $

TnT Kitchen. 101 West First; (541) 886–7705. For something different, have a buffalo burger. This small restaurant also serves dynamite homemade cinnamon rolls. $

Where to Stay

IN BAKER CITY

Best Western Sunridge Inn. 1 Sunridge Lane; (800) 233–2368 or (541) 523–6444. An outdoor pool waits for you in the summer, and an indoor spa will warm your bones during the cold winter months. $$–$$$

Eldorado Inn. 695 Campbell Street; (800) 537–5756 or (541) 523–6494. A restaurant and indoor pool are among the amenities here. Pets are welcome. $$–$$$

Rodeway Inn. 810 Campbell Street; (800) 228–2000 or (541) 523–2242; www.quality inn.com. The inn serves continental breakfast and welcomes pets. $$–$$$

Super 8. 250 Campbell Street; (541) 523–8282. Laundry facilities, an indoor pool, and a spa pool help make family stays here more comfortable. $$–$$$

Union Creek Campground. Located on State Highway 7 on the shores of Phillips Reservoir about 20 miles southwest of Baker City; (541) 523–4476. Fifty-eight campsites for tent and trailer camping. The swimming beach is a great place for your kids to enjoy a summer dip while Mom and Dad soak up some of this area's seemingly endless sunshine (in the summertime, that is). $

IN BURNS

Hotel Diamond. 10 Main Street; take State Highway 205 south toward Frenchglen; (541) 493–1898. This century-old hotel has both charm and tradition. Adjacent to the Malheur Wildlife Refuge, it receives regular visits from deer and great horned owls. The restaurant serves breakfast, lunch, and dinner. $$–$$$

Silver Spur Motel. 789 North Broadway; (800) 400–2077 or (541) 573–2077. Twenty-six units. A health club, microwaves, and refrigerators make this a convenient place for families to settle in for a day or more. Best of all, they offer a full breakfast buffet. $$

IN ENTERPRISE

Best Western Rama Inn & Suites. 1200 Highland Avenue; (800) RAMA–INN or (541) 426–2000. Continental breakfast is offered, plus an indoor pool, spa, and exercise room. Pets are welcome. $$–$$$

Lick Creek Campground. 29 miles southeast of Enterprise on Forest Road 39, Wallowa Mountain Loop Road; (541) 426–4978; www.fs.fed.us/r6/w-w. At the 5,400-foot elevation, nights are chilly, but the views from the ridge above the campgound are terrific. You can fish or hike from this campground, which also has trailer sites and drinking water. $

Wilderness Inn. 301 West North Street; (541) 426–4535. This newly remodeled inn has private saunas, kitchenettes, and an adjoining restaurant. $$

IN FRENCHGLEN

Frenchglen Hotel. Located on State Highway 205, 62 miles south of Burns; (541) 493–2825 or (800) 551–6949; www.oregonstateparks.org. The hotel provides lodging and meals for visitors coming to Malheur to enjoy bird-watching and wildlife. Breakfast, lunch, and dinner are served daily to residents and drop-in guests. Be sure to make reservations for dinner. $–$$$

IN JOHN DAY

Budget 8 Motel. 711 West Main Street; (541) 575–2155. Fourteen units. Your family will settle in nicely here, with a restaurant and laundry services plus an outdoor pool for those hot summer days. $$–$$$

John Day Sunset Inn. 390 West Main Street; (541) 575–1462. Forty-three units. You'll find a restaurant here, plus laundry facilities, an indoor pool, and a sauna pool. $$–$$$

Lands Inn Bed and Breakfast. 45457 Dick Creek Road, Kimberly; (541) 934–2333; www.landinn.net. Located 10 miles northeast of Fossil Beds National Monument headquarters off State Highway 19, this bed-and-breakfast has two quaint cottages for rent. $$–$$$$

Riverside School House Bed and Breakfast. 28076 North River Road (County Road 61); located 6 miles east of Prairie City, 19 miles east of John Day; (541) 820–4731; www.riversideschoolhouse.com. Here's a bed-and-breakfast that will give your children a new experience in going to school. Originally a one-room schoolhouse, it is now part of a working cattle ranch. $$$–$$$$

IN JOSEPH

Collett's Cabins. 84681 Ponderosa Lane; (541) 432–2391 or (866) 432–7300; www .collettscabins.com; e-mail: info@colletts cabins.com. Cabins with linens, utensils, microwave, fridge, coffeepot, and barbecue. Sleeps from two to eight. Artist-owners provide artwork in rooms and sell art supplies in the gift shop. $$–$$$$

Flying Arrow Resort. 59782 Wallowa Lake Highway; (541) 432–2951; www.flying arrow resort.com; e-mail: flyinga@oregon trail.net. Twenty units. This family-oriented resort with all the amenities—heated swimming pool, hot tub, sundecks, and barbecues—is open year-round. Cabins range from rustic to modern, with one to four bedrooms. Most are located on the Wallowa River, and all are fully equipped. $$$–$$$$

IN LA GRANDE

Anthony Lakes Recreation Area. Baker Ranger District, on Forest Road 73; (541) 523–4476. You can camp at Anthony, Mud, and Grande Ronde Lakes. Campgrounds are available for tents and trailers, and there are boat ramps for nonmotorized craft. $

Hilgard Junction State Park. Located on the Grande Ronde, at the edge of the Blue Mountains, take I–84 northwest about 9 miles to the Highway 244 turnoff and head west about 0.25 mile; (800) 551–6949; www.oregonstateparks.org. The park lies along the path taken by pioneers on the Oregon Trail, and you can use the interpretive panels to share some of its history with your children. $

Lehman Hot Springs. P.O. Box 187, Ukiah, OR 97880; (541) 427–3015. If you plan ahead, you can camp or rent a cabin or tepee here. A large swimming pool heated from a natural hot spring and a mineral

bath adjacent to the pool will keep the whole family content for hours. $$$–$$$$

Stang Manor Inn. 1612 Walnut Street; (541) 963–2400. A stay at this small B&B will add to your list of memorable travel experiences. The stately Georgian manor was the home of a local lumber baron in the 1920s and is furnished with antiques. The spacious grounds are ideal for children to let off pent-up energy. $$–$$$$

Super 8. 2407 East R Avenue at the I–84/Highway 82 interchange; (800) 800–8000 or (541) 963–8080. Sixty-four units. The simple rooms are comfortable, and the indoor pool and spa pool offer a nice respite after a day of outdoor activities. $$–$$$

IN PENDLETON

Emigrant Springs State Heritage Area. Located near the summit of the Blue Mountains off I–84, 26 miles southeast of Pendleton; (541) 983–2227 or (800) 551–6949; (800) 452–5687 for reservations. Your family can stay in the Totem Bunkhouse, with two bunk beds (four single beds) in each of two units. It's available year-round for winter cross-country ski holidays and summer camping. The campground offers a self-guided nature trail, a kitchen shelter in the day-use area, a horse camp with two corrals, and a horse trail that doubles as a cross-country ski trail in winter. $$

Holiday Inn Express. 600 Southeast Nye Street; (541) 966–6520 or (800) HOLIDAY. Indoor and outdoor spa and indoor swimming pool are offered. Continental breakfast is served. $$–$$$$

7 Inn. I–84 exit 202 and Barnhardt Road; (800) 734–7466 or (541) 276–4711. Continental breakfast is served. Kitchenette and laundry services are available. Pets are welcome, too. $–$$$

IN THE WALLOWAS

Eagle Cap Chalets and Park at the River RV Park. 59879 Wallowa Lake.Highway; (541) 432–4704; www.eaglecap chalets.com. Twenty chalet rooms, twelve cabins, five condos, plus full RV hookups (no tent camping). All rooms and cabins have TV, coffeepot, microwave, and fridge. Indoor pool and spa at chalet. $–$$$$

Wallowa Lake Lodge. 60060 Wallowa Lake Highway; (541) 432–9821; www .wallowalakelodge.com; e-mail: info@ wallowalake.com. Lodge rooms and rustic cabins are for rent. Open year-round (weekends only mid-October through Memorial Day) for all-weather recreation, the lodge has a dining room for breakfast and dinner, and you can order picnics to go. $$–$$$$

For More Information

Baker County Visitor & Convention Bureau. 490 Campbell Street, Baker City, OR 97814; (800) 523–1235 or (541) 523–3356; www.visitbaker.com.

Eastern Oregon Visitors Association/ Oregon Trail Marketing Coalition. P.O. Box 1087, Baker City, OR 97814; (800) 332–1843 or (541) 523–9200; www.eova.com.

Grant County Chamber of Commerce. 281 West Main Street, John Day, OR 97845; (800) 769–5664 or (541) 575–0547; www .grant county.cc; e-mail: grant@grant county.cc.

Harney County Chamber of Commerce. 76 East Washington, Burns, OR 97720; (541) 573–2636; www.harneycounty.com; e-mail: burnscc@centurylel.net.

Joseph Chamber of Commerce. P.O. Box 13, Joseph, OR 77846; (800) 585–4121 or (541) 432–1015; www.josephoregon.com; email: cjdays@oregontrail.net.

La Grande–Union County Visitors and Convention Bureau. 102 Elm Street, La Grande, OR 97850; (800) 848–9969 or (541) 963–8588; www.visitlagrande.com; e-mail: info@unioncountychamber.org.

Pendleton Chamber of Commerce/ Visitors & Information Center. 501 South Main Street, Pendleton, OR 97801; (800) 547–8911 or (541) 276–7411; www.pendletonchamber.com; e-mail: info@pendleton-oregon.org.

Wallowa County Chamber of Commerce. P.O. Box 427, 936 West North Street, Enterprise, OR 97828; (800) 585–4121 or (541) 426–4622; www.wallowa countychamber.org; e-mail: chamber@ wallowacountychamber.com.

Index

About the Author

Cheryl McLean is an Oregon native who spent a great deal of her childhood exploring the state on family vacations. She received a bachelor's degree in English from Oregon State University and a master's degree in journalism from the University of Oregon. Cheryl worked for several years as a stringer, writing travel articles for *Sunset Magazine*'s northwest office. She also taught writing at Western Oregon State College before starting her own design and publishing company. She is the author of *Oregon's Quiet Waters: A Guide to Lakes for Canoeists and Other Paddlers* (Jackson Creek Press). Since 1979 she has served on the book and journal editorial boards of CALYX Books, a women's literary press. Cheryl lives in Corvallis, Oregon, with her husband and daughter.